Daniel Boone and the Wilderness Road

Biography of a Great American Explorer

By H. Addington Bruce

Published by Pantianos Classics

ISBN-13: 978-1-78987-460-0

First published in 1910

Contents

Preface v

Chapter One - The Youth of Daniel Boone 7

Chapter Two - Boone's First Campaign 13

Chapter Three - Dark Days on the Border 21

Chapter Four - Boone's explorations in Kentucky 27

Chapter Five - The People Who Followed Boone 36

Chapter Six - Westward ho! 43

Chapter Seven - The Building of the Wilderness Road 51

Chapter Eight - Boone as a Law-Maker 56

Chapter Nine - The Passing of Transylvania 66

Chapter Ten - War-Time in Kentucky 74

Chapter Eleven - The Campaigning of George Rogers Clark 84

Chapter Twelve - Boone among the Indians 95

Chapter Thirteen - The Last Years of the War 105

Chapter Fourteen - Pioneering in Watauga 116

Chapter Fifteen - From Watauga to the Cumberland 124

Chapter Sixteen - Annals of the Wilderness Road 131

Chapter Seventeen - Kentucky after the Revolution 140

Chapter Eighteen - Boone's Last Years 151

Daniel Boone

From a painting by Chester Harding, owned by Colonel Reuben T, Durrett, of Louisville, Kentucky

Preface

In his old age, though in no spirit of boastfulness, Daniel Boone declared that "the history of the western country has been my history." Undoubtedly, of all the men who took part in the winning of the early West, none played so conspicuous a role as Boone, or a role of such extensive usefulness. His services to his country began in the bitter struggle of the French and Indian War, that colossal conflict which definitely eliminated France as a factor in New World colonization. It was he, more than any other man, who made England's colonists acquainted with the beauty and fertility of the vast and well-nigh unoccupied region between the Alleghenies and the Mississippi. To his bold pioneering the United States owes one of its greatest highways of empire — the famous Wilderness Road, along which so many thousands of home-seekers passed in the first peopling of the West. Throughout the stormy years of the Revolution, he was preeminent in the defence of the infant settlements which he had done so much to plant in the country beyond the mountains. And, finally, after the Revolution, when the American people had begun to take possession of the new territory gained and held for them by him and his fellow-pioneers, Boone once more entered upon his self-imposed mission of pointing the way for his countrymen to the land of the setting sun; and, having crossed the Mississippi, died as he had lived — in the very forefront of civilization.

The attempt, therefore, to write such a book as the present — which is intended to serve the double purpose of a biography of Daniel Boone and a study of the first phase of the territorial growth of the United States — finds ample justification in the facts of Boone's career. On the biographical side the effort has been made not only to give as complete and accurate an account of Boone's life as is now possible, but also to estimate and make clear his specific contributions to the progress of the nation; while on the historical side my chief aim has been to describe the process of expansion in its military, political, economic, and social aspects. This has necessitated a somewhat detailed examination of the characteristics of the people who won the West, and the measures they took — notably in the organization of the Watauga, Transylvania, and Cumberland settlements — to establish the institutions of civilized society in their isolated wilderness communities. But I have endeavored to accomplish this portion of my task without causing the reader to lose sight of the great central figure of the narrative. In any event, I believe that only by gaining an understanding of the life and spirit and ideals of the sturdy folk of the frontier, is it possible to appreciate Boone's place in history and the bearing of the early westward movement on the subsequent development of the United States.

I am, of course, under obligations to previous writers, particularly to Boone's leading biographers, Dr. Reuben Gold Thwaites and Dr. John M. Peck; to the distinguished author of "The Winning of the West"; to the early historians of Kentucky and Tennessee; to the contributors to the excellent Filson Club publications; and to Professor A. B. Hulbert, author of the "Historic Highways of America" series of monographs. I am further indebted to Dr. Thwaites for helpful advice, as also to Professors Edward Channing and Albert Bushnell Hart, of Harvard University, and Colonels Reuben T. Durrett and Bennett H. Young, of Louisville, Kentucky. I would also thank Captain Edward M. Drane, of Frankfort, Kentucky, for assistance in illustrating my book, and Mr. T. Gilbert White, of New York, for permission to reproduce his two beautiful paintings now in the Kentucky State Capitol. Much valuable material to which I could not otherwise have had access — especially in the way of rare copies of early Western newspapers — has been placed at my disposal by the authorities of Harvard University Library, for whose sympathetic cooperation I desire to express sincere gratitude. And, as in all my undertakings, I owe much to the wise counsel and aid of my wife.

H. ADDINGTON BRUCE.

Cambridge, Mass.,
April 4, 1910.

Chapter One - The Youth of Daniel Boone

DANIEL BOONE, as every schoolboy knows, is the typical American backwoodsman. He was never so much at home as when treading the pathless wilderness, rifle in hand, in quest of game or of the pioneer's mortal foe, the wily Indian. Always Boone kept in the forefront of civilization, pointing the way for its advance but never allowing it quite to overtake him. Not city streets, but the mountain, the forest, and the prairie were his habitat. And he came honestly by his unquenchable passion for the wild and open life of the backwoods and the border.

He was born in a log-cabin, remote from the refinements and allurements of civilization; and he had for parents plain, simple country folk, accustomed to hardships and at all times preferring the freedom of the frontier to the crowded, hurried, worried existence of the town. His mother was the daughter of an unassuming Welsh Quaker, John Morgan. His father, who bore the odd name of Squire, was an Englishman by birth, a native of the obscure Devonshire village of Bradninch. Although bred a Quaker, Squire Boone seems to have had in his veins a touch of the longing for excitement and adventure that sent Hawkins and Drake and those other old-time sea-dogs of Devon on their epoch-making voyages. At all events, when scarcely in his teens, he became profoundly interested in reports of the Quaker paradise said to have been established by William Penn on the other side of the Atlantic.

It was unfortunately the case that in England, and even in New England, Quakers were subject to bitter and bloody persecution, and many of them led most wretched lives. In Penn's dominions, on the contrary, according to the story which in time found its way to the farthest corners of the old country, not only were Quaker refugees absolutely free from molestation by religious bigots, but they were on the friendliest of terms with the native Indians, were making the wilderness to blossom like the rose, and were in every way living amid the most delightful surroundings.

His curiosity roused to a high pitch, young Boone one fine day took ship for Philadelphia, in company with a brother, George, and a sister, Sarah. Their immediate object was to verify the rumors they had heard, and to determine for themselves the fitness of Pennsylvania as a place of residence for the entire family, their father having signified his willingness to emigrate if the outlook seemed promising.

To us of to-day this sailing of Squire Boone — whose American-born son was to serve as guide to the American people in the first stage of the wonderful westward march that has carried them to the shore of the Pacific and beyond — cannot but seem a most noteworthy occurrence. Yet history is silent concerning it. The ship that carried the youthful Boones was not a *Mayflower* or a *Susan Constant*. It was simply one of many others employed in the emigrant trade, and even its name and the port of its departure have long since passed into oblivion. Whether the crossing was smooth or rough, whether the Boones enjoyed it or regretted ever having set foot aboard, it is impossible to say. The probability is that they were herded together in unpleasant quarters with a small army of fellow-emigrants, — for people were already flocking to Pennsylvania, — and that they were heartily glad when they saw the low, thin, blue line indicating land ahead. At an uncertain date in the years 1712, 1713, or 1714 their ship swung in between the capes of the Delaware, proceeded up the river, on whose banks were still visible the ruins of Sweden's ill-fated experiment in colonization three-quarters of a century before, and eventually landed the ardent, hopeful Boones in Philadelphia.

It needed only a few months of travel and exploration to convince them that rumor had not unduly exaggerated the beauties and riches and advantages of Pennsylvania. In high good humor brother George hurried back to bring out their father and mother and the younger children; sister Sarah gave a favorable ear to the advances of a matrimonially inclined German, and, as Mrs. Jacob Stover, became the mistress of a rude but perpetually neat cabin home in what is to-day Berks County; while Squire Boone, for his part, roamed with all the restlessness of youth through the country about Philadelphia, eventually choosing for his home the frontier hamlet of North Wales, and settling down to the hard life of a Pennsylvania backwoodsman.

It was in North Wales that he met Sarah Morgan, and it was on the 23d of July, 1720, that they were married in a Quaker meeting-house and in accordance with the simple Quaker ceremony. A family tradition, quoted by Dr. Reuben Gold Thwaites, Daniel Boone's latest and best biographer, pictures Squire Boone as "a man of rather small stature, fair complexion, red hair, and gray eyes"; while his wife was "a woman something over the common size, strong and active, with black hair and eyes."

There was no honeymoon — merely the rough and boisterous yet sincere rejoicings after the backwoods fashion, and then the young couple laid aside their wedding garments, and plunged once more into the business of life. Very poor they were, yet very happy, and their happiness was soon increased — as likewise their cares and responsibilities — by the advent of children, four of whom were born to them during the dozen years they remained in the North Wales country.

At the end of that time Squire Boone had saved enough money to buy a farm of his own, and he decided to remove to Oley Township — in the modern Berks County — where now lived not only his sister Sarah but his parents and several younger brothers and sisters. The Boones, indeed, were sufficiently numerous in that part of Berks to give the name of Exeter to one of its townships, in honor of the ancient Devonshire city that stood only a few miles from their native village.

In Oley Township, then, in the beautiful valley of the Schuylkill, and for what would seem to us a ridiculously small sum. Squire Boone became the owner of a tract of two hundred and fifty acres. Most of it was in woodland, — that is to say, the hardest sort of work would be necessary to make it fit for cultivation, — but Boone's arms were strong and his heart courageous, and with right good-will he began to make a clearing. Erelong the smoke from another cabin was rising above the trees of Oley Township, a token to all who saw it that one more pioneer family had joined in the labor of conquering that portion of the Pennsylvania wilderness.

In this cabin, Nov. 2, 1734, Daniel Boone made his initial appearance on the stage of life. Had he been a first-born his arrival might have been accounted an event, and something made of it. But being only a sixth child, — another had been born since the departure from North Wales, — he was regarded from so distinctly matter-of-fact a point of view that nothing whatever is known with respect to his infancy. It may safely be taken for granted, though, that he was left pretty much to shift for himself as soon as he was able to go about on hands and knees. This was a way pioneer mothers had, and that it was not a bad way is clearly evidenced by the sturdiness of their deer-stalking, Indian-fighting sons.

It may also be reasonably conjectured that the little Daniel's infantile amusements included playing with his father's powder-horn, tugging at his father's rifle as it lay carelessly thrown on a settee after the return from a hunt, or staring fixedly and eagerly at it when it reposed in its accustomed place against the wall. If, as is said, the child is father of the man, these toys must have held Daniel Boone's attention at an unusually early age.

Certainly, he was still a very small boy when he began to give indications of the remarkable fondness for hunting which was characteristic of him even in extreme old age. It is difficult to realize that his birthplace, only a few miles south of the progressive city of Reading, and in the heart of one of Pennsylvania's most populous counties, boasting, as it does, close upon one hundred and seventy-five thousand inhabitants, was in the days of Boone's boyhood a grim, sparsely settled frontier region, abounding in game of every description. Against the smaller sort of creatures — squirrels and chipmunks and birds — he soon declared war, tracking them in imitation of a veteran huntsman, and slaying them with a knob-rooted sapling, which he learned to hurl with remarkable dexterity.

This, too, when he was not more than ten years old. A little later — to be precise, at the age of twelve — his father surprised and delighted him with the gift of a light rifle. Gone forever was the knob-rooted sapling, thrown aside in the exuberance of his joy at this wonderful present. He was a man now, a man full grown, he told himself, for did he not carry the weapon of a man? And he patted its stock fondly, and peered eagerly through the undergrowth in search of some fierce beast of prey to overcome.

In point of sheer fact, for all his feelings of bigness and self-importance, he was just a freckled, barefoot, ragged little urchin, who frequently gave his parents a great deal of trouble by neglecting his duties as herd-boy in order to play Nimrod in the surrounding forest. He, they knew, could take care of himself, but the cattle required attention, and it sometimes was no easy matter to ascertain where they had strayed. But it was impossible long to be angry with him, so intensely earnest was he in his hunting expeditions; and, recognizing this, his parents, instead of scolding him, turned his fondness for hunting to good account by commissioning him to provide the wild meat for the family table. They could have found no occupation more congenial to him, and none better calculated to train him for his life-work. He became an unerring shot, an expert woodsman, acquainted with the ways of furred and feathered life, and schooling himself admirably in many another text-book of nature.

Of schooling as most boys know it, however, he had next to none. The majority of his biographers assert that he went for a time to an "old field" school, where he acquired the rudiments of "book learning" in the form of easy lessons in the spelling-book and Psalter, together with some slight instruction in writing and arithmetic. One author even goes so far as to give imaginary details of his school life, including an obviously fanciful account of a singular and reprehensible trick played by Boone and some fellow-pupils on their schoolmaster, who is described as a worthless drunkard. Of course Virtue, as typified in these fascinating juvenile vagabonds, triumphed over Vice, the learned but dissolute pedagogue.

The truth seems to be that, at all events in the role of scholar, Boone never saw the inside of a schoolroom; but was indebted for such education as he received to his mother and a young sister-in-law, the wife of his much older brother Samuel. Both of these devoted instructors, although they must have found in the restless, nature-loving, active boy a most difficult pupil, took pains enough, as we shall see, to enable him in after-life to write interesting, if badly spelled letters; and to earn his living as a surveyor.

He also received some manual training of a useful sort. His great-grandfather on the paternal side had been a blacksmith, his grandfather — who died in Berks County when Daniel was in his tenth year — a weaver; and both of these occupations were followed by his father as soon as the farm was sufficiently cleared to permit of his devoting some part of his attention to interests other than agricultural. He kept half a dozen looms at work making "homespun" for his neighbors and for the Philadelphia market, and the cheery blaze of his forge was a welcome sight to tired travellers after a day's journey through the forest. As between the two — the loom and the forge — Daniel infinitely preferred the latter; but, we are told, only because it enabled him to repair broken rifles and traps. Everything was subordinated to his zeal for the life out doors, and each succeeding year he awaited with growing impatience the approach of winter as the happy season when he would be free to give full rein to his passion for the chase.

For, from the time he was thirteen he made it his custom to spend every winter hunting. All through Berks County, and far into the forests and mountains beyond, he wandered, exploring the country so thoroughly that for miles roundabout there was scarcely a foot of territory unknown to him. The Blue Mountain and South Mountain ranges became as familiar to him as the undulating hills of his father's Oley farm. Many a day he climbed Penn's Mount, near the site of Reading, and from its summit beheld the snow-laden clouds gather over the far-extending valleys. Sometimes, laden with furs, he journeyed down the Schuylkill to Philadelphia, then a most picturesque little city, with its Tudor cottages, its orchards, its gardens, and its bustling waterfront, where ships were constantly coming and going, bringing in all manner of strange people from foreign parts, and taking out the rich produce of the New World.

Thus his life passed until he reached his sixteenth year — an irresponsible, roaming, care-free life, but in its own way stimulating to ambition and not devoid of achievement. At sixteen there was no better woodsman in all eastern Pennsylvania than Daniel Boone. Thanks to the wise policy of William Penn and his Quaker successors in the governing of Pennsylvania, it had not been necessary for him, while thus serving his apprenticeship in the forest, to match his wits against those of the Indian, as would have been the case had his boyhood been spent in almost any other part of the frontier. He saw plenty of Indians, but they were always friendly. Nevertheless, as though with an instinctive forewarning of what the future had in store for him, he gave himself to a most careful study of their traits and habits.

This — like the pursuit of the deer, the bear, and the wolf — meant hours of patient trailing and of hawk-like watching from the concealment afforded by thicket, log, and stump. It was a fascinating game, — this mimic hunt of unsuspecting warriors, — and it aided immeasurably both in the success that Boone afterwards won as an Indian fighter, and in the formation of his character. It developed in him remarkable powers of observation, it increased his self-confidence and self-reliance, and it accustomed him to the exercise of great self-control.

Still more, it awoke a desire to penetrate to those distant wilds whence the Indians emerged, as by magic, whenever they came to visit the Pennsylvania settlements. To spur the same desire was the knowledge that the game which he was so fond of hunting was rapidly disappearing from Berks County before the advance of civilized man. It is easy, therefore, to understand the satisfaction with which Boone one day heard his father announce his intention of disposing of his Pennsylvania lands and removing to the Yadkin Valley in North Carolina, five hundred miles and more to the southwest, one of the richest farming sections of the colonial South, and, at that time, a veritable paradise for game.

Just why Squire Boone should wish to abandon the pleasant home which he had built up with such painful effort, does not appear. [1] Nor is there anything to show why he chose the distant Yadkin Valley as his future place of abode. But to us these are matters of comparative unimportance. The great point is that the removal was determined on, and that its outcome, in due course of time, was to give Daniel Boone an unsurpassed opportunity to distinguish himself as an explorer and path-finder of the wilderness — an opportunity which it may safely be said would never have been his had he remained in Berks.

Some time in the spring of 1750 the start for North Carolina was made, the caravan of canvas-covered wagons that carried the family of Squire Boone pushing on as rapidly as possible to Harper's Ferry and the Valley of Virginia, that magnificent tableland which extends for three hundred miles between the Blue Ridge and the Alleghanies from the Potomac to the Iron Mountains in the extreme southwest section of the State after which the valley is named. Few details of the journey have been preserved, but it is known that Boone acted as hunter and scout for the caravan, and that the valley's charms proved so attractive that all thoughts of haste were laid aside. There is a story, though based only on tradition, that the travellers camped for many months, perhaps even for a year, on Linnville Creek, near Harrisonburg, in Rockingham County, Virginia. Wherever they lingered, it was not until the late autumn of 1751 that they crossed the Blue Ridge near the dividing line between Virginia and North Carolina and found themselves within striking distance of their destination.

This was reached when they arrived at the forks of the Yadkin, in Davie County, North Carolina. Here, as Squire Boone's practised eye at once perceived, a region of splendid possibilities from a farming standpoint offered itself to all comers; and casting about, he soon selected a claim where Dutchman's Creek empties its waters into the North Yadkin, and once more began the arduous task of conquering the forest and transforming weedy wastes into profitable fields.

As for young Daniel, we may feel confident that whenever the opportunity offered, he would steal away from the wood-chopping and the ploughing to enjoy a day's hunt. Although a century and a half has elapsed since the crack of his rifle first woke the echoes of the Carolina mountains, the Old North State can still offer attractions to the hunter of big game. At the time of Boone's coming it teemed, from the Piedmont region westward, with beasts and birds of every description. The buffalo, the elk, the Virginia deer, the bear, the panther, the wildcat, wolf, and fox wandered through the meadows and cane-brakes about its rivers, or took their repose amid the cool shades of its rocky heights. Here, in truth, as Boone enthusiastically told his father and his more phlegmatic brothers, was hunting worth the name.

In imagination it is no difficult matter to see him, his five foot ten of sinewy, buck-skinned manhood stretched at full length behind a fallen log, finger on trigger, ear alert, blue eyes gleaming, thin lips doggedly compressed, a healthy glow on his cheek. Or, it may be, cutting his way through a tangle of undergrowth, leaping silently from rock to rock across the bed of a fast-running mountain stream, and buoyantly clambering from ridge to ridge of some bristling mountain wall. Never, they say, was there such a hunter on the Yadkin, or one who so enjoyed the hunter's life. Young, ardent, tireless, burdened with few cares and carrying them lightly, Daniel Boone found these first years in North Carolina pleasant indeed.

But the time for a rude awakening was drawing near. All too soon he would have the realities of life thrust upon him, would discover that it is made up of something besides the hunt, the feast, and the frolic. For, while he was light-heartedly tracking the sullen bear to its lair, and merrily dressing the freshly slain venison, the clouds of a terrible war were steadily gathering to sweep at last in a bloody storm along the entire frontier.

[1] It is suggested by Dr. Thwaites that possibly Squire Boone moved from Pennsylvania because "the choicest lands of eastern Pennsylvania had at last been located," and "the outlook for the younger Boones, who soon would need homesteads, did not appear encouraging." But this seems scarcely an adequate explanation, particularly in view of the great fertility of the Schuylkill Valley, which Squire Boone would ordinarily be reluctant to abandon even for the sake of the "younger Boones." Perhaps the inrush of "foreign" immigrants, of the non-English-speaking Dunkards and Mennonites and Schwenckfelders, who flocked into Berks County between the years 1720 and 1750, may have had something to do with his removal. Or there may have been some connection between the removal and the fact that both Squire Boone and his son Israel were "disowned" by the Society of Friends — Squire in 1748, or but two years before his departure to North Carolina. There was by no means a general Boone exodus from the vicinity. I have seen a list of Exeter Township taxables for 1759, and in it occur the names of Joseph, James, William, Benjamin, and John Boone.

Chapter Two - Boone's First Campaign

LATE in the summer of 1754, or about the time Squire Boone and his family were beginning to feel at home in their new surroundings, startling news reached the settlers of the Yadkin Valley. The French, it seemed, had come down from Canada into the Ohio country, and had built forts there, notwithstanding that England laid claim to all that territory. Governor Dinwiddie, of Virginia, the colony most interested in sustaining the English claim, — since, indeed, it had a claim of its own to the Ohio country, based on the terms of its ancient charter, — had sent troops under a young Virginia officer, George Washington, to build forts for England and dislodge any Frenchmen that might be found. There had been a short but spirited conflict. First Washington had surprised, attacked, and defeated a French force. Then he, in turn, had been attacked, overwhelmed by numbers, and compelled to capitulate, being permitted, however, to march his men back to Virginia. To the Yadkin Valley people, and to the English colonists generally, this sounded very much as though war were inevitable.

The prospect was not altogether displeasing to the younger and more reckless and adventurous settlers. But those of mature experience, and particularly the dwellers along the border, viewed it with undisguised alarm. They knew only too well the horrors of a war with the French and their Indian allies — the night attack, the sanguinary raid, the scalpings, the torturings, the burnings. And, as the graybeards among them whispered to one another, the chances were that the impending struggle would outdo in bitterness and violence everything that had preceded it. For it would mean more, far more, than the determination of ownership of the Ohio Valley — it would determine whether England or France was to be the arbiter of the destinies of America, and whether the colonists of England were to remain forever cooped up in the narrow strip of territory between the mountains and the sea, or should be free to pass the mountains and possess themselves of the glorious and almost unoccupied country that lay beyond.

This was the question at issue, a question of peculiar interest to us, studying, as we are, the first phase in the territorial expansion of the American people. When young George Washington fired that first shot of the French and Indian War in the gloomy depths of the trans-Alleghany glades, he rang the curtain up on the last act of one of the most fascinating and tragic dramas of world-history, and a drama that had been in progress long before Washington or any other colonist of Washington's time had seen the light of day. Its opening act — or, more accurately, the prologue to its opening act — dated as far back as the first settlement of America by Englishmen and Frenchmen, and its plot was conditioned from the outset by the radically different motives that brought the English and the French into the New World.

The English, in the vast majority of cases, had crossed the ocean to win homes for themselves in a country where they would be free from the crushing disabilities — the religious persecutions, political discriminations, and economic inequalities — under which they had labored in their native land. The French had been inspired scarcely at all by the homebuilding spirit. Desire to amass wealth, love of adventure, and missionary zeal were their great motives. As a consequence, the two peoples acted very differently when they reached America. The English established themselves in compact settlements along the coast, and began industriously to till the soil. The French gave themselves to exploring and fur-trading, and dispersed far and wide, making friends of the Indians, trafficking with them, and Christianizing them.

In less than a decade after the founding of Quebec, a French missionary friar of the Recollet order was laboring among the Lake Huron savages. Only a few years more, and the daring young Norman, Jean Nicolet, had penetrated as far west as Wisconsin. A little later, and before the close of the first half of the seventeenth century, the black-gowned Jesuits were planting the Cross among the Indians of Sault Ste. Marie. In a word, France was rapidly establishing a title to the ownership of the vast interior region of the North American continent.

All this time the English colonists had made next to no progress so far as territorial expansion was concerned, their "farthest west" as late as 1660 being only a few miles from the coast, in the upper valley of the Connecticut. But, as the authorities in Quebec saw clearly enough, they were rapidly outdistancing the inhabitants of New France in point of population, the increase being at the rate of nearly thirty to one in favor of the English. This meant that, if they continued to increase in the same proportion, it could only be a question of time before they would overflow into territory claimed by France. In fact, there had already been an armed invasion of Arcadia by volunteer soldiers from New England.

Louis XIV., king of France, vigorously attacked the problem thus presented to him, dissolving, in 1663, the colonization company that had hitherto mismanaged the affairs of New France and sending out rulers of his own choosing, men who were, like King Louis himself, zealous to exalt the fleur-de-lis. Chief among these were the famous Talon and the still more famous Frontenac.

Under their leadership there at once began a systematic development of what historians have called the "hinterland movement." It involved nothing less than the exploration and occupation of the entire Mississippi Valley, and the construction of a chain of forts and trading-stations designed to connect the mouth of the Mississippi with the mouth of the St. Lawrence, and to oppose an effectual barrier to the English colonists if they attempted to cross the mountain wall that stretched for hundreds of miles between the coastal strip and the Mississippi country. A beginning, and a magnificent beginning, was made to this ambitious project with the explorations of Marquette and Joliet, La Salle and Tonti, Iberville and Bienville. And at the same time, both to weaken the English and to divert their attention from these inland operations, the rulers of New France embarked on a policy of armed aggression, enlisting the services of Indian allies for a series of murderous border raids.

Thus opened in 1689 the memorable Seventy Years' War. You will not find it under that name in the histories, where it is usually treated as a succession of different wars, called respectively King William's War, Queen Anne's War, King George's War, and the French and Indian War. All these, however, were parts of one and the same conflict, broken by intermittent truces, such as the Peace of Aix-la-Chapelle, which lasted just long enough for the combatants to recover their breath. Up to the French and Indian War the English colonists were, in the main, left to fight their battles by themselves — a circumstance which had not a little to do with weakening their attachment to the mother country. But they more than held their own with the French, and steadily extended their settlements closer to the mountain wall, even venturing upon explorations in the forbidden country on the other side of it. Finally a day came when the supreme trial of strength could no longer be avoided. In

1748, the year of the signing of the Treaty of Aix-la-Chapelle, a company was organized in Virginia for the express purpose of planting an English colony in the Ohio Valley, and in the same year English settlers raised their cabins on the banks of the Greenbrier River in West Virginia, the first of that race to make a home on a west-flowing American stream. At once the French took alarm, and the following year sent a representative, Céloron de Bienville, to traverse the Ohio Valley and take formal possession of it in the name of the king of France, driving out all English settlers and traders encountered by him, and making sure of the allegiance of the native inhabitants. But Céloron's expedition was of little effect, the English traders among the Indian villages of the Ohio paying no attention to his warnings and threats, and the Indians showing themselves for the moment none too well disposed towards the French.

The situation was completely changed, however, by the arrival at Quebec of a new governor, the Marquis Duquesne de Menneville, who brought with him the most positive instructions to vindicate the title to the Mississippi Valley claimed by France by virtue of La Salle's discoveries, and of possession as exemplified in the old French trading-stations in the Illinois country and elsewhere. In accordance with these instructions, Duquesne sent out a body of troops to construct and garrison a number of forts along the alleged boundary-line between the dominions of the two rival Powers. It was this that had occasioned the expedition commanded by Washington, and it was thus that, after more than half a century of indecisive warfare. Frenchman and Englishman at last stood face to face, conscious that the time had arrived for a fight to the death.

All through the winter of 1754-55, following Washington's defeat, there were intimations of the approaching storm. The Ohio Indians, and particularly the Shawnees, showed themselves hostile to the English traders, who promptly took refuge in the older settlements east of the mountains. The Indians of the Valley of Virginia, hitherto, as a rule, on friendly terms with the white settlers, became sullen and treacherous, and ultimately withdrew altogether from the valley, to return to it only as frenzied, blood-thirsting raiders. Here and there, along the border, were occasional outbreaks, swift and sudden descents which left a faint, but still significant, trail of blood and ashes. The Yadkin country, where the Boones dwelt, was practically free from such alarms, for it was only at a later date that the Indians of the South took the war-path in the interests of the French. But with reports of murder and rapine coming to them from none too distant quarters, the settlers along the Yadkin awaited anxiously the news of the raising of a punitive expedition strong enough to suppress the pernicious activities of the French and their Indians.

Among those most ardently hopeful that such an expedition would soon be organized was Daniel Boone. It is said, in fact, that he was so eager to be up and at the enemy that he hurried to Pennsylvania and passed the winter in scout duty on its exposed frontier. This is not impossible, but it is rather unlikely, for it was only on occasions of extreme crisis that the frontiersmen of that time were wont to rally to the protection of a remote locality. They were too well aware that at any moment the foe might strike an unexpected blow at their own homes, and they had no fancy to leave their loved ones at the mercy of the painted savage. This, rather than callous indifference to the sufferings of others, is the true explanation of the absence of united action on the part of the people of the border in times of war — although, it is proper to add, it scarcely suffices to explain the dissension manifest among the colonists generally from the beginning to the end of the Seventy Years' War, and at all times handicapping greatly the operations against the French.

Nor does it altogether explain why North Carolina, when the call finally came for volunteers to aid in avenging Washington's defeat and driving the French back to Canada, sent a scant hundred men to represent her, under the command of Captain Edward B. Dobbs, son of the governor of the province. [1]

With this North Carolina contingent went Daniel Boone. He was then less than twenty-one years old, and was probably the youngest among the entire hundred, nearly all of whom were backwoodsmen like himself. By forced marches the little regiment made its way northward until, some time in May, 1755, it arrived at Fort Cumberland, which had been built only the previous autumn at the juncture, in western Maryland, of Wills Creek and the Potomac River. It was from this point that the punitive expedition planned to march against the French stronghold of Fort Duquesne, at the forks of the Ohio, where Pittsburg stands to-day.

Although the distance from Fort Cumberland to Fort Duquesne was only eighty miles as the crow flies, the way led through an almost trackless wilderness of mountain and forest, river and swamp, so difficult that the French were confident the English could never traverse it.

They did not take into their reckoning the commander chosen to lead the expedition against them, a typical English bull-dog named Edward Braddock, a soldier of many European campaigns, of a brutal and domineering disposition, but conceded even by his enemies to be a man of dauntless courage. General Braddock had been despatched from England with two regiments — the Forty-fourth and the Forty-eighth — for the special purpose of establishing English sovereignty in the valley of the Ohio, and he had already given signal proof of his masterfulness by the way in which he succeeded in wringing troops and supplies from reluctant colonial authorities. [2] His one great defect was a stubborn self-will, so extreme as to render him deaf to suggestions, immovable in his own beliefs and decisions, and incapable, as was fatally demonstrated, of knowing when he was beaten.

It was also unfortunate — though not at all exceptional, for the feeling was shared by almost every English officer who played any prominent part in the French and Indian War — that he betrayed an open contempt for the colonial troops. Besides the two regiments of regulars and a detachment of marines, his wilderness army eventually included volunteers from New York, Maryland, Virginia (four hundred and fifty picked marksmen, under Washington), and the Carolinas. Of these he spoke and wrote in most slighting terms, lamenting that their "slothful and languid disposition renders them very unfit for military service." Naturally, language such as this — and the volunteers doubtless heard its equivalent in blunter phraseology — would not tend to make him a popular commander; nor would the severity with which he drilled them, day after day, in the open space about Fort Cumberland.

Still, being fair-minded men, they unquestionably would set down to his credit his evident desire to make the expedition a success in every particular; and they also would not overlook the fact that he had paid them the compliment of selecting the popular young George Washington as one of his chief staff officers. Besides they saw clearly enough that, whatever his faults, Braddock was of fighting stuff, and could be depended upon to satisfy their desire to come to close grips with the French. So that it is likely they took a more favorable view of him than many who did not know him at all have since done. At any rate, they responded with alacrity when, early in June, the command was given to break camp and begin the march to Fort Duquesne.

It is not necessary to enter into the details of this journey across the mountains, by a path so narrow that a regiment of engineers and woodchoppers had to lead the way and build a road which in after years, under the name of "Braddock's Road," was to become one of the great arteries of communication between the East and the early West. What Is of importance, from our point of view, is to note that Daniel Boone, instead of being allowed to accompany his North Carolina comrades, was compelled to follow humbly in the rear of the long, winding procession, having been assigned to the duties of a wagoner and mechanic, on the strength of his blacksmithing experience. This was not making war as he had dreamed of making it. Yet it had its compensations.

Not the least of these was the opportunity it gave him for long talks with men who, as hunters or traders, had an intimate knowledge of the Indian country beyond the mountains through which Braddock's column was slowly toiling. Most of all he took pleasure in the astonishing tales of a certain John Finley, who, for the sake of barter with the savages, had visited their villages on the Ohio, and had even penetrated into regions more remote. To Boone's eager demand whether good hunting was to be had, Finley replied that the hunting there, particularly in the country south of the Ohio, was the best in the world.

Two years before, he then explained, he had visited this country, and had found it a second Garden of Eden, blessed with the richest of soils and the balmiest of climates, with noble forests and luxuriant expanses, where thousands of buffalo and other big game browsed. The Indians called this wonderful country "Kentucky," and preserved it as a hunting-ground nominally open to all. So bitter, though, were the tribal animosities and jealousies that as often as not hunting-parties were transformed into war-parties at a moment's notice, and Kentucky became the scene, not of a hunt, but of a battle. Hence, for all its beauty, it was a dark and bloody land, and one where the white man would instantly be deemed an interloper. Finley himself, it appeared, had been obliged to return to the settlements sooner than he desired, because of the evident resentment of the Indians at his having dared to visit Kentucky.

Fascinated, Boone absorbed his companion's word-pictures. Neither of them realized that, as they trudged along side by side, or chatted together in the quiet of the evening, they were making history of a world-wide interest. Not for a moment did they dream that their chance meeting in Braddock's ill-starred campaign was to be the means of bringing one of them imperishable renown. They only knew that they had taken a warm liking to each other, and that in Kentucky they had found a theme of mutual interest. Both of them were young, confident, and high-spirited. The daring of Boone found counterpart in the Scotch-Irish ardor of Finley. And thus it came about that from discussing Kentucky they passed to planning a journey to it. From North Carolina, Finley told Boone, it could be reached by an Indian trail that ran northwestward until it left the mountains at Cumberland Gap. There was yet another route by canoe down the Ohio River to the mouth of a stream which itself bore the name of Kentucky and watered the delectable land. Perhaps after the French had been driven from Fort Duquesne they might find opportunity to voyage to Kentucky by the river route.

In this, however, as they were all too soon made aware, they were doomed to bitter disappointment. The farther Braddock's expedition advanced, the slower its progress became, until the stern-faced backwoodsmen themselves began to fear that the goal would never be reached, and that the confidence of the French in the inaccessibility of their position would be justified. But Braddock, bull-dog Braddock, refused to turn back. For once, though, he listened to the advice of others, and on Washington's suggestion split his column in two, leaving the less able-bodied troops to act as a reserve. Thus relieved, he again pushed towards Fort Duquesne, but still at so slow a pace that Washington, burning with impatience as well as with a fever which had for a time totally incapacitated him, afterwards complained that instead of proceeding vigorously "they were halting to level every mole-hill, and to erect bridges over every brook, by which means we were four days in getting twelve miles."

Nevertheless, the very fact that he was able to advance his troops the twelve miles, was sufficient proof that Braddock was accomplishing what many had declared to be impossible. In Fort Duquesne the news of his approach caused great dismay. Expected reenforcements had failed to arrive, and the commandant, Contrecoeur, could see no way to avoid a surrender, especially after the discovery that his Indians were panic-stricken at the enemy's successful passage of the mountains. There was no use, he told himself, in offering resistance; he would simply be overwhelmed.

Thoroughly despondent, he shook his head hopelessly when one of his young captains, a daredevil named Beaujeu, asked leave to take troops and Indians, and make a last-ditch stand against the English, then less than ten miles from the fort. The Indians, Contrecoeur feared, would not lend their aid, and he had no wish to see his garrison cut to pieces.

But Beaujeu was as shrewd as he was brave. Donning savage costume, painting himself, and throwing an Indian gorget about his neck for good luck, he visited the encampment where the red men were gloomily awaiting the capitulation.

"Brothers," cried he, "I am told that you refuse to march with me against the enemy. But I will face the foe, even if I must go alone. And that, I know, you will never suffer. Come! Up and follow me!"

For a moment, silence. Then a mad outburst of shouts and cheers. If it be true, as has been said, that the great Ottawa war lord, Pontiac, was at Fort Duquesne that day, there is no need to seek further for the first chieftain to respond to Beaujeu's gallant appeal.

Headlong down the narrow trail to the Monongahela the young captain raced at top speed, followed by a motley host of Indians, Canadians, and French regulars, some eight hundred in all. It was then high noon of the 9th of July. Between two and three o'clock on the upland trail in the midst of the Turtle Creek ravine, they encountered the English.

Beaujeu, coming unexpectedly on Braddock's engineers, who were busy at their road-building, stopped short and waved his hat. Instantly the Indians, leaping to this side and that, buried themselves in the dense thickets that encumbered the trail. Then, as the retreating engineers and the advancing main body of the English came together in a confused mass on the narrow trail, the rain of bullets began — thick, fast, deadly.

In vain Braddock tried to form his men for a charge that should clear the underbrush of the hidden foe. The first attack had completely disorganized his regulars; while the colonial troops, skilled Indian fighters all, had instinctively broken ranks and begun fighting from cover. Braddock's men, falling like leaves in an autumn gale, sought to profit by their example; but Braddock himself, notwithstanding the expostulations of Washington, beat them back into the open with the flat of his sword, vainly urging them to form and charge.

He was demanding the unattainable. Time and again, in little squads that offered a splendid target to the French and Indian marksmen, the redcoats plunged into the ravine, many of them never more to retrain the trail.

Beaujeu had fallen almost at the first fire, but now there were many eager to take his place, and the allies did not lack for leadership. Braddock, for his part, was here, there, and everywhere, until at last he too dropped with a mortal wound. Sir Peter Halket, second in command, lay dead, with the corpse of his son lying across his own. Still the rain of bullets continued, and still the doomed army battled magnificently in a vain effort to stave off the inevitable. When, however, late in the afternoon, the retreat was ordered, a natural reaction set in; and, seized with an insane panic, the survivors fled back to the reserves.

Beyond the Monongahela, which was recrossed by but a pitiful fraction of the advance column, there was no pursuit; but still they fled. And, their terror infecting the reserves, the panic grew, until finally all the remnants of Braddock's beaten army were in full flight, stumbling and staggering along the rugged road towards the protecting stockade of Fort Cumberland.

What Daniel Boone was doing all this time, we have no means of knowing. But now, for a moment, we catch a glimpse of him among the fugitives, on the back of one of his wagon-horses, galloping at top speed. It was hardly a glorious ending to his first campaign, and his bitterness and chagrin can readily be imagined. Yet he would have found ample consolation could he but have pierced the veil of the future and beheld the notable events, growing directly or indirectly out of this disastrous experience, in which he was to fill the leading role.

[1] It has been quite generally believed that there were two companies from North Carolina in the Braddock expedition, one under Dobbs, and another under Captain Hugh Waddell, but as Mr. G. A. Ashe has shown in his recently published "History of North Carolina," Waddell's company did not join Braddock, but served as a guard along the North Carolina frontier.

[2] Until recently it has been customary to sneer at Braddock and abuse him unsparingly, placing at his door all responsibility of the crushing defeat in the Turtle Creek ravine. But modern research has made it clear that had it not been for colonial backwardness in cooperating with him, history might have had an altogether different story to tell. Explicit instructions had been sent by the Home Government, requiring the raising of troops and money, the procuring of supplies, and the opening of roads, prior to Braddock's arrival in America. So little attention was paid to these instructions that Braddock was obliged to organize the expedition practically single-handed. This meant a loss of much valuable time.

Chapter Three - Dark Days on the Border

THE immediate result of Braddock's defeat was to expose the frontier to all the horrors of Indian warfare. Colonel Dunbar, who had succeeded to the command, in the face of frantic protests by the frontiersmen of Virginia, Maryland, and Pennsylvania, hurried his surviving regulars from Fort Cumberland to comfortable quarters in Philadelphia, and left the savage allies of the French at liberty to harass and plunder the outlying settlements. Only George Washington, then as ever a heroic figure in the annals of the country, remained to organize the unhappy border folk into some semblance of an effective military force.

Braddock's Road, which it had been so fondly hoped would prove a highway to the mastery of the Ohio Valley, now formed a dread line of communication between the victorious French and the helpless settlers. At an early day following the disaster in the ravine, the commandant of Fort Duquesne could truthfully report that he had destroyed the border settlements over a tract of country thirty leagues wide, reckoning from the line of Fort Cumberland, and that the villages of his Indians were full of prisoners.

Even in the extreme South — that is, in the Carolinas and Georgia — there were rumors that the native tribes, and more especially the Cherokees, were growing restive, and were likely to take the war-path at any time. This led to the building of several stockaded forts of the type which Mr. James Lane Allen has aptly called "rustic castles." Both rustic and castle-like they looked, with their stout, sharply pointed, twelve-foot palisades and their three-storied blockhouses. One, Fort Prince George, stood on the upper waters of the Savannah River, near its source; another. Fort Loudon, on the Little Tennessee, about thirty miles from the present town of Knoxville; a third. Fort Dobbs, not far below the forks of the Yadkin. These three forts guarded the approach from the southwest, and all of them were garrisoned to a fair strength. After which, the Southern borderers quietly awaited the development of events.

Soon, nothing untoward occurring, they resumed their pastoral mode of life, cultivating their farms and herding their sheep and cattle as usual. To this the Yadkin Valley settlers, Daniel Boone among them, — for he had returned home immediately after the fatal ending of the Braddock campaign, — proved no exception. Boone himself, with an unwonted energy and steadfastness, lent a hand in the daily tasks of his father's farm, ploughing, seeding, and harvesting with the utmost diligence. For the present, chastened by his experiences with Braddock, he had lost all disposition to roam, and if he still secretly cherished the dreams that had been inspired by Finley's romantic stories, he rigorously subdued them. Besides, he was now urged to earnest effort by the greatest of human motives, for he had fallen in love.

In the Yadkin settlements, at the forks of the Yadkin, and thus quite near the Boone homestead, lived a Scotch-Irish family of Bryans, a simple, primitive people, of strong passions and big hearts. Among the younger Bryans was a black-eyed, rosy-cheeked lass named Rebecca, who made a conquest of Daniel Boone almost at first sight. She was only fifteen when they plighted their troth, and but two years older when Daniel's father, in his capacity of justice of the peace, read the service that made them man and wife. For a time they found a home in a rude cabin on the Boone farm, but before long Daniel set up a cabin of his own on land a few miles distant. Here, the following year, a son, James, was born to them; and two years afterwards another son, whom they named Israel.

Meanwhile the proud husband and father toiled like the proverbial beaver, sowing and reaping his crops, raising livestock, hunting wild animals for the sake of their meat and furs, and occasionally adding to his always meagre income by serving as a wagoner in one of the caravans that from time to time wound through the foot-hills to the markets of the coast, where the backwoods products were exchanged for salt and iron and other necessaries. Some smithing he did also, and possibly took his turn at the loom, as he had done in the by-gone days of his boyhood in Pennsylvania.

Thus he passed his time, happily and hopefully, if laboriously, until the early spring of 1759, the year which before its close witnessed the historic battle on the Plains of Abraham, when Wolfe, by the conquest of Quebec, sounded the death-knell of French authority in America. All through the winter there had been signs that the Carolina frontiers could not expect much longer to escape the fury of the Indians. In 1758 the Cherokees, instigated by French emissaries and also influenced by a well-grounded fear that the English intended some day to possess themselves of the tribal lands on the Little Tennessee, had gone raiding in the Valley of Virginia with deadly results. In April, 1759, they forced an entrance into the fertile Yadkin and Catawba valleys, destroyed crops, burned cabins, murdered settlers, and dragged their wives and children into a cruel captivity.

So sudden and severe was the blow that the stricken people had no opportunity to rally for an organized resistance, much less undertake an offensive campaign. Abandoning their farms, they hastened for shelter to the strong stockade of Fort Dobbs, or to hurriedly constructed "houses of refuge"; or else, if they could possibly find the means to do so, fled with all their belongings to the settlements in the tide-water country. This was the course followed by the Boones, or at least by Squire Boone, his son Daniel, and their respective families. Squire, it is said, went to Maryland. Daniel took Rebecca and their infant children to eastern Virginia, where he found employment at his old occupation of wagoner.

It was not in his nature, however, to remain in a stranger's land, and leave to others the task of defending his hearth and home. So soon as he had satisfied himself that his little family would not be exposed to want, he returned to the border, where he found thrilling events in progress. The Cherokees had laid a desperate siege to Fort Dobbs, but had been gallantly beaten off by its garrison under the command of Colonel Hugh Waddell, one of the foremost Indian fighters of his day. They had then renewed their depredations in small war-parties, ultimately gathering in force to attack Fort Prince George.

In the meantime a British army officer, Colonel Montgomery, had organized a strong punitive expedition. It included two regiments of regulars, fresh from their victories in Canada, and several hundred Carolina backwoodsmen, led by Waddell. With Waddell went Daniel Boone. A swift march to Fort Prince George resulted in its instant relief, and the destruction of a number of Cherokee villages in the country round about it. At one of these.

Little Keowee, the troops effected a night surprise, and tradition has it that not one of the warriors found there was left alive. Then Montgomery hurried his soldiers across the mountains, resolved to deal a decisive blow to the more important Indian towns on the Little Tennessee.

But he had underestimated the desperate valor of the Cherokees, now fighting for their very existence. Although the English column was almost two thousand strong, they did not hesitate to lay an ambush for it. Beneath the fragrant laurels and behind the mossy rocks of a steep mountain road they hid themselves, while their spies kept them constantly informed of the approach of the unsuspecting soldiers. Not a rifle cracked, not a war-whoop was heard until the invaders were well within the trap set for them. Then, at a signal, a sheet of flame burst from the verdant roadside, and exultant shouts from six hundred savage throats went echoing down the narrow gorge.

It was a complete surprise — far more of a surprise than that experienced by poor Braddock. But, rallying his men, many of whom had fallen dead or wounded at the first volley, Montgomery fought bravely for a full hour. The Indians, no less brave, and having the advantage of knowing every inch of the ground, were not to be shaken off, but hung like leeches to the flanks of the stricken column, which at last was forced to retreat back to Fort Prince George, dogged every step of the way by the triumphant and vindictive Indians.

Nothing but the poor marksmanship of the Cherokees, and the courageous rear-guard defence of Waddell's borderers, averted a disaster comparable with that sustained by Braddock. As it was, Montgomery lost twenty men killed and seventy-six badly wounded; and, abandoning all thought of further chastising the savages, marched his regulars from Fort Prince George to Charleston, whence he presently embarked with them for New York. Once more the frontier of Georgia and the Carolinas lay at the mercy of the copper-colored foe.

But instead of following up this advantage, and immediately plundering and ravaging as before, the Cherokees first of all turned their attention to the conquest of Fort Loudon, which stood a solitary English outpost in the very heart of the Cherokee country and one hundred and fifty miles from the nearest white settlement. For some weeks the garrison, which numbered in all two hundred regular soldiers, made a determined resistance; but the surrender of the fort was ultimately forced by the failure of the food supply. It was stipulated that the soldiers should be allowed to march out under arms, and proceed unmolested to Fort Prince George or to the Virginia settlements, whichever they preferred. Nevertheless, when only fifteen miles from Fort Loudon, they were attacked by the Cherokees, and either killed or taken prisoner. Accounts differ as to the loss of life, the estimates ranging from thirty to two hundred slain.

Whatever the exact figure, this most treacherous massacre proved the undoing of the Cherokees, for it aroused the colonial authorities to the necessity of taking drastic measures to stem the Indian tide that now threatened to engulf every outlying settlement. A joint invasion of the Cherokee country was decided on by the governors of Virginia, North Carolina, and South Carolina, and by June of 1761 two armies were on the march. One, consisting chiefly of Scotch regulars and South Carolina militia, and commanded by a Highlander, Colonel James Grant, advanced against the towns on the Little Tennessee by way of Fort Prince George. The other approached the same destination from the north, and was composed of Virginia and North Carolina backwoodsmen under Colonels Byrd and Waddell. In this second army Boone again found a place, serving once more under the valiant Waddell. But he was destined on this occasion to witness little or no fighting, for Grant anticipated Byrd and Waddell in meeting the Cherokees, whom he fought on the very battle-ground where Montgomery had been so disastrously repulsed the previous year.

Establishing themselves on a hill, the Indians for three hours successfully resisted every attempt at dislodgment, and at the same time numbers of them harassed the army by a galling fire from the bushes and rocks. For a while it almost seemed as though their bravery would be rewarded with another victory. But at eleven o'clock — the engagement having begun at eight in the morning of June 11 — they suddenly gave way, and a running battle followed until two in the afternoon with little damage to either side. All told, indeed, the loss to the whites was only between fifty and sixty men killed and wounded, while the Indians suffered little more severely. Still the battle was in the truest sense a "decisive" one.

It taught the Cherokees that their only safety lay in making peace as quickly as possible. Submitting to Grant, they submitted also to Byrd and Waddell, and after some tedious negotiations a treaty of amity was signed on Nov. 19. By its provisions the Cherokees were to remain in possession of their ancestral lands, and were to cease from troubling the whites for all time to come — or, to put it in the poetic phraseology of Indian treaty makers, they were to "keep the chain of friendship bright so long as rivers flow, grasses grow, and sun and moon endure."

It was a noteworthy treaty, ending a noteworthy war. Hewatt and Ramsay and other early historians have described this struggle between the Cherokee and the Carolinian as one among "the last humbling strokes given to the expiring power of France in North America." It was that, and it was more, since it had an important bearing on the opening up of the unoccupied country west of the mountains. As has been stated. Fort Loudon was situated one hundred and fifty miles in advance of the nearest white settlement. Between it and the Carolina borders lay a difficult but fertile expanse of mountain and valley practically unexplored prior to the Cherokee War. The successive campaigns of Montgomery, Grant, Byrd, and Waddell revealed this territory in all its richness, proved that it was not so inaccessible as had generally been supposed, and aroused in many frontiersmen the desire to make their homes in a region where nature's gifts were so bountiful.

Consequently, after the signing of the Cherokee Treaty, and the more far-reaching Treaty of 1763, by which France formally relinquished her American claims, there was great activity along the southwest frontier. Settlements became more numerous in the Valley of Virginia and the Piedmont section of the Carolinas, there was a constant edging westward by the more daring pioneers, and hunting parties for the first time penetrated the mountain fastnesses in which the buffalo and bear and deer had taken refuge from the oncoming wave of civilization.

In this mid-mountain hunting no one was so conspicuous as Daniel Boone. The Cherokee campaigning had reawakened all his latent passion for adventure, and although he brought his family back to the Yadkin as soon as peace had been made sure, he found it impossible to resume the humdrum life of the stay-at-home farmer. More than ever he relied on the products of the chase to supply him with a livelihood, and since game had become scarce in the Yadkin Valley, he of necessity, as well as choice, embarked on long and perilous hunting-trips. As early as 1760 he was threading his way through the Watauga wilds, where the first settlement in Tennessee was afterwards established. [1] In 1761, at the head of a hunting-party which crossed the Alleghanies that year, "came Daniel Boone from the Yadkin, in North Carolina, and travelled with them as low as the place where Abingdon now stands, and there left them."

Three years later he was once more in the Tennessee country. It was on this occasion that he is reported to have cried, while gazing from a Cumberland Mountain peak at a herd of buffalo grazing below: "I am richer than the man mentioned in scripture, who owned the cattle on a thousand hills — I own the wild beasts of more than a thousand valleys!"

In the following year — 1765 — he actually carried his explorations as far south as Florida, and almost made up his mind to settle at Pensacola. Had he done so, the chances are that nothing more would have been heard of him. Assuredly, he would never have won fame as the great pilot of the early West. But, dissuaded by his wife, he abandoned this plan, and once more gave himself whole-heartedly to the pursuit of the big game of the mountain ranges.

Sometimes he took with him his oldest son, James, then a boy of eight. More frequently he journeyed in absolute solitude, pressing restlessly forward on the trail of the retreating beasts of prey. Always, he noted, this led him towards the west; and erelong there recurred to his mind the glowing tales he had heard from the trader Finley in the sad days of Braddock's campaign. It must be to Kentucky, the hunter's paradise, that the wild animals were fleeing. He had vowed to visit Kentucky. Now, if ever, while the Indians were at peace with the whites, was the time to fulfil that vow.

But, as he soon discovered, it was no easy matter to reach Kentucky. In the autumn of 1767 he made his first start, accompanied by a friend named Hill and, it is thought, by his brother, Squire Boone, named after their brave old father who had died two years before. The route followed was from the Yadkin to the valleys of the Holston and Clinch, and thence to the head waters of the West Fork of the Big Sandy. Boone's plan was to strike the Ohio, and follow it to the falls of which Finley had told him. But they had only touched the eastern edge of Kentucky when they were snow-bound and compelled to go into camp for the winter. Attempting to renew their journey in the spring, they found the country so impenetrable that they soon abandoned all idea of entering and exploring it by that route, and made their way back to the Yadkin, laden with the spoils of the winter's hunting.

Whether, if left to himself, Boone would again have endeavored to find a way into Kentucky, there is no means of knowing. But just at this juncture, and guided, it would seem, by the finger of Fate, there unexpectedly appeared in the Yadkin Valley the one man best calculated to hold him to his purpose — the trader, John Finley.

[1] Until a few years ago there stood on the bank of Boone's Creek, a tributary of the Watauga River, a beach tree bearing on its time-incrusted bark a hunting-knife inscription which testified that "D. Boon cilled a bar on this tree in the year 1760."

Chapter Four - Boone's explorations in Kentucky

WITH the advent of John Finley in the Yadkin Valley that part of Boone's career which really belongs to history may be said to have begun. He was then in his thirty-fifth year, and, as the reader will have perceived, had as yet done little in the way of actual achievement. Two of the three military campaigns in which he had taken part had been miserable failures, and for the rest his life had been spent in a desultory way, differing only in degree from that of hundreds of other young borderers.

Yet his roaming and hunting, his incessant wandering, and his attentive studying of the ways of nature had constituted the best of apprenticeships for his future labors. And it is precisely because of this that such emphasis has been laid in the preceding pages on the events of what may fairly be called his probationary period.

He found Finley enthusiastic as ever with regard to Kentucky, and entirely willing to act as guide to an exploring party. It was then too late in the year to attempt to cross the mountains, but Boone promised himself an early start with the coming of spring, and at once began to seek among his neighbors for fellow-travellers. In this he had the efficient cooperation of Finley, who remained on the Yadkin all winter as Boone's guest, and contrived to make the long winter evenings pass most pleasantly with stories of his own adventures in the forests and canebrakes of Kentucky. Added to the effect of such tales, from the standpoint of securing volunteers for the enterprise, was the fact that the dwellers along the Yadkin, in common with many of their fellow-settlers throughout the Piedmont region of North Carolina, were growing restless and discontented under conditions which presently led to an outbreak of civil war.

There had been a rapid increase in population since the close of the Cherokee War, and with the newcomers had appeared not merely the farmer and hunter and trader but also the tax-collector. Corrupt officials and cunning lawyers preyed upon the simple frontiersmen until, driven to desperation by a sense of wrongs which the courts seemed unwilling to correct, the men of the border united in an armed protest known in history as the War of the Regulation. This is not the place to give a narrative of its tumultuous events, [1] but it is important to recognize the influence it exercised on the opening up of the West. It made men eager to hazard the perils of the remote wilderness, in preference to remaining in settled communities where injustice was rampant. Especially did it contribute to the first settlement of Tennessee. And, although its crisis had not been reached at the time of Finley's sojourn with Boone, the situation had become sufficiently acute to account for the readiness with which volunteers stepped forward in response to Boone's appeal.

Among those offering their services was Boone's brother, Squire. It was wisely determined, however, that he should remain at home to harvest his own and Daniel's crops, and should then follow them across the mountains with fresh horses and an additional supply of ammunition. As finally selected the exploring party included Finley, Boone, a brother-in-law of Boone's named John Stuart, and three other Yadkin settlers, Joseph Holden, James Mooney, and William Cooley.

All six were resolute, hardy men, expert shots, and equal to every emergency. With the exception of Finley, it is believed that they were all men of family, but there is nothing to show that their wives raised any objection to their departure on a journey which, under the most favorable conditions, was certain to prove more or less perilous. They were true border women, at a moment's notice capable of "playing the man for their people." They relied implicitly on their husbands' good judgment, and were ever ready to adopt any course of action that promised to mitigate the hardships of frontier existence.

On the 1st of May, 1769 — a truly memorable May Day in the annals of American exploration — the start was made from the Yadkin. [2] Each man was mounted on a good horse, and led a second horse equipped with that useful if rude contrivance, the pack-saddle. Each was well armed, and dressed in the regulation garb of the frontiersman — deerskin shirt and trousers, light cap and moccasins, and belt bristling with tomahawk, hunting-knife, powder-horn, and bullet-pouch. Picturesque, indeed, they must have looked, as they turned in their saddles, to wave a farewell, and then disappeared, one after another, at a bend in the road.

Overhead, the sun beamed down upon them with the genial warmth of spring; beneath, babbling merrily away in a blossom-hidden gorge, a mountain brook cheerily wished them good luck; while all about them a companionable whispering came from the forest trees, fresh and lusty in their new garbs of green. As the travellers may well have told one another, it was a glorious morning for the commencement of a glorious enterprise.

But much of gloom and rigor lay before them. Not many miles, and they were compelled to turn from the beaten road and follow winding, scarcely discernible Indian paths along the ridges and through the valleys of the North Carolina mountains. And soon history itself loses sight of them. Boone, in the curious "autobiography" which the first Kentucky historian, John Filson, [3] wrote for him, simply says that "after a long and fatiguing journey through a mountainous wilderness, in a westward direction," they found themselves on the Red River in Kentucky. From other sources it is gathered that their route lay across the Blue Ridge and Stone and Iron mountains, and through the valleys of the Holston and the Clinch into Powell's Valley, where they discovered Finley's promised trail through Cumberland Gap, and, following it, came at last into Kentucky.

Once there, they quickly realized that it was all that Finley had painted it. "We found everywhere," Boone told Filson, "abundance of wild beasts of all sorts. The buffalo were more frequent than I have seen cattle in the settlements, browsing on the leaves of the cane, or cropping the herbage on these extensive plains, fearless, because ignorant of the violence of man. Sometimes we saw hundreds in a drove, and the numbers about the salt springs were amazing." And, according to Filson, he added in a rhapsody of enthusiasm: —

"One day I undertook a tour through the country, and the diversity and beauties of nature I met with ...expelled every gloomy and vexatious thought. Just at the close of day the gentle gales retired, and left the place to the disposal of a profound calm. Not a breeze shook the most tremulous leaf. I had gained the summit of a commanding ridge, and, looking round with astonishing delight, beheld the ample plains, the beauteous tracts below. On the other hand I surveyed the famous river Ohio, that rolled in silent dignity, marking the western boundary of Kentucky w4th inconceivable grandeur. At a vast distance I beheld the mountains lift their venerable brows, and penetrate the clouds."

These, it is as well to point out, are Boone's words only as they have come down to us in the peculiar phraseology of Filson. But they depict accurately enough the profound impression made on the simple frontiersman and his companions by the magnificent scenery of Kentucky and the numerous evidences of its great natural wealth. Journeying leisurely along the so-called

Boone's First Glimpse of Kentucky
From the painting by T. Gilbert White, in the Kentucky State Capitol.

"Warriors' Path," — a rough highway opened up by Indian war-parties in their movements back and forth between the Ohio country and the villages of the South, — the explorers before the end of June established a permanent camp on a tributary of the Kentucky River in what is now Estill ^Jounty. Then, being practical men, and having a keen desire to profit as much as possible from their daring venture, they at once started hunting.

Swiftly the days passed, and with each succeeding day their store of furs grew larger, so abundant and unwary was the game. The hunter's paradise of their dreams had, in truth, become a reality. But they were fated to learn that, as Finley had warned Boone when he first told him about Kentucky, it was not altogether without its evils. Indian "signs" began to multiply, and more than mere "signs."

It was the custom of the adventurers to hunt singly or in couples, and as a general thing Boone and his brother-in-law, Stuart, paired together. One day they left camp as usual, intending to explore the country along the banks of the Kentucky. All went well until just before sunset when, as they were about to ascend a small hill, they found themselves surrounded by a band of Shawnees, who evidently had been watching them for some time from the shelter of a thick cane-brake. They were given no chance to defend themselves, but were seized, hurled to the ground, and pinioned securely.

Among the Shawnees was one who could speak a little English, and by him the captives were presently informed that they must guide the Indians to their camp. In the hope, perhaps, that their comrades would effect a rescue they complied, but such was the cunning of the Shawnees that Finley and the rest were taken prisoners as Boone and Stuart had been, without striking a blow. Unable to resist, but protesting vigorously, they watched the Indians plunder the camp of everything it held — furs, provisions, horses, traps, rifles, and ammunition. They were told that they were trespassing on land which belonged exclusively to the red men, and which the latter were determined to keep forever as their own; and they were warned that did they venture to set foot in it again, their lives would pay the penalty. After which, to their infinite relief, they were released, given just enough food to carry them back to the settlements, and ordered to leave Kentucky at once.

It was Finley's advice that they should take the hint, and make the best of their way over the mountains; and in this Cooley and Mooney and Holden concurred. But Boone and Stuart, infuriated at the idea of returning poorer than they had left home, bluntly refused to flee. They intended, they said, to make an effort to recover their property; and, after a cautious pursuit, they actually succeeded in entering the Shawnee camp and making away with four horses. Two days later, the Shawnees having given chase as soon as they missed the horses, Boone and his brother-in-law were captives once more.

There was no talk now of releasing them. On the contrary they were given to understand that they would be taken to the Shawnee villages on the Scioto River, in the Ohio country, and there punished as their temerity and ingratitude deserved. But for the time being they were not treated unkindly, and Boone's active mind was soon revolving projects for escape. In his boyhood, as will be remembered, he had made a careful study of Indian characteristics, and his experiences in the Tennessee mountains, during and after the Cherokee War, had rounded out his knowledge so completely that there were few so well equipped as he to outwit the wiliest of savages. Bidding Stuart keep up his courage and do nothing to irritate the Shawnees, Boone strove earnestly to win their confidence. Soon, so artfully did he work upon them, their watchfulness relaxed, and the prisoners were granted an unusual degree of liberty.

Thus seven days passed. On the night of the seventh day, having decided that the attempt at escape must be made before crossing the Ohio, Boone waited until he was sure that every Indian in camp had fallen asleep. Then, creeping along the ground so cautiously that not a twig snapped beneath him, he gently aroused Stuart, who, like the Shawnees, was slumbering soundly. Together, and keeping well out of the glow of the camp-fire, the two plucky backwoodsmen secured rifles, bullets, and powder, and, their moccasined feet making never a sound, vanished ghost-like into the darkness of the surrounding cane-brake.

Meanwhile Finley, Cooley, Mooney, and Holden were homeward bound, convinced that Boone and Stuart had perished in their rash attempt. At the same time Squire Boone, in company with a hunter named Neely, whom he had accidentally encountered while crossing the mountains, was hurrying westward along the Warriors' Path, bringing with him horses and supplies, as had been agreed. Not far from Cumberland Gap the two parties met, and Squire learned from Finley the news of the supposed death of Boone and Stuart. It was decided to return East without delay, and East all six would undoubtedly have gone but for the sudden and welcome arrival of the two fugitives, who staggered into camp one day, weary and famished and in tatters. [4]

Exhausted though he was, Boone's spirit remained unbroken. The glamour of the wilderness was full upon him, and moreover he had no desire of returning empty-handed after his year on the Kentucky. So soon as he learned of Squire Boone's presence with the new equipment, he declared his intention of hastening back to lay in another store of furs. To this. Squire, scarcely less adventurous than Daniel himself, gave a ready assent; and Neely, too, expressed his cordial approval, as did Stuart. But Finley protested that, for the present, he had had enough of Kentucky — the Indians were aroused and angered, and might at any time fall upon them. This was the view of the others, who continued homeward with Finley, while the Boones, Stuart, and Neely were soon afterwards building a new camp not far from the scene of the recent adventure.

It would have been well for one of them had he taken Finley's advice and abandoned an enterprise which had thus far proved most unprofitable. As before, Daniel Boone and Stuart hunted together, frequently separating during the day to meet at nightfall at some appointed rendezvous. One evening, shortly after their return to the Kentucky, Stuart failed to appear, and he was still missing at sunrise. Boone, greatly alarmed, began a search for him, and before night came upon the embers of a fire not more than a day old.

But he could find no other trace of his brother-in-law, and Neely and Squire Boone were equally unsuccessful when they joined in the hunt. Reluctantly it was concluded that Stuart had either been killed by Indians, or had accidentally shot himself. He was too good a backwoodsman, as they were well aware, to lose his way. Five years afterwards, but not until then, the mystery of his disappearance was partially cleared when Boone, while on a hunting trip in the same vicinity, discovered in a hollow sycamore tree a few human bones and a powder-horn marked with Stuart's name. But he did not require this long-hidden evidence to convince him that Stuart had indeed perished — the first, as Roosevelt has put it in his "The Winning of the West," of the thousands of human beings with whose life-blood Kentucky was bought.

Soon afterwards Neely started home, satisfied with his share of the winter's hunting. This left the two Boones alone in the wilderness. Only a little later, and but one Boone remained in it — the indomitable Daniel. Their ammunition had become almost exhausted, and they had decided that Squire should go home with the horses, dispose of the furs they had already collected, and return with the means for further hunting. On the first of May, a year to a day since the departure from the Yadkin, Squire silently wrung his brother's hand, swung himself into the saddle, and set off down the lonesome Warriors' Path.

It has been charged that Daniel Boone, in thus electing to hold himself remote from kith and kin, and lead a solitary existence among the Kentucky cane-brakes, displayed a singular lack of human sympathy, and still more a callous disregard for the feelings of his wife and children. As a matter of fact, though not an emotional man he was devotedly attached to his family, and it was out of regard to their interests, as well as in accord with his characteristic fondness for the untrammelled life of the forest, that he permitted his brother to travel alone to the Yadkin.

Both the Boones had been obliged to go into debt to equip themselves for the expedition; and the furs which Squire took with him would only in part discharge their indebtedness. By remaining in Kentucky Daniel would save time and money in many ways. He could not, to be sure, do much hunting, for he would have to be careful of his ammunition until Squire returned; but he could keep things shipshape at the camp, repair rifles, mend traps, and otherwise occupy himself to good purpose.

Most important of all, he would have leisure to make extensive explorations during the best season for studying the topography and resources of Kentucky. If he had not done so before, Boone had by this time definitely determined to remove his family from North Carolina to this glorious land of enchantment, where, as he phrased it, "a man might have elbow-room and breathing-space." It did not need a prophet to predict that before many years Kentucky, although as yet quite unoccupied, would become a seat of white settlement. As early as 1754, or the year of Washington's capitulation to the French, pioneer families had ventured across the Alleghanies and established homes on a river in northwestern Virginia. In the Southwest the limits of white habitation had been extended to Powell's Valley, in the shadow of the Cumberland Mountains. The conquest of the French, the growth of population, and the introduction, more especially in the Carolinas, of laws which, if not intrinsically unjust, were rendered so by the manner of their enforcement, had all combined to stimulate the trend westward. Boone had no desire to be a laggard in the rear of this movement. He preferred to be among its leaders. And accordingly, soon after his brother had left him, he gave himself seriously to the task of selecting a future home.

At first, as he afterwards admitted, he felt unutterably lonely — a circumstance which is itself strong evidence to the falsity of the charge that he was lacking in natural affection. "I confess," he told Filson, "I never before was under greater necessity of exercising philosophy and fortitude. A few days I passed uncomfortably. The idea of a beloved wife and family, and their anxiety upon the account of my absence and exposed situation, made sensible impressions on my heart. A thousand dreadful apprehensions presented themselves to my view, and had undoubtedly disposed me to melancholy, if further indulged." But his strong will and the genial influence of the beautiful Kentucky Maytime overcame all feelings of depression. Every day presented some new attraction to him. Whether walking through the luxuriant wilds that have since been transformed into the famous Blue Grass region, tracing the course of some broad-flowing stream, or traversing the twilight depths of a primeval forest so thickly leaved that scarce a ray of sunlight filtered through, he found much to occupy his thoughts.

Adventures he had in plenty and of a kind to increase his knowledge of woodcraft and of the Indians with whom he was later to come so often into conflict. Shawnees, Cherokees, Chickasaws, and other tribesmen wandered near his path. Sometimes he found indications that his camp had been visited during his absence, and on such occasions he slept for many nights afterwards in thicket or canebrake, fearing lest an attempt might be made to surprise him. Once he encountered a band of savages and escaped from them only by leaping down a precipice into a river and swimming to the opposite bank. Frequently he sighted other bands, but always managed to elude them. At least one Indian fell a victim to his skill with the rifle, being shot down while fishing in the Kentucky.

In his wanderings he travelled as far as the Falls of the Ohio, where he discovered, at the site of the future Louisville, a fur-trade stockade of which Finley had told him. And, no doubt, as he stood there, he thought of his old friend, hopefully anticipating the day when they should again be hunting together in marvellous Kentucky. Perhaps he fancied that Finley might return with Squire, but when Squire did return, towards the end of July, he c'ame alone. [5] He had had an uneventful but most successful journey, had sold the furs at a substantial profit, and brought the good news that Daniel's wife and children were well. The rest of the summer and the early fall the brothers spent in hunting and exploring, this time moving in a southwesterly direction into the country between the Green and Cumberland rivers. Some time in October, Squire again went home, carrying with him many deerskins; but he was back in Kentucky before the end of the year, and there both he and Daniel remained until the following March.

Then, having previously met and spent some weeks with a party of Virginia hunters who, it appeared, had been for six months and more in different parts of the country west of the Cumberland Mountains, the Boones finally broke camp for the return to the Yadkin. As on the outward journey, their route was by way of the Warriors' Path, Cumberland Gap, and Powell's Valley. And in Powell's Valley, to their surprise and bitter disappointment, they were overtaken by the danger which they had so warily avoided in uncivilized Kentucky.

Riding cheerily along, only a few miles from the westernmost settlements, they were captured by a war-party of Northern Indians returning from a raid against Cherokee and Catawba villages, were robbed of their hard-earned pelts and everything else they possessed, and were sent on their homeward way poorer than when the long hunt had first begun, two years before.

The Indians could not, however, rob them of the knowledge gained concerning the fertile lands beyond the mountains. Infuriated but not disheartened, mingling curses against all red men with fervid vows to return to Kentucky and make good their losses, the brothers hastened to the Yadkin, where, as may be imagined, they found the heartiest of welcomes. And there, for the moment, let us leave them, while we turn to make the acquaintance of the people who, stirred by the reports which they and other adventurers brought home, were soon to burst the mountain barrier and spread themselves through the groves and glades and prairies concealed from view by its craggy heights.

[1] The most authoritative and scholarly account of the War of the Regulation is contained in Professor John S. Bassett's "The Regulators of North Carolina," a monograph published as part of the annual report of the American Historical Society for 1894. Professor Bassett gives references to the earlier, and mostly partisan, literature on the subject.

[2] It should be clearly understood that Boone was by no means the first white man to enter Kentucky. As has been said, Finley had visited it in 1752, and possibly again in 1767. And it was visited by white men long before Finley's day. There is even reason to believe that it was entered and partially explored as early as 1671 by a company of Virginians under Captain Thomas Batts. La Salle was

another seventeenth-century visitor to Kentucky. A French expedition is reported to have been at Big Bone Lick in 1735, and seven years afterwards two Virginians, John Howard and Peter Sailing, likewise anticipated Boone, as did Dr. Thomas Walker in 1748. It was Boone's distinction, however, to obtain a more thorough knowledge of the country than did any of his predecessors, and to be the first man to turn that knowledge to practical account. If not the first in point of time, he was the first explorer of Kentucky in the true meaning of the term.

[3] An interesting character in the annals of Kentucky and Ohio. He was one of the founders of Cincinnati, to which he gave the curious name of Losantiville. In 1788, while on a surveying expedition, he was killed by Indians. His name is perpetuated in the celebrated "Filson Club," the Kentucky organization devoted to research in the early history of that State, and to whose publications all students of American history are greatly indebted.

[4] In its essentials this account of Boone's first captivity follows the version given by Dr. Thwaites. It differs in important respects from that of earlier writers, but Dr. Thwaites had the advantage of being able to utilize the invaluable Draper collection of Boone manuscripts, preserved in the library of the Wisconsin State Historical Society, and for that reason his version is to be preferred.

[5] So far as is known Boone and Finley never met after the latter's departure from Kentucky, as recorded above. In fact, with that departure Finley steps off the stage of authentic history. Dr. Thwaites says that after leaving Boone, he went to visit relatives in Pennsylvania, but what became of him afterwards is unknown. I believe, however, that I have possibly succeeded in tracing his subsequent movements to some extent. The records of Lord Dunmore's War in 1774 show that there was a John Finley who volunteered under Captain Evan Shelby from Watauga. This same John Finley took part in the Cherokee wars of 1776-80. And in 1808, when the town of Huntsburg, Ohio, was founded, the first settler, Stephen Pomeroy, found a trader and trapper named John Finley living in a hut on the bank of a creek now known as Finley Creek. This Finley told Pomeroy that he had been with Boone in Kentucky and had fought under Wayne. He enlisted in the War of 1812, returned to Huntsburg after the war, but about 1818 left there, removing, it is thought, to Maryland. He was then a very old man. For this information I am indebted to Mr. W.W. King, of Huntsburg, a great-grandson of Stephen Pomeroy. Of course, there is in all this no positive identification, but it seems at least possible that the John Finley of Watauga, the John Finley of Huntsburg, and the John Finley of Boone's expedition were one and the same.

Chapter Five - The People Who Followed Boone

THE first settlement of the early West — by which is meant the settlement of Kentucky and Tennessee — was essentially the work of the frontier inhabitants of Virginia, North Carolina, and South Carolina. It differed in important respects from the initial colonization of the country, and most of all in being carried through mainly by native-born Americans in whom the dominant racial strain was not English or Dutch or German, or any of the other nationalities which contributed so largely to the settlement of the seaboard colonies. It was none of these — it was Scotch.

Yet here, again, a distinction has to be made. For the men who were to the fore in the movement across the mountains, and in the teeth of hardship, privation, and suffering won a foothold for civilization in the trans-Alleghany wilderness, were in most cases not of direct Scotch extraction. They were the descendants of Scottish people who, many years before, had moved from their native country to Ireland, settling especially in North Ireland. Meeting with persecution, they, or their children and grandchildren, had in time migrated from Ireland to the New World, bringing with them a mixture of both Scotch and Irish traits — for which reason, to distinguish them from people of pure Scotch or pure Irish ancestry, writers have called them Scotch-Irish. It is an awkward term, but it seems impossible to devise a better.

They had representatives in America within a comparatively short time after the colonization of Virginia and Massachusetts, but it was not until the closing years of the seventeenth century and the opening of the eighteenth that Scotch-Irish immigration began in earnest. It flowed in, generally speaking, through two ports, Philadelphia and Charleston, and by 1730 had reached considerable proportions. In the one year 1729 nearly six thousand Scotch-Irish entered the port of Philadelphia, and every year for long thereafter saw a constant increase in their numbers.

By choice and of necessity, for the lands along the coast were even then rather thickly settled, these late-comers moved inland, forming large if widely scattered communities in the "back counties" of Pennsylvania and the Carolinas. Being a restless, enterprising, and aggressive folk, those who located in Pennsylvania got on none too well with the sedate Quakers and phlegmatic Germans who formed the bulk of the population in that colony, and in consequence they either built their cabins in outlying districts, or moved southward along the open table-land of the Valley of Virginia. As early as 1736 there were isolated Scotch-Irish families in the Valley, and as time passed a strong current of Scotch-Irish immigration set in, journeying from Pennsylvania through the Valley of Virginia, and thence to the hills and meadows of the Piedmont section of North Carolina.

Meanwhile, the Scotch-Irish who had come in by way of Charleston likewise moved inland, passing southward to the hill country of Georgia, or northward into the Carolina uplands. In this way, notwithstanding the presence of English, German, French Huguenot, and other settlers, the Scotch-Irish element by 1750 was sufficiently numerous to give color and tone to the entire frontier as far north as Pennsylvania. The other colonies, too, had quotas of Scotch-Irish, as evidenced by the giving of such names as Londonderry, Dublin, and Antrim to New Hampshire towns; and Orange and Ulster to New York counties. But nowhere did the Scotch-Irish make their presence so strongly felt as on the borders of the Carolinas and Virginia.

There they were indeed the chief factor in developing the institutional life of the country. Like their ancestors, the ancient Scotch Covenanters, who had suffered much for conscience' sake, they were a profoundly religious people, of the Presbyterian faith. They were also strong believers in the virtue of education, if only to enable their children to read the Bible for themselves. The schoolmaster was an early adjunct of a Scotch-Irish settlement; and when, for any reason, a schoolmaster was not to be had, the children were taught their letters at their mother's knee. It is true that as a rule their schooling was of a primitive sort, confined to the rudiments of reading, writing, and arithmetic. But this was ample for the needs of the simple life which the vast majority of Scotch-Irish settlers led.

Everything about them, in fact, was characterized by a rugged, outright simplicity. In an old and now almost forgotten book — Joseph Doddridge's "Notes on the Settlement and Indian Wars of the Western Parts of Virginia and Pennsylvania" — there is a crude but graphic picture of their customs and manners, drawn from life by one of themselves. "Most of the articles in common use," says Doddridge, "were of domestic manufacture. There might have been incidentally a few things brought to the country for sale in a primitive way, but there was no store for general supply. Utensils of metal, except offensive weapons, were extremely rare and almost entirely unknown. The table furniture usually consisted of wooden vessels, either turned or coopered. Iron forks, tin cups, etc., were articles of rare and delicate luxury. The food was of the most wholesome and primitive kind. The richest meat, the finest butter, and best meal that ever delighted man's palate, were here eaten with a relish which health and labor only know. The hospitality of the people was profuse and proverbial.

"The dress of the settlers was of primitive simplicity. The hunting-shirt was worn universally...and was usually made of linsey, sometimes of coarse linen, and a few of dressed deerskin. The bosom of this dress was sewed as a wallet, to hold a piece of bread, cakes, jerk, tow for wiping the barrel of the rifle, and any other necessary for the hunter or warrior. The belt, which was always tied behind, answered several purposes besides that of holding the dress together. In cold weather the mittens, and sometimes the bullet-bag, occupied the front part of it. To the right side was suspended the tomahawk, and to the left the scalping-knife in its leathern sheath.

"A pair of drawers, or breeches and leggins, were the dress of the thighs and legs, and a pair of moccasins answered for the feet much better than shoes. These were made of dressed deerskin. They were generally made of a single piece, with a gathering seam along the top of the foot, and another from the bottom of the heel, without gathers, as high as the ankle joint. Flaps were left on each side to reach some distance up the leg. Hats were made of the native fur; the buffalo wool was frequently employed in the manufacture of cloth, as was also the bark of the wild nettle."

Reading this description, one can readily appreciate the stir of lively curiosity aroused in Philadelphia, Williamsburg, and Charleston whenever a backcountry settler "came to town" from his home among the mountains. The women dressed as simply as the men; their garb a linsey gown, which they spun and dyed and fashioned themselves. For headgear they wore huge sunbonnets, and on their feet moccasins like the men, or else went barefoot, as was largely their custom in the summer.

In a word, the Scotch-Irish settler who took possession of the mountain frontier, and thence moved onward to the conquest of the early West, was conspicuously devoid of everything that made for ease and comfort. Remote from the older and more populous communities near the sea, he led his own life, a hard, cheerless existence in many ways. To begin with, enough space had to be cleared in the untrodden forest for the building of the cabin home and the sowing of the first crop of corn. Until this was done, he and his wife and little ones perforce lived in the canvas-covered wagon, prototype of the prairie schooner of later times, which had carried them to the scene of their chosen habitation. And when the cabin was raised, with the willing help of neighboring pioneers, the struggle for a livelihood had only commenced.

Week in and week out, for years together, the backwoodsman and his wife — no less brave than he, and gladly sharing his unending labors — toiled to extend their area of cultivation, increase their products, and win a few scant comforts for their later years. However poor, they were an ambitious folk, these backwoods people. They had not come into the wilderness to bury themselves, to stagnate, to take life shiftlessly. And thence it was that where all had once been savage waste, tenanted only by the wild beast or the wandering red man, there soon or late arose progressive settlements, each with its church and schoolhouse, its mill and forge.

Cut off as he was from ready intercourse with the markets and manufactures of the tide-water country, every backwoodsman necessarily did much besides cultivate his farm. We have seen how Squire Boone and his son Daniel were weavers and blacksmiths as well as farmers. Among the settlers there were also carpenters, coopers, wheelwrights, wagonmakers, rope-makers, wine-makers, tailors, traders, surveyors, teachers. Every settler was of course a hunter, at all events in the days of the first conquest of the wilds, since he was obliged to depend on game for his meat supply. This taught him to be expert with the rifle, and was excellent training for the grim days when he had to use the rifle to withstand the Indian raider. It taught him, too, as every requirement of his laborious existence taught him, to be self-reliant, resourceful, ready to take long chances, and to yield to no obstacle however difficult or dangerous it seemed.

Here we approach one of the most important phases of the influence exercised on the backwoodsman by the nature of his environment. Whether he was Scotch-Irish or English or German or French Huguenot, there was bred in him just those characteristics which make for an efficient democracy. His struggle with, and conquest of, the wilderness gave him a pronounced individualism; and at the same time his perpetual sense of isolation, and of dangers shared in common by his fellow-pioneers, increased his human sympathy, and invested the backwoods people as a whole with a keener feeling of solidarity than less exposed communities could boast.

To put it otherwise, the backwoodsman was the typical "man in the state of nature," depicted by the political philosophers of the seventeenth and eighteenth centuries; and he vindicated those theorists who maintained that "man in the state of nature" would voluntarily and effectively organize for mutual defence and for the preservation of his "natural rights." To the backwoodsman all men were free and equal, and should have due regard to the freedom and equality of their fellows. He further believed that the function of government was to insure universal freedom and equality, and that for this purpose no better form of government could be devised than a government by the people themselves. Hence the readiness with which, to give an illustration, the Scotch-Irish backwoodsmen of both North and South Carolina formed "associations" in the time of the Regulation — just previous to the outbreak of the War for Independence — to correct what they viewed as intolerable interference and injustice on the part of the colonial authorities.

More impressive still is the example of the backwoodsmen who came together to form the Watauga Association, the first written constitution drawn up and adopted by any community west of the Alleghanies. The Watauga country lay in the eastern part of the present State of Tennessee, and comprised the forest-clad valleys of the Clinch, the Holston, the Watauga, the Nolichucky, and those nu-

James Robertson –
The "Father of Tennessee"

merous other streams which eventually unite to form the Tennessee River. Until 1769 this region was without a single white inhabitant. In that year at least one borderer, William Bean, from Virginia, settled with his family on Boone's Creek, a tributary of the Watauga; and it is believed that at about the same time several other families came in from North Carolina. In any event, a steady, if at first insignificant, volume of immigration began in 1770, from Virginia and North and South Carolina. [1]

By 1772 several little settlements, or stations as they were often called, had been established, their population including not a few who afterwards won lasting fame in the history of the early West. Chief among these were James Robertson and John Sevier, the former justly celebrated as the "Father of Tennessee," the latter the renowned "Nolichucky Jack of the Border," and the hero, according to his biographer, James R. Gilmore, of thirty-five battles, every one of which was a victory. Both were native-born American borderers, Robertson being of Scotch-Irish lineage and Sevier of Huguenot ancestry.

The great majority of the Watauga settlers were Scotch-Irish, and were a plain, substantial, right-minded people. But, as has always been the case in border communities, there were some evil-doers among them — "refugees from justice, absconding debtors, and horse-thieves." Preying both on their fellow-whites and on the Cherokee Indians, whose villages stood to the south of the Watauga country, these scoundrels soon became a great menace to the peace and progress of the settlements. They were literally beyond the pale of the law, for although Watauga was a part of North Carolina the jurisdiction of that colony had not been extended beyond the mountains, and consequently there were no courts or officers of justice to deal with those deserving punishment.

The settlers themselves, however, were equal to the emergency, and this without resorting to "lynch law." Robertson, Sevier, and a few others consulted together and decided that, pending the extension of colonial authority, they would form a government of their own. A call was issued for a general convention, and early in the spring of 1772 the settlers met at Robertson's house. The result of their deliberations was the holding of an election at which the people of the different stations chose an assembly of thirteen representatives. The thirteen, in their turn, met and elected five of their number as a committee, or court, clothed with full authority to administer the public business of the community.

They were empowered — by "articles of association," the text of which has unfortunately been lost [2] — to settle all disputes, enforce law and order, appoint minor officers of justice, and also appoint the officers of the local militia to be organized in accordance with the articles of association. They were to meet at stated intervals as a regularly constituted tribunal, and in the performance of their duties were to follow as far as possible the laws of Virginia. This last provision was due to a mistaken belief of the Wataugans that their territory instead of being part of North Carolina was within the limits of Virginia.

As thus constituted the government of Watauga would seem, on a surface view, to have been oligarchic rather than democratic, government by a few rather than government by the people. But such was not actually the case, since the committee of five retained throughout their existence as an executive-judicial body a keen appreciation of their status as representatives of the popular will. In 1776, for example, we find Sevier stating in the petition addressed by him, in the name of the Wataugans, to the Provincial Council of North Carolina: —

"Finding ourselves on the frontiers, and being apprehensive that, for the want of a proper legislature, we might become a shelter for such as endeavored to defraud their creditors; considering also the necessity of recording deeds, wills, and doing other public business, we, by consent of the people, formed a court for the purposes above mentioned, taking (by desire of our constituents) the Virginia laws for our guide, so near as the situation of affairs would admit. This was intended for ourselves, and was done by the consent of every individual."

The government thus established endured for more than four years, or until North Carolina, in response to the petition just quoted, annexed Watauga under the name of the District of Washington. It was, of course, a makeshift government, but it bore striking evidence to the intrinsic worth and good sense of its framers. And they, be it remembered, were not men trained for the exercise of legislative, executive, and judicial functions. They were not skilled in the formulation of codes, or versed in the intricacies of legal procedure. They were simply backwoodsmen — wielders of the axe and followers of the plough. Yet they displayed an inborn and wonderful capacity for self-government, and a singular ability in devising governmental methods and processes best fitted to meet their needs.

Whence they derived this capacity and ability, it is impossible to say fully. But this much may be said — that they owed it in no small measure to the religion which the Scotch-Irish immigrant had brought with him from Ireland. Presbyterianism had become the creed of the border, and Presbyterianism, with its democratic principles of church polity, was emphatically a training school in political science for the humblest layman as well as the best educated clergyman.

Here, then, is a foremost Scotch-Irish contribution to the foundation-building of the West; and, for the matter of that, to the growth of the American governmental system as we know it to-day. If for this alone, the Scotch-Irishman of the border backwoods should always be held in honorable remembrance.

Not that he was without his faults. Progressive and thrifty, his thrift sometimes developed into an unpleasant penuriousness. As one of his eulogists has wittily remarked, he kept the Sabbath and all else that he could lay his hands on. To a ready appreciation of his political rights he added an almost abnormal tendency to insist on his personal rights. He was over-ready to take offence, and when aggrieved, fought like a wildcat. Many repulsive pictures of border fights have been preserved, with their eye-gouging and nose-biting, their rough-and-tumble wrestling and kicking. Moreover, the Scotch-Irish backwoodsman's proneness to quarrel and fight was intensified by his love of strong drink. A writer who has made a special study of the Scotch-Irish in colonial North Carolina says that nearly every farm of any size had a distillery attached, and that much of the corn grown was marketed in liquid form. He adds: —

"A punch bowl and glasses were found among the effects of the Rev. Alexander Craighead, founder of the earliest churches of the Mecklenburg region.

Whiskey played a great part on funeral occasions, and especially at 'vendues,' when it was supposed to put the buyers in good humor and was charged to the estate disposed of. The tavern on the public road was a famous institution of these early days, and the variety of the liquors sold reminds one of the English inns that Dickens has portrayed." [3]

Still, for all his defects, the Scotch-Irish backwoodsman compels warm admiration. His virtues far outweighed his vices. And it needed a stalwart, rugged, restless, persevering, and fighting people to conquer the wilderness and the savage, and win the West for civilization. If the Scotch-Irish took with them across the mountains their quick temper and the whiskey bottle, they also took the Bible and the spelling-book, an unquenchable devotion to liberty, splendid courage, and soundly democratic institutions. In the War for Independence they played a noble part, and from that day to the present their descendants have been found zealous in the service of the nation. Scotch-Irish blood has coursed in the veins of many a President of the United States, and of a long line of Cabinet officers, Supreme Court Justices, Senators, Representatives, and State Governors and Legislators. Great, in truth, is the debt which America owes to the Scotch-Irish of the border.

[1] Mainly, it would seem, from North Carolina, especially after the battle of Alamance, when Governor Tryon so signally defeated the Regulators.
[2] Our knowledge of the Watauga Association is based chiefly on a petition addressed to the Provincial Council of North Carolina, by John Sevier, in the name of the inhabitants of Watauga. It is printed in J. G. M. Ramsey's "Annals of Tennessee."
[3] Rev. A. J. McKelway's "The Scotch-Irish of North Carolina," in *The North Carolina Booklet*, vol. IV.

Chapter Six - Westward ho!

WHEN Daniel Boone returned to the Yadkin in the spring of 1771, he fully expected to remove his family to Kentucky within a very short time. But circumstances, the exact nature of which does not appear from the surviving records, so retarded his plans that more than two years passed before he was able to make a start. In all probability the chief cause of delay was the War of the Regulation, for, after the battle of Alamance, — which was fought May 16, 1771, — many Regulators abandoned their homes and fled, as already stated, to the Watauga country. This made land cheap in many parts of Piedmont North Carolina, and rendered it difficult for Boone to sell his farm, as he was obliged to do in order to equip himself for the journey.

In the interval he paid at least two visits to Kentucky, and there is reason to believe that on the second of these he definitely selected the site of his future home. From both visits he returned more enthusiastic than ever with respect to the possibilities of the country beyond the mountains, and so loudly and persistently did he sing its praises that a number of his neighbors, and even distant settlers, became fired with the desire of seeing it for themselves. Thus it happened that when his preparations were at last complete, and he bade farewell to the Yadkin Valley, Sept. 25, 1773, he found himself at the head of a fairly large caravan, which was to be considerably augmented en route by immigrants from the Valley of Virginia and Powell's Valley.

It speaks volumes for the courage and hardihood of Rebecca Boone and other women in the party that they unhesitatingly embarked on the long pilgrimage. Little danger was apprehended from the Indians, as the various tribes had been comparatively quiet since Pontiac's futile uprising of 1763-65 and the subsequent treaties explicitly recognizing the territorial rights of the natives. But in every other respect the journey was certain to prove arduous in the extreme. For the greater part it would have to be made by narrow and brier-choked trails, often precipitous and involving difficult ascents and descents of the successive ridges. This meant that only the absolute necessaries for existence could be transported, and that the women and children as well as the men would have to travel on horseback or afoot. Instead of sleeping comfortably of nights in the familiar canvas-covered wagon, they would be obliged to camp in the open wilderness, sheltered at most by tent-cloth or bedcoverings stretched between upright poles. Their food would be meagre, unless the hunting proved good; and did the weather turn stormy, the hardships of the journey would be increased a thousandfold. [1]

Yet the emigrants, men and women alike, faced the prospect with buoyant hopefulness. Leading their pack-horses, and driving a few cattle ahead of them, they journeyed cheerfully westward, their immediate destination being Powell's Valley, where they were to await the home-seekers from that section and from the more northerly Valley of Virginia. Five families accompanied the Boones, and if every family was as large as Daniel's, the caravan must have been of really imposing dimensions. For, besides James and Israel, the two children whose births have already been noticed, Daniel and Rebecca had by that time been blessed with six sons and daughters, including Susannah, then thirteen years old; Jemima, eleven; Lavinia, seven; Rebecca, five; Daniel Morgan, four; and John, a mere infant in arms.

Until Powell's Valley was reached the journey was without incident. There was no thought that deadly danger lurked ahead — that, in fact, the travellers were now about to undergo an experience so tragic as to postpone for many months the settlement of Kentucky. Boone, as had been arranged, went into camp, pending the arrival of the expected additions to his party. At the same time he ordered his son James to ride across country with two other men for the purpose of obtaining extra supplies from a Clinch River settler named Russell. It was not many miles to Russell's place, and the supposition was that the trip there and back could be made between sunrise and sunset.

However, while returning in company with several Clinch River people who had volunteered their assistance in carrying the supplies, Boone's messengers lost the trail when within three miles of the encampment, and were obliged to pass the night in the forest. It so happened that their supper-fire attracted the attention of a band of Shawnees, homeward bound after a hunt or a raid against the Cherokee villages on the Little Tennessee. The temptation to secure some scalps was too strong to be resisted. Surrounding the unsuspecting sleepers the Indians waited until dawn, and then made their attack, with rifle and tomahawk. Resistance was impossible, so sudden was the onslaught, and no quarter was given. Even as they sprang to their feet, half-dazed and groping for their fire-arms, the doomed victims sank back, pierced with bullets or brained by a war-hatchet. Only two, a Clinch River settler and a negro slave belonging to Russell, escaped the carnage. The rest, seven in all, and James Boone among them, were left weltering in their blood.

The grief of Daniel and Rebecca Boone over the loss of their first-born, who had grown into a stalwart, intelligent, most attractive youth of seventeen, may be better imagined than described. Leaving the weeping mother to the kindly ministrations of the other women in the party, Daniel, grim and silent, rode forward to the scene of the massacre, guided by the two survivors. He had long been familiar with Indian warfare; had, as we know, been himself an Indian captive, but this was the first time that the actuality of the Indian menace had been brought directly home to him. Hitherto he had taken Indian hostility to the white man as a matter of course and had reckoned with it in an impersonal way. Henceforward he could not but feel, as felt hundreds of borderers whose loved ones had fallen beneath the red man's hand, that every Indian was the incarnation of all that was devilish, treacherous, and malignant, and should be treated accordingly.

It is easy for us who have never known the horrors of the ambuscade, the raid, and the torturing at the stake to condemn the spirit of unreasoning revenge with which the frontiersmen were too often swayed in their dealings with savages. But let us in imagination put ourselves in their place — let us stand, as Boone stood that chill October morning, gazing at the mangled remains of a beloved son — and we shall be far more likely to sympathize than to condemn. [2]

A few words of prayer, and the bodies of young Boone and his companions were tenderly consigned to their last resting-place. Then the men from the Yadkin returned to camp to deliberate as to their future course. By this time their fellow-immigrants from the Valley of Virginia and Powell's Valley had arrived, forty strong, and it was Boone's opinion that they could safely proceed. But the others demurred. To them it seemed probable that the Shawnee attack was the precursor of a general Indian uprising, and they held it madness to cut themselves off from all relief and run the risk of annihilation. Let us, they argued in substance, await developments; and in the spring, if peace remain unbroken, we can complete the journey. In vain Boone, who had staked his all on the Kentucky venture, pleaded and expostulated with them. They were obdurate, and, as the sequel proved, were wisely obdurate.

From the Great Lakes to the Gulf of Mexico unrest and suspicion were once more taking possession of the Indian peoples, as a result of the increasing evidences of the intention of the English colonists to enter in and occupy the rich Mississippi Valley. This was what the old friends of the Indians, the French, had predicted would come to pass; and it was to check the borderers' westward tendency that Pontiac had organized his great conspiracy. Following Pontiac's conspiracy, it is true, the Indians themselves had promoted the westward movement when, in 1768, the chieftains of the powerful Iroquois Confederacy, by the Treaty of Fort Stanwix, ceded to the English all of their claims to land south of the Ohio as far as the Tennessee. Possibly they imagined that the King's Proclamation of 1763, forbidding English settlement beyond a certain distance from the sea, [3] would operate to preserve this region from white occupation. If they so imagined, they were speedily undeceived.

Not only did hunters like Boone range through it, but prospective settlers and land-speculators, regardless of the King's Proclamation, began to stake out claims. Still further complicating the situation was the fact that many tribes denied the validity of the Iroquois cession, and asserted what Finley had told Boone when they first met in Braddock's campaign — namely, that the country between the Ohio and the Tennessee was a no-man's land, open to all the tribes for hunting purposes. Irritated and alarmed, the Shawnees, Delawares, Cherokees, and other Western and Southwestern Indians needed only a slight excuse to harry the frontier.

Ample provocation was found in the wanton murder by border ruffians of the entire family of the Mingo chieftain, Logan, an Indian of really admirable characteristics and long a friend to the white man. As in the days of Pontiac, the war-belt and the blood-stained hatchet were hurried from tribe to tribe, and soon a number of simultaneous raids on widely separated settlements gave notice that many chieftains had taken up Logan's cause, and that another struggle between the red man and the white was inevitable.

It was evident, too, that the Virginia frontier was destined to suffer most severely, and the governor of Virginia, the energetic and forceful Lord Dunmore, at once issued orders for the raising of troops to crush the uprising in its inception by carrying the war into the enemy's country. And, with a consideration not always found in colonial governors, Dunmore also ordered that messengers be sent to warn several surveying parties known to be at work in the wilds of Kentucky.

At first it was thought that word might best be sent to them by way of Fort Pitt (the former Fort Duquesne, which Braddock had in vain attempted to capture) and down the Ohio River to the Falls of the Ohio. But it was discovered that the Shawnees had established so close a blockade that navigation of the Ohio was impossible. Instructions were then hurried to Watauga, directing the employment of "two good woodsmen" to proceed into Kentucky by the Cumberland Gap route. Obviously this was a mission that called not alone for courage and endurance but for a thorough knowledge of the country, and the authorities at once thought of Boone, who was recognized by them as knowing more about Kentucky than any other man in all the colonies.

Ever since the failure of his home-seeking expedition, Boone had been living in a deserted cabin on the Clinch, where he had found the greatest difficulty in supporting his family. He did not need a second invitation to accept this opportunity of securing some sorely needed money. Taking with him an experienced hunter, Michael Stoner, he started for the Gap about the end of June, 1774, and within ten days was in the heart of Kentucky. On or before July 8 he made the discovery that the Shawnee attack of the previous year had robbed him of the honor of planting the first Kentucky settlement, for he found thirty-five men, under the leadership of James Harrod, engaged in laying out a town in the section subsequently included in Mercer County. [4] Warning them of the danger to which they were exposed, Boone and Stoner continued overland to the Falls of the Ohio, hunting out and notifying the surveying parties for whose safety Dunmore had been so commendably concerned. After a brief rest at the Falls, the homeward journey was begun, and exactly two months after they had left the Clinch Valley the plucky adventurers were once more with their relatives and neighbors, having in the interval completed a tour of many hundreds of miles through a practically unbroken wilderness.

Nor did Boone return worn out by this strenuous feat. Hearing that Sevier, Robertson, and other Wataugans were marching to join the army that Lord Dunmore had raised, he started after them with a number of volunteers from the Clinch and Powell's Valley. But he was met by orders to assist in the defence of the southwestern border, which had been weakened by the departure of the Wataugans. For this reason, and only for this reason, he failed to participate in the great battle of Point Pleasant, Oct. 10, 1774, when the allied Indians, led by the famous Cornstalk, suffered overwhelming defeat after an all-day struggle, described by some as the most fiercely contested battle ever fought between the Indian and the white. But he none the less contrived to enhance his reputation as an Indian-fighter by the bravery with which he repelled raid after raid against the settlements about the Clinch. "Mr. Boone," the commanding officer of the district reported, "is very diligent at Castle's Woods, and keeps up good order." Dr. Thwaites, who examined with the utmost care the correspondence relating to Lord Dunmore's War, found that it contained numerous complimentary allusions to Boone. All of which, of course, redounded to his advantage. His fame spread even to the tide-water settlements; in the comfortable town house, as in the bleak log-cabin, tales of his exploits were recited, usually with ultrasensational elaborations; and by the time the war was at an end, there were few men of the border so well known as he.

Among those who heard of him was a certain Richard Henderson, of North Carolina, a man of very different type from the borderers. Born in Virginia, he removed to North Carolina when a boy of ten, making his home in Granville County, where his father gained appointment to the unpopular but remunerative post of sheriff. Young Henderson himself, when old enough, became a constable, and afterwards under-sheriff, and in this way obtained more or less insight into the aims and methods of the office-holding oligarchy, or "ring," that then dominated county government in western North Carolina.

What he saw seems to have aroused in him a strong desire not so much to correct the manifold abuses, which in time led to the Regulation Movement, as to turn them to his own advantage. Under existing conditions, as he clearly perceived, no class of men had better opportunities for "getting on in the world" than did lawyers. He improved a somewhat neglected education, procured a few law-books, and after twelve months of diligent study was admitted to the bar. Thereafter he made rapid progress, built up a profitable practice, and in 1768, at the age of thirty-five, was appointed a justice of the North Carolina Superior Court.

It was about this time that the Regulation troubles became acute, and before long Judge Henderson came into collision with the Regulators. In the fall of 1770, while hearing cases at Hillsborough, his court-room was invaded by a mob, some minor officials were beaten, and Henderson himself was so terrorized that during the night he mounted a fast horse and galloped out of town. A month or so later his house, barn, and stables were burned.

After such treatment he naturally would have less sympathy than ever for the grievances and aspirations of the frontier people from whose ranks the Regulators had been recruited. He had this much in common with them, however, that he was bold, enterprising, and profoundly interested in the opening up of the West. But his was the interest of a speculator, not of a home-seeker, and it was coupled with a high-soaring and extraordinary ambition; for he dreamed of nothing less than emulating the achievements of Lord Baltimore, William Penn, and other colonial founders of earlier times. He would establish in faraway Kentucky a proprietary colony whose inhabitants should look up to him as their overlord, and from him take title to their lands.

The mere fact that Richard Henderson could conceive such a scheme marks him out as a man of superlative self-confidence. But it was by no means a scheme altogether to his credit. He knew perfectly well that Kentucky was a part of Virginia, and that it also came within the provisions of the King's Proclamation of 1763. Nevertheless, he steadily if quietly went ahead with his plans. It was his idea to purchase Kentucky from the Cherokees who, he asserted, were its rightful owners; and in order to obtain funds for this purpose he formed a company which he called the Transylvania Company, in

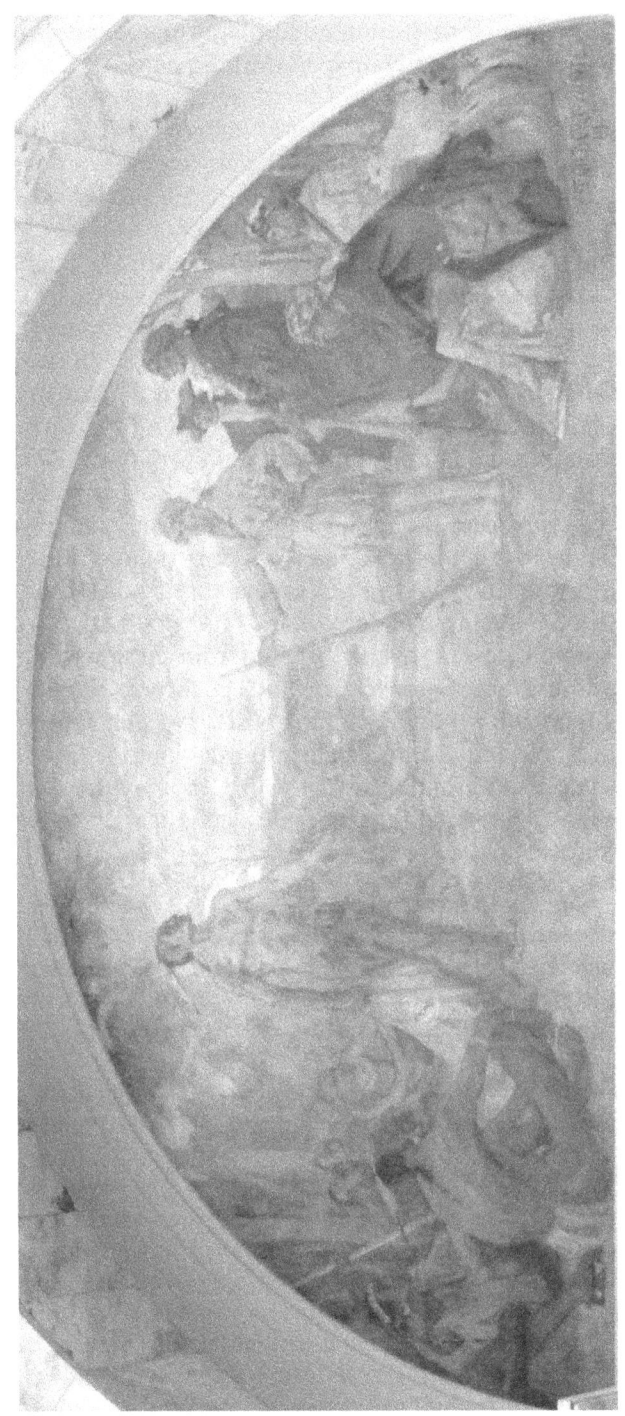

The Sycamore Shoals Treaty
From the painting by T. Gilbert White, in the Kentucky State Council.

accordance with the name he intended giving his colony. John Williams, Leonard Bullock, James Hogg, Nathaniel Hart, David Hart, Thomas Hart, John Luttrell, and William Johnston, all of them North Carolinians, were the men whom he prevailed upon to venture money in his risky undertaking.

This necessary preliminary completed, he visited the Watauga country and sought out Boone, [5] who, when the nature of the project was explained to him, readily agreed to guide Henderson to the Cherokee towns on the Little Tennessee. The Cherokees, for their part, enthusiastically approved Henderson's designs. They would willingly relinquish their Kentucky claims, as also their pretensions to a strip of land giving access to Kentucky, provided only that the compensation were satisfactory. Early in 1775, accordingly, the tribesmen gathered at the Sycamore Shoals, on the Watauga, and by treaty ceded to the Transylvania Company — for a consideration variously stated to have been two thousand pounds in lawful money of Great Britain, ten thousand pounds worth of merchandise, and but "ten wagons loaded with cheap goods, some firearms, and spirituous liquors" — their shadowy claims to all the country between the Kentucky and the Cumberland.

To no purpose did the governor of Virginia and the governor of North Carolina unite in denouncing Henderson and his associates as an "infamous company of land pirates." At a safe distance from these wrathful functionaries, and secure in the knowledge that both governors would be too busily occupied in coping with the rising spirit of independence to follow up their threats, Henderson calmly continued his preparations.

And, as a first and all-important measure, he engaged Daniel Boone to cleave a road through the wilderness, and select a seat of government for the proposed colony.

[1] In another volume, "Woman in the Making of America," I enter in more detail into this phase of the territorial expansion of the United States. It seems to me that the notable part played by women in the growth of the nation has not been sufficiently recognized, and the book to which I refer endeavors in some part to make clear just what the United States of to-day owes to its heroic women of the past.
[2] The reader who would obtain a clear insight into the borderer's point of view is recommended to consult the opening sketch — "The Pioneer" — in James Hall's "Tales of the Border."
[3] The exact purpose of the Proclamation of 1763 has been a subject of lively controversy among historians. Until quite recently, it was commonly represented as being intended to restrain the colonists from passing beyond the political and economic control of England, and was accounted a coercive measure constituting one of the grievances which led to the Revolution. But modern research indicates that it was in reality designed to maintain peace between the colonists and the Indians, by guaranteeing to the latter that they should not, for a time at any rate, be disturbed in their possession of the Western lands. It was thus a wise and salutary, rather than a consciously repressive, measure. For an informative discussion of this subject see G. H. Alden's "New Governments West of

the Alleghanies before 1780."

[4] The present town of Harrodsburg, known in earlier times as Harrodstown and Oldtown. Lewis Collins, in his "History of Kentucky," dates the beginning of this first Kentucky settlement about the middle of June, 1774. But, as Harrod and his companions, in consequence of Boone's warning, and of an attack by Indians, left Kentucky shortly after Boone's visit to them and did not return until the following spring, Harrodsburg was permanently settled less than a month before Boone founded the historic settlement at Boonesborough. James Harrod in many ways closely resembled Boone, and became one of the most picturesque characters in early Kentucky. Collins, following Morehead, thus describes him: "Possessing qualities of a high and generous nature — tall, erect, and commanding in his personal appearance — bold, resolute, active, and energetic — inured to the life of a backwoodsman, familiar with its dangers, and capable of supporting its hardships — he was singularly adapted to the position that he was to occupy. His open, manly countenance — his mild and conciliating manners — all conspired to render him the idol of his associates. Expert in the use of the rifle, he was a successful hunter, and a skilful and dangerous antagonist of the Indian...If he received information that a party of hunters had been surprised by the savages, 'let us go out and beat the red rascals,' was his instantaneous order; and the command and its execution were synonymous with him...Of a restless and active temperament, the dull routine of life in a station was unsuited to him. He loved, like Boone, the free and unrestrained occupation of a hunter."

[5] It has often been stated that Boone acted as Henderson's agent long before this occasion; and that, in fact, it was as an employee of Henderson that he undertook his exploration of Kentucky in 1769. But I have been unable to discover any satisfactory evidence that Henderson even knew Boone until some time after the latter's return from Kentucky in 1771. Moreover, the claim has been recently made to me, by Professor Archibald Henderson, of the University of North Carolina, a descendant of Judge Henderson, that in developing his Transylvania project and purchasing Kentucky from the Cherokees, he acted under the advice of an eminent English jurist "in the closest confidence of the King," and that he therefore regarded his enterprise as having the royal sanction. This view of the case, I understand, Professor Henderson will soon set forth in a biography of Richard Henderson. That, whatever his motives, Judge Henderson played an important part in promoting the early westward movement is beyond question, and for this he is deserving of full credit. Without his backing Boone would not have been able to open up his famous pathway to the West, - the Wilderness Road, - and had it not been for Henderson and the Transylvania Company, the settlement of Kentucky would have been of far less rapid growth than it actually was.

Chapter Seven - The Building of the Wilderness Road

WHEN Daniel Boone undertook to open up a road between the border settlements and the interior of Kentucky, it was impossible for him to foresee the important place this rugged highway was to hold in the history of the territorial expansion of the American people, and the fame that would consequently accrue to him as its builder. He could have had no idea that within a few years it would be sought out and followed by a continuous stream of humanity, of thousands of men and women — aye, and little children — hurrying westward to lay the foundations of powerful, progressive commonwealths; and that these westward-hurrying people would cross the mountains not as British subjects, but as the sons and daughters of a free and independent republic whose limits and influence it was to be their part to extend. Nothing of this could Boone know, as he returned with Henderson from the treaty-making at the Sycamore Shoals. But he could and did perceive plainly that after five years of futile effort the time had come for the realization of his fondest hopes, and with good-will he set about the task of recruiting a party of roadmakers.

So liberal were the terms offered to settlers by the Transylvania Company that he found little difficulty in securing volunteers. Squire Boone was one who agreed to accompany him, and another was his companion on the Dunmore mission, Michael Stoner. There were others to enlist under him who afterwards attained more or less distinction in Kentucky history — men like Richard Callaway, William Bush, David Gass, and Felix Walker. All together, a company of "thirty guns" was organized, almost every man of whom was a trained woodsman and Indian fighter.

It was intended by Henderson and his partners that the road should begin within easy access of the principal route of travel through the Valley of Virginia, and to carry out this plan the party rendezvoused at Long Island, in the Upper Holston, just south of the present line between Virginia and Tennessee. According to an autobiographical statement left by Felix Walker, and almost our only source of information as to the events of the journey, the road-builders before starting explicitly agreed to put themselves "under the management and control of Colonel Boone, who was to be our pilot and conductor through the wilderness to the promised land." After which the making of the Wilderness Road began, March 10, 1775.

From the Holston, Boone struck out for Cumberland Gap, following as direct a line as possible by way of Clinch River and Powell's River, both of which were crossed without difficulty. Indeed, as far as the Gap, and for some miles beyond it, Boone's chief task consisted in skilfully directing the path so as to avoid abrupt descents or arduous climbs, though this was far from being entirely possible, owing to the mountainous nature of the country. Aside from this, all that he deemed it necessary to do was to indicate the way by blazing trees, and to cut down the undergrowth so that it could not spread during the summer and choke the trail.

Thus, from the standpoint of the hardy backwoodsman accustomed to tasks from which others would shrink, there was little to test the mettle of the road-builders until after they forded Rockcastle River in southeastern

Kentucky. Nor, up to that point, had they experienced anything more adventurous than a bear-hunt. But from the time they crossed the Rockcastle, both difficulties and adventures began to multiply. To reach their destination — an open expanse in the heart of the future Blue Grass country, near the juncture of the Kentucky River and Otter Creek, and chosen by Boone years before as an ideal spot for settlement — they were obliged to turn northward from the Rockcastle, [1] and at once plunged into a region of dead brushwood, through which not even the buffalo had penetrated.

Every foot of the advance, for the next twenty miles, had to be won by the most painful effort; and, after chopping and burning their way through the brush, the road-makers entered a scarcely less difficult cane-brake country, where the hatchet again found constant employment. Still they courageously persevered, slowly but steadily pressing forward, until the welcome moment when, in the language of Felix Walker: —

"We began to discover the pleasing and rapturous appearance of the plains of Kentucky. A new sky and strange earth seemed to be presented to our view. So rich a soil we had never seen before — covered with clover in full bloom. The woods were abounding with wild game — turkeys so numerous that it might be said they appeared but one flock, universally scattered in the woods. It appeared that nature, in the profusion of her bounty, had spread a feast for all that lived, both for the animal and rational world. A sight so delightful to our view and so grateful to our feelings almost inclined us in transport to kiss the soil of Kentucky — in imitation of Columbus, as he hailed and saluted the sand on his first setting foot on the shores of America." Their troubles and labors forgotten, Boone and his comrades hastened forward, eager to begin the settlement at Otter Creek, and confident that nothing would occur to delay them. But they were sadly mistaken. On the night of March 24, while encamped near Silver Creek, in the present Madison County, and not more than fifteen miles from their goal, they were surrounded by an Indian war-party. It had not seemed necessary to Boone to post sentinels, as he had every reason to believe that there would be no danger from the Indians. By the Treaty of Fort Stanwix, as was said, the Six Nation Indians had abandoned their claims to Kentucky; by the treaty ending Lord Dunmore's War the Shawnees and other Northwestern tribes had taken similar action; and the friendship of the Cherokees had been secured, for the time being, by the Treaty of the Sycamore Shoals. It was not in Indian nature, however, to permit the unopposed advance of the white man, or forego an opportunity to avenge the defeat at Point Pleasant, and consequently the savages who chanced upon Boone's camp in Kentucky resolved, if possible, to annihilate his company.

Just before sunrise, after a night of patient waiting, they silently took position behind the trees about the camp. Not an inkling of their presence did the road-makers obtain, until aroused from sleep by a chorus of ear-splitting yells and a volley of musketry. Luckily for them, the Indians aimed too high, and the loss of life was small. One man was killed instantly, another was wounded so badly that he died three days later, and a third, no other than Felix Walker, was severely but not fatally wounded. This was the extent of the casualties, and while several of the whites, under the impression that they were greatly outnumbered and that resistance would be useless, fled back along the road they had so laboriously carved out, the rest, under the leadership of Boone, rallied and put the Indians to flight.

Fearing that the attack was part of a pre-concerted plan to prevent the occupation of Kentucky, and that the assailants would soon return with reenforcements, Boone at once ordered his men to begin work on a fort, and before nightfall they were securely protected by a stout stockade, square in form, and built of logs six or seven feet high, with but one narrow opening. That day and the next passed without incident, but on the third day the alarm was given that a man had been sighted skulking through the woods.

Finger on trigger, the road-builders awaited the expected attack, only to discover, to their great relief, that the man who had so startled them was not an Indian but one of the fugitives from their own camp. The same day the second victim of the surprise died, and his death so unnerved a number that they begged Boone to return to Watauga before a similar fate overtook the entire company. Boone's reply was a stubborn, bitter negative. [2] He was resolved that, come what might, he would not again acknowledge failure in his efforts to gain lodgment in Kentucky. He had also begun to surmise, as was actually the case, that the Indian attack had been the work of a small band of marauders, and that no assault in force need be feared. Convinced, though, by the attitude of his companions that many of them would desert him unless relief soon arrived, he despatched a messenger to carry to Henderson the following urgent and interesting missive: —

"After my compliments to you I shall acquaint you with our misfortune. On March 25 a party of Indians fired on my company about half an hour before day, and killed Mr. Twetty and his negro, and wounded Mr. Walker very deeply, but I hope he will recover. On March 28, as we were hunting for provisions, we found Samuel Tate's son, who gave us an account that the Indians fired on their camp on the 27th day. My brother and I went down and found two men killed and sculped, Thomas McDowell and Jeremiah McPhelters. I have sent a man down to all the lower companies, [3] in order to gather them all to the mouth of Otter Creek.

"My advice to you, sir, is to come or send as soon as possible. Your company is desired greatly, for the people are very uneasy, but are willing to stay and venture their lives with you, and now is the time to flusterate the intentions of the Indians, and keep the country, whilst we are in it. If we give way to them now, it will ever be the case. This day we start from the battleground, for the mouth of Otter Creek, where we shall immediately erect a fort, which will be done before you can come or send — then we can send ten men to meet you, if you send for them.

"N.B. — We stood on the ground and guarded our baggage till day, and lost nothing. We have about fifteen miles to Cantuck [the Kentucky River] at Otter Creek."

This letter is dated April 1, and after writing it Boone and the majority of his company began the last stage of their journey, leaving three or four to care for Felix Walker until, five days afterward, he was sufficiently recovered from his wound to be carried forward in a litter. Little actual road-making remained to be done, since from Silver Creek the route merged in a great buffalo trace — as trails were then usually called — worn smooth by the constant tramping of the heavy beasts to and fro from the Big Lick of the Kentucky, whither they went, as the name implies, to lick impregnated ground around a salt spring.

Indeed, even as they approached their journey's end, the men from beyond the mountains heard a continuous, dull, rumbling sound. Boone, who understood its cause, bade them hurry to the top of a little eminence, looking down from which they beheld with astonishment a herd of two or three hundred buffalo lumbering awkwardly from the Lick and across the Kentucky River, followed by young calves that played and skipped about in blissful unconsciousness of the fate which would soon be theirs, now that the white man had come to take possession of Kentucky.

Looking from the eminence, too, the pioneers glimpsed a magnificent panorama, stretching off to the north and west across the verdant, rolling country that in later times was to be covered with the "blue grass" to which Kentucky owes so much of its prosperity. As yet all was wilderness, with never an indication of the marvels to be wrought through the intelligence of man. But it did not need a practised eye to perceive that Boone had brought his followers to a land of wondrous fertility. Even in the barrens about the salt lick vegetation was striving to assert itself and filling every nook and corner where it could hope to evade the deadly hoof-beats of the buffalo. The foliage of the forest trees, whether of the giant oak or the feathery elm, was fast adorning the ample boughs, which drooped with a fascinating grace. The ground, moss-carpeted, or dotted with the first wild flowers of spring, invited the weary road-makers to rest, and, sinking down, they gave themselves to undisturbed enjoyment of the scene before them.

When they arose at Boone's bidding, it was to descend a gentle slope to a beautiful level in a sheltered hollow. Open towards the Kentucky, which coursed with quiet dignity beneath a precipitous bank, the level was well wooded as it receded inland. Here, as Boone indicated with a wave of his hand, was the end of his Wilderness Road — of the narrow, blood-won path that stretched back for two hundred miles, through cane-brake and thicket, open plain and mountain gorge, to the Watauga settlements.

[1] Had they continued in a westerly direction they could have followed an Indian trail to the Falls of the Ohio. It was this trail which Benjamin Logan took not long afterwards, and by so doing gave his name to another and most important

branch of the Wilderness Road. It ultimately became the main-travelled road for those entering Kentucky by way of the Ohio, and for those wishing to traverse Kentucky and go still farther north. The importance of Boone's Branch lay in the access it gave to the Blue Grass region. Both branches, however, are associated with Boone's memory, and deservedly.

[2] Felix Walker's comment on Boone's management of the expedition is well worth quoting: "In the sequel and conclusion of my narrative, I must not neglect to give honor to whom honor is due. Colonel Boone conducted the company under his care through the wilderness with great propriety, intrepidity, and courage; and was I to enter an exception to any part of his conduct, it would be on the ground that he appeared void of fear and of consequences — too little caution for the enterprise. But let me, with feeling recollection and lasting gratitude, ever remember the unremitting kindness, sympathy, and attention paid to me by Colonel Boone in my distress. He was my father, my physician, and friend; he attended me as his child, cured my wounds by the use of medicines from the woods, nursed me with paternal affection until I recovered, without the expectation of reward."

[3] The reference is to the Harrodstown settlers and other homeseekers who had wandered in ahead of Boone's road-making party. It has been estimated that at that time more than one hundred white men were scattered in small companies through the country about the upper waters of the Kentucky. But the great majority fled to Watauga or western Virginia at news of the activity of the Indians. The attack of March 27, to which Boone refers in his letter, was evidently delivered against the camp of one of these little parties. Boone's letter, it may be added, is quoted from Collins's "History of Kentucky," where we find it explained that "with the exception of the words *sculped* and *flusterated* the bad spelling has been corrected." It seems more than likely that there has also been some editing. Boone, though by no means illiterate, was not what one would call an expert letter-writer, and was always far more at ease with the rifle than with the pen.

Chapter Eight - Boone as a Law-Maker

WHILE Boone and his companions were industriously engaged in the erection of a group of cabins in the sheltered level by the Kentucky, a picturesque cavalcade was slowly drawing near to them. At its head rode Richard Henderson. To do full justice to the promoter of the Transylvania Company, it must be said that, whatever his faults, he had in him not a little of the stuff of which empire-builders are made. He was determined that the foundations of his mid-wilderness colony should be securely laid, and that he would himself superintend at least the first stages of its organization. More than a week before Boone's messenger met him, he had begun the long journey westward, with an escort which numbered some fifty persons by the time it reached the Kentucky.

Originally, it comprised but a personal, or official, following that included two of Henderson's partners, Nathaniel Hart and John Luttrell; his brothers,

Nathaniel and Samuel Henderson; a legal representative of the Cherokees named John Farrar; an adventurous Virginian, William Cocke, afterwards famous in Tennessee history as soldier, legislator, and judge; a few prospective settlers, and several slaves. But it constantly received accessions by the way. In Powell's Valley, where Henderson arrived March 30, he was joined by the future renowned Indian fighter, Benjamin Logan, and by a party of immigrants from Virginia, among whom was Abraham Hanks, the maternal grandfather of Abraham Lincoln.

Slow progress was made until April 7, when, a few miles to the east of Cumberland Gap, the messenger from Silver Creek arrived with the dismal news of the attack on Boone's camp. Almost at the same time word was received that five travellers had been slain by the Indians while endeavoring to enter Kentucky. This alarming intelligence caused some of Henderson's followers to turn back, but it had quite the contrary effect on Henderson himself, as he feared that unless he soon brought up support Boone's roadmakers would abandon Kentucky, and the Transylvania enterprise would come to an untimely end.

It did not diminish his fears to meet, a few hours after passing through the Gap, a party of forty fugitives who declared that the Indians were out in force. Dreading lest at any moment he might also meet Boone in flight, he called for a volunteer to ride ahead and carry news of his coming. For this hazardous service Cocke promptly offered himself, and, "fixed off with a good Queen Anne's musket, plenty of ammunition, a tomahawk, a large cuttoe knife, a Dutch blanket, and no small quantity of jerked beef," [1] he galloped away amid the plaudits of the company, many of whom, on Henderson's showing, would gladly have galloped in the opposite direction had not shame restrained them. But, perceiving no signs of the enemy, the panic gradually subsided, excepting perhaps on the part of the slaves, who imagined they saw a painted "Injun" behind every bush. Henderson himself, who had too much at stake to retreat, labored ceaselessly to restore confidence and hasten the advance.

Beyond meeting an occasional fugitive, nothing of further moment occurred until April 15, when a serious difference of opinion arose between Logan and the Transylvania partners, the upshot being that Logan and a friend named Gillespie left the main party at the Rockcastle, and turned westward to take up their residence in Lincoln County, some miles to the southwest of Boone's settlement. Logan's departure was not at all to Henderson's liking, and still less was an interview he had the following day with James McAfee, a Harrodstown settler, who, with his brothers Robert and Samuel, was hurrying eastward to escape the expected Indian avalanche. These McAfees had been among the first to visit Kentucky after the Boone-Finley expedition of 1769, and, like Boone, Logan, and Harrod, they became prominently identified with its early settlement. They hailed from Virginia, and were typical backwoodsmen.

Henderson, after vainly endeavoring to persuade them that the danger from the Indians was greatly exaggerated, explained the purpose of his presence in Kentucky, and offered liberal terms of settlement if they would turn back with him and take up land in the Transylvania grant. To which James McAfee, who seems to have understood the situation better than most of the borderers, bluntly replied that Virginia, not the Transylvania Company, had the disposal of Kentucky lands. Samuel and Robert McAfee, however, were sufficiently impressed by Henderson's glib exposition of the Cherokee sale, to disregard their brother's advice and throw in their fortunes with the Transylvanians.

It was an incident, though, that cast a damper over the spirits of the Transylvania partners, arguing as it did possible opposition on the part of other borderers, such as James Harrod, who had already taken possession of land within the limits defined by the Sycamore Shoals Treaty. But their thoughts were almost immediately diverted into more pleasant channels by the appearance of Michael Stoner, sent by Boone to let Henderson know that all was going well, and to assist him with a relay of fresh packhorses. Henderson also learned from Stoner that Cocke had reached "Fort Boone" in safety, and that Felix Walker was rapidly recovering from the wound sustained in the surprise at Silver Creek.

April 20, [2] two days after they had been joined by Stoner, and after having been travelling for more than a month over a road that had proved for most part "either hilly, stony, slippery, miry, or bushy," the three Proprietors of Transylvania and their attendant retinue rode proudly into Boone's little settlement, where they were received with a salute of twenty-five guns. An hour later the entire company sat down to a banquet, of which the principal viands were cold water and lean buffalo meat.

Before nightfall, spurred possibly by dread of interference from Virginia, Henderson turned his attention to the task of allotting land for immediate settlement, and at once made the distinctly embarrassing discovery that Boone and his companions had preempted the choicest locations for themselves. Rather than have trouble, the tactful Proprietor decided to leave them in undisturbed possession and appease the rest by locating the site of the capital of Transylvania, not in the sheltered level chosen by Boone, but some little distance from it, on a commanding elevation overlooking the Kentucky.

The work of clearing away the trees and undergrowth began without delay, and in little more than a week's time the foundations were laid for a large fortified "station" to which, fittingly enough, the name of Boonesborough was given. Not a vestige of it remains to-day, but fortunately a plan, drawn by Henderson himself, has been preserved, and from this it appears that Boonesborough was a typical palisaded village of the pioneering period. It consisted of nearly thirty one-story cabins, arranged in a hollow square and enclosed by a log stockade, part of which was formed by the backs of the cabins. At each corner stood a two-story blockhouse, the second story projecting about two feet over the lower, so that the inmates could shoot from above upon an enemy attempting to scale the stockade, which was entered by only two gates, one opening towards the buffalo lick, the other towards the river. Stockade, cabins, and blockhouses were provided with little portholes for rifles. It was a rude system of defence, but it answered admirably the requirements of Indian warfare.

Of course the building of Boonesborough took time, but Henderson found much to keep him busily engaged while its construction was in progress. As already stated, there were earlier settlers within the limits of the Transylvania Purchase, settlers at Harrodstown and also at Boiling Spring, which might almost be called a suburb of Harrodstown, since it was quite near that place and had likewise been founded by James Harrod. Besides these two settlements, a party of Virginians, under the command of Captain John Floyd, had quite recently established themselves on Dick's River, some thirty miles southwest of Boonesborough. Floyd was an official surveyor for Virginia, and it seemed altogether likely that he would refuse to recognize the validity of the purchase from the Cherokees. But when he visited Boonesborough, early in May, he came in the friendliest mood imaginable, assuring Henderson that if good terms were offered to him and his comrades, they should gladly become citizens of Transylvania. Otherwise, they would remove across the Kentucky and settle on land not included in the Cherokee grant. Similarly, James Harrod, speaking in behalf of the settlers at Harrodstown and Boiling Spring, expressed willingness to take title from the Transylvania Company.

Greatly relieved by this agreeable solution of a problem that had worried him not a little, Henderson bent his energies to the no less difficult task of organizing a government for his colony. He had seen enough of the backwoodsmen — whom he seems to have heartily disliked, for he describes them in his journal as "a set of scoundrels who scarcely believe in God -or fear a Devil, if we were to judge from most of their words, looks, and actions" — to know that they would insist on having a voice in the management of affairs.

The question was how to reconcile their instinctive desire for self-government with his determination to keep the supreme authority in the hands of himself and his partners. If they intrusted to a popular assembly the power of making and executing laws, it was quite conceivable that legislation fatal to the interests of the company might be enacted. The only feasible course, as it seemed to him, was to frame a semi-autocratic, semi-democratic scheme of government, giving an outward semblance of sovereignty to the "people" but withholding its realities. It was a plan ill-adapted either to the temper of the times or to the conditions of life in the wilderness, and it was foredoomed to failure. But it promised well enough at first, and is of the greatest importance to students of American history, since out of it grew Kentucky's first constitution, and the first meeting of a fully organized legislature west of the Alleghenies.

The settlers, as may be imagined, were delighted with the announcement that it was proposed to convene a representative assembly with delegates from each of the four settlements, Boonesborough, Harrodstown, Boiling Spring, and Floyd's settlement, to which the name of St. Asaph had been given. Elections were held about May 20, and on May 23 the delegates gathered at Boonesborough, where the fort was still so far from completion that they were obliged to meet in the open, under a giant elm. [3]

Boonesborough was represented by six delegates, and each of the others sent four. With few exceptions the electors had chosen the real leaders of their respective communities, the men who had been conspicuous for their efforts to carry civilization westward. The Boonesborough delegation included Daniel and Squire Boone, William Cocke, Richard Callaway, William Moore, and Richard Henderson's brother Samuel, the last-named having been elected probably out of compliment to the chief Proprietor. From Harrodstown came Thomas Slaughter, Dr. John Lythe (a clergyman of the Church of England), Valentine Harman, and James Douglas. James Harrod headed the delegation from Boiling Spring, and was accompanied by Nathan Hammond, Azariah Davis, and Isaac Hite, two of whom, Davis and Hite, had been associated with Harrod in the founding of both Harrodstown and Boiling Spring. John Floyd, of course, was a delegate from St. Asaph, which also sent John Todd, Samuel Wood, and Alexander Spotswood Dandridge. It is well to bear these names in mind, for we shall meet with them again, and some of them quite frequently, in connection with later events of importance.

A low platform had been built at the foot of the great elm, and around this the delegates grouped themselves, some seated on the turf, others on logs, and others standing erect, leaning on their rifles. It was a picturesque assemblage, and an assemblage of serious-minded men, very much in earnest. No more striking commentary on the spirit in which they came together can be found than in the fact that they invited Dr. Lythe to open the proceedings by a prayer for divine guidance in their deliberations.

Following this, they elected Thomas Slaughter as their presiding officer, and then waited in a body on the three Proprietors — Henderson, Hart, and Luttrell — to notify them that the "Transylvania House of Delegates" had been formally organized, and would be pleased to hear any suggestions they might have to make. At this announcement — which, needless to say, had been prearranged — Henderson mounted the platform and, in a resonant voice and with no small dramatic effect, read aloud a carefully prepared address.

Printed in full in Mr. Ranck's "Boonesborough" it constitutes a most interesting document. It reveals Henderson's constant and well-grounded fear of "foreign" intervention, his anxiety to vindicate the rightfulness of the cession by the Cherokees, and his intense desire to conceal from the representatives of the people of Transylvania the subordinate part which he intended they should play in the government of the Colony.

He began by artfully flattering their well-known democratic prepossessions, and by emphasizing in glowing language the influence which the laws drawn up by them might be expected to have. "If prudence, firmness, and wisdom," he assured them, "are suffered to influence your counsels and direct your conduct, the peace and harmony of thousands may be expected to result from your deliberations... You, perhaps, are fixing the palladium, or placing the first corner-stone of an edifice, the height and magnificence of whose superstructure is now in the womb of futurity, and can only become great and glorious in proportion to the excellence of its foundation." He reminded them — and the sentiment was no doubt received with an outburst of applause — that "all power is originally with the people." He vehemently insisted that they had the right to make laws for the regulation of their conduct, "without giving offence to Great Britain or any of the American Colonies, without disturbing the repose of any society or community under Heaven."

Adverting to the official opposition to the Sycamore Shoals Treaty, he especially denounced the proclamation of Governor Martin of North Carolina, as falsely "placing the proprietors of the soil at the head of a lawless train of abandoned villains, against whom the regal authority ought to be executed"; and he urged the delegates to enact such laws as would disprove utterly the charge that Transylvania had been founded as "an asylum for debtors and other persons of desperate circumstances."

This naturally led him to speak of the measures which he regarded as essential to the welfare of the community. Courts would have to be established for the punishment of criminals, as also for "the recovery of debts, and determining matters of dispute with respect to property, contracts, torts, injuries, etc." No less important was the organization of a militia system. It was quite true that as yet there had been no recurrence of the Indian alarm, but, Henderson warned his hearers, it could only be a question of time when they would be involved in a war with the savages.

"I am persuaded," said he, "that nothing but their entire ignorance of our weakness and want of order has hitherto preserved us from the destructive and rapacious bands of cruelty, and given us an opportunity at this time of forming some defensive plans to be supported and carried into execution by the authority and sanction of a well-digested law." He also referred to the need for a game law, pointing out that the buffalo and other food-giving and fur-bearing animals were rapidly disappearing as a result of the settlers' wasteful methods of hunting. [4] In conclusion, he reiterated the great interest felt by the Proprietors in the welfare of Transylvania, and their intention of cheerfully concurring "in every measure which can in the most distant and remote degree promote its happiness or contribute to its grandeur."

Highly satisfied with his address, the delegates set about giving effect to its recommendations, and, backwoodsmen though most of them were, went to work with a noteworthy regard for parliamentary usage. Committees were appointed to draw up and report bills, and when brought in, the bills were debated, referred back, and amended before being put on final passage. In this law-making Daniel Boone was conspicuous. He was chairman of the committee intrusted with framing a law for the preservation of game, and he also sponsored a measure of great historic interest — a bill for improving the breed of horses. Little did the rugged road-maker and pioneer dream that in this bill lay the germ for Kentucky's future fame as the land, par excellence, of fine horses.

Relics of Daniel Boone
Rifle, Hunting Shirt, Powder Horn, Tomahawk, and Hunting Knife, owned by Colonel Reuben T. Durrett

Other bills passed during the brief session — it lasted less than a week — related to the establishment of a militia and tribunals of justice, the regulating of legal fees and of the issuance of writs of attachment, and, finally, "an act to prevent profane swearing and Sabbath breaking." Here, in truth, we catch a glimpse of the Covenanter spirit, of the sound religious principles which these rough-and-ready frontiersmen brought with them from their cabin homes of the Virginia and Carolina border.

But the principal event of the session was the signing of a compact between the Proprietors and the representatives of the people. This was the colony's constitution, and the earliest document of the kind — barring the Watauga Articles of Association, which have not come down to us — recorded in the annals of the West. According to the "Journal of the House of Delegates," it was drawn up by a committee consisting of Representatives Todd,

Lythe, Douglas, and Hite; but to judge from the evidence afforded by its provisions, it must have been prepared under the watchful eye of Richard Henderson. It unmistakably surrendered the control of public business to the Proprietors, and left the House of Delegates with the shadow rather than the substance of authority. Yet it contained some praiseworthy features, particularly a clause declaring for religious toleration. It is not a long document, and is well worth reprinting.

"Whereas," it opens, "it is highly necessary for the peace of the Proprietors and the security of the people of this Colony, that the powers of the one and the liberties of the other be ascertained; We, Richard Henderson, Nathaniel Hart, and J. Luttrell, on behalf of ourselves as well as the other Proprietors of the Colony of Transylvania, of the one part, and the representatives of the people of said Colony, in convention assembled, of the other part — do most solemnly enter into the following contract or agreement, to wit: —

"That the election of delegates in this Colony be annual.

"That the Convention may adjourn, and meet again on their own adjournment; Provided, that in cases of great emergency, the Proprietors may call together the delegates before the time adjourned to; and, if a majority do not attend, they may dissolve them and call a new one.

"That, to prevent dissension and delay of business, one Proprietor shall act for the whole, or some one delegated by them for that purpose, who shall always reside in the Colony.

"That there be perfect religious freedom and toleration; Provided, that the propagators of any doctrine or tenets evidently tending to the subversion of our laws, shall, for such conduct, be amenable to, and punished by, the civil courts.

"That the judges of the superior or supreme courts be appointed by the Proprietors, but be supported by the people, and to them be answerable for their malconduct.

"That the quit-rents never exceed two shillings per hundred acres.

"That the Proprietors appoint a sheriff, who shall be one of three persons recommended by the court.

"That the judges of the superior courts have, without fee or reward, the appointment of the clerks of this colony.

"That the judges of the inferior courts be recommended by the people, and approved by the Proprietors, and by them commissioned.

"That all other civil and military officers be within the appointment of the Proprietors.

"That the office of surveyor-general belong to no person interested or a partner in this purchase.

"That the legislative authority, after the strength and maturity of the Colony will permit, consist of three branches, to wit: the delegates or representatives chosen by the people; a council, not exceeding twelve men, possessed of landed estate, who reside in the Colony, and the Proprietors.

"That nothing with respect to the number of delegates from any town or settlement shall hereafter be drawn into precedent, but that the number of representatives shall be ascertained by law, when the state of the Colony will admit of amendment.

"That the land office be always open.

"That commissions without profit be granted without fee.

"That the fees and salaries of all officers appointed by the Proprietors, be settled and regulated by the laws of the country.

"That the Convention have the sole power of raising and appropriating all public moneys, and electing their treasurer.

"That, for a short time, till the state of the Colony will permit to fix some place of holding the Convention which shall be permanent, the place of meeting shall be agreed upon between the Proprietors and the Convention.

"To the faithful and religious and perpetual observance of all and every of the above articles, the said Proprietors, on behalf of themselves as well as those absent, and the chairman of the Convention, on behalf of them and their constituents, have hereunto interchangeably set their hands and affixed their seals, the twenty-seventh day of May, one thousand seven hundred and seventy-five."

Thus, the taxing power was the sole governmental faculty of any importance bestowed on the representatives of the people. Otherwise there was scarcely any check on the Proprietors, who could fill the courts and other civil offices with functionaries of their own choosing, could select military officers subservient to their wishes; and, by resorting to the clause providing for the dissolution of the Convention might so manoeuvre that even the popular branch of the legislature would be "packed" in their interest. It was, in fine, an excellent framework for the creation of an oligarchic system not unlike that under which Henderson and several of his Transylvania partners had flourished in North Carolina. But, as the Regulator Movement had demonstrated in the case of the North Carolina system, the oligarchic and the autocratic could not hope to endure in the free air of the border.

For the present, however, no objections were raised, and the delegates brought their labors to a close by participating in a singular but impressive ceremony, intended probably to confirm them in the idea that all who would settle in Transylvania must purchase their land from the Company. As was said at the beginning of this chapter, Henderson had been accompanied from Watauga by a lawyer named Farrar, retained as the representative of the Cherokees. On the morning after the signing of the compact, Henderson, standing under the huge elm, read to the delegates the title deed executed by the Cherokees, and called upon Farrar to complete the cession of the soil by performing the ancient feudal ceremony of "livery of seisin." Stooping down, the lawyer cut out a piece of the luxuriant turf and handed it to Henderson, pronouncing as he did so the legal formula by which possession of the soil was specifically "delivered" to the Transylvania Proprietors.

The next day, Sunday, May 28, the representatives from Harrodstown, Boiling Spring, and St. Asaph started for their homes, but before their departure all attended divine service, conducted by Dr. Lythe beneath the shade of the giant elm. "It was," as Mr. Ranck finely says, in his history of Boonesborough, "a religious event absolutely unique. Most of the usual accessories of the service were wanting, from echoing church bell and 'long drawn aisle' to pealing organ. No woman was there to join in litany or hymn, no child to lisp 'amen.' Only men were present — Dissenters as well as Episcopalians — for common dangers had drawn them together, and this one chance for public worship was eagerly seized by pioneers who were as strong in simple faith as stout in heart."

As was the custom, prayers were said for the king and royal family of England. It was the first and last time such prayers were publicly recited on the soil of Kentucky. Within a week new-comers from the East brought the long-delayed tidings of the battle of Lexington. From settlement to settlement the news flew like wild-fire, to create in each a furore of excitement and enthusiasm. Nor can we believe that the liberty-loving sons of the unfettered frontier would have huzzaed one whit less loudly could they have foreseen the woes which the struggle for independence was to bring upon them.

[1] From a letter written by Henderson, June 12, 1775, to his partners, giving an account of his experiences on the road. This letter is printed in full, together with Felix Walker's narrative, the "Journal of the Transylvania House of Delegates," and much other valuable source material, in George W. Ranck's "Boonesborough," one of the best of the excellent Filson Club publications.

[2] This date is worth noting, as it was just one day after the raid on Concord and the battle of Lexington. It is certainly an interesting coincidence that the opening gun in the struggle for independence should have been fired at practically the time when the expansion of the American people may be said to have begun in earnest.

[3] Henderson, in his journal, under date of May 14, gives a graphic description of this historic tree: "About fifty yards from the place where I am writing and right before me to the south (the river about fifty yards behind my camp, and a fine spring a little to the west) stands one of the finest elms that perhaps nature ever produced in any region. This tree is placed in a beautiful plain surrounded by a turf of fine white clover, forming a green to its very stock to which there is scarcely anything to be likened. The trunk is about four feet through to the first branches which are about nine feet high from the ground. From thence above, it so regularly extends its large branches on every side at such equal distances as to form the most beautiful tree that imagination can suggest. The diameter of its branches from the extreme ends is one hundred feet — and every fair day it describes a semi-circle, on the heavenly green around it, of upward of four hundred feet, and any time between the hours of ten and two, one hundred persons may commodiously seat themselves under its branches. This divine tree, or rather one of the many proofs of the existence from all eternity of its divine Author, is to be our church, state-house, council-chamber." Clearly, there was a strong strain

of the romantic and the sentimental in Judge Richard Henderson of North Carolina.

[4] On this point there is a luminous reference in Henderson's journal, under date as early as May 9. "We found it very difficult at first," he records, "to stop great waste in killing meat. Some would kill three, four, five, or half a dozen buffaloes and not take half a horse load from them all. For want of a little obligatory law our game as soon as got here, if not before, was driven off very much. Fifteen or twenty miles was as short a distance as good hunters thought of getting meat, nay sometimes they were obliged to go thirty, though by chance once or twice a week buffalo was killed within five or six miles."

Chapter Nine - The Passing of Transylvania

WITH the adjournment of the House of Delegates the people of Boonesborough settled down to the everyday life of the frontier, cultivating the corn and vegetables which they had planted at the time of their arrival, completing the construction of their dwelling-places, and going on long hunts. There were numerous departures, both of settlers who, like Daniel Boone, wished to bring out their families, and of others, such as William Cocke, who had journeyed to Kentucky more in a spirit of adventure and curiosity than as true home-seekers.

Boone was among the first to leave, setting out June 13 in company with a number of young men sent by Henderson to obtain fresh supplies from the Watauga settlements. He found his wife and children well, and late in the autumn returned with them. A few days afterwards Richard Callaway, who had gone East on a similar mission, arrived at Boonesborough with Mrs. Callaway and their boys and girls, together with several other immigrants and their families. To Boone's wife and daughters, however, as he often recalled with pride, belongs the honor of having been the first white women to set foot on the banks of the Kentucky.

Meantime, Henderson and Luttrell had started for North Carolina in order to confer with their partners regarding the future of Transylvania. The American Revolution had by this time made such progress that no danger was to be apprehended from the representatives of the British Crown either in Virginia or North Carolina, and although Henderson was well aware that the recently created patriot government of Virginia would be unwilling to forego Virginia's claim to the whole of Kentucky, he was hopeful of being able to persuade the Continental Congress to recognize the validity of his purchase from the Indians.

Should the Congress take such action it would, he felt, establish for all time the right of the Transylvania Company to dispose of, as its members saw fit, the seventeen million acres embraced in the Cherokee Cession. In any event, something had to be done to relieve the Proprietors of the perpetual anxiety created by the knowledge that at any time Transylvania might be overrun by an army of immigrants unwilling to pay for the land on which they chose to settle, and basing their refusal on the prior right of Virginia to the country.

Arriving in North Carolina about the middle of September, Henderson immediately called a general meeting of the Company. It was held at the little town of Oxford, in Granville County, with seven of the nine partners present, the absentees being David Hart and his brother Nathaniel, who had remained at Boonesborough to keep a watchful eye on the trend of events. After taking action on several matters of a personal or purely commercial character — such as fixing the terms under which future settlers could obtain land, appointing John Williams as the Company's permanent representative in Transylvania, and voting Daniel Boone a gift of two thousand acres in recognition of "the signal services he has rendered to the Company" — the Proprietors gave their undivided attention to the all-important problem of successfully combatting the almost certain opposition of Virginia.

It was boldly resolved to endeavor to secure Transylvania's admission as the fourteenth Colony in the Revolutionary Union, and for this purpose the partners selected one of their number, James Hogg, to lay before the Continental Congress a memorial in which, after a preamble setting forth their firm belief in the legality of the purchase, and their determination "to give it up only with their lives," they expressed an earnest desire to be considered "as brethren engaged in the same great cause of liberty and of mankind," and concluded by saying: —

"From the generous plan of liberty adopted by the Congress and that noble love of mankind which appears in all their proceedings, the memorialists please themselves that the United Colonies will take the infant Colony of Transylvania into their protection; and they, in return, will do everything in their power, and give such assistance in the general cause of America as the Congress shall judge to be suitable to their abilities. Therefore the memorialists hope and earnestly expect that Transylvania may be added to the number of the United Colonies, and that James Hogg, Esq., be received as their delegate, and admitted to a seat in the honorable the Continental Congress."

An instructive side-light on the men who composed the Transylvania Company is afforded by the fact that they did not hesitate to turn Hogg's delicate mission to money-making purposes. "Resolved," reads one of the resolutions adopted at the same meeting, "that Mr. Hogg be empowered to treat and contract with any person or persons who may incline to purchase lands from the Company, and that he be allowed his expenses for transacting the above business."

Excepting the suave Richard Henderson, Hogg was perhaps the best-fitted of them all for this sordid combination of diplomacy and land-jobbing. He was a shrewd, canny Scot, with an eye ever open to the main chance; he was a man of good appearance and plausible manner, and he was abundantly endowed with what, in the slang of the present day, would be described as "nerve." [1] When he reached Philadelphia, he found Congress absorbed in the serious work of reorganizing and providing for the patriot army, but this did not prevent him from thrusting himself and his affairs upon its attention. He sought out John Adams, Samuel Adams, Silas Deane, and other leading men, and by sheer persistency interested them in Transylvania.

They examined the maps he had brought with him from North Carolina, listened carefully to his detailed recital of the circumstances attending the purchase from the Cherokees, the building of the Wilderness Road, and the settling of Boonesborough, and gave their cordial approval to the democratic manner in which the settlers had been brought together in convention for the purpose of framing the laws of the Colony. But they made it plainly evident that they would not countenance any proprietary form of government. Silas Deane, ever an enthusiast in the cause of liberty and democracy, was even at the pains of drawing up an outline scheme of government for the new Colony, based on the Connecticut system.

"You would be amazed," wrote Hogg to Henderson, "to see how much in earnest these speculative gentlemen are about the plan to be adopted by the Transylvanians. They entreat, they pray, that we make it a free government, and beg that no mercenary or ambitious views in the Proprietors may prevent it. Quit-rents, they say, is a mark of vassalage, and hope they will not be established in Transylvania. They even threaten us with their opposition if we do not act upon liberal principles when we have it so much in our power to render ourselves immortal. Many of them advised a law against negroes."

But, besides the obnoxious proprietary element in the government of Transylvania, there was an insuperable obstacle to recognizing the new Colony, even though Virginia should make no protest. At that time all hope of a reconciliation with the mother country had not been abandoned, and as the Adamses pointed out to Hogg, Congress would be greatly handicapped in its efforts towards a peaceful adjustment if it received into the Union a Colony established on land purchased from the Indians by private individuals, for such a purchase was expressly forbidden by the King's Proclamation of 1763.

"We have petitioned and addressed the king," said they, "and have entreated him to point out some mode of accommodation. There seems to be an impropriety in embarrassing our reconciliation with anything new; and the taking under our protection a body of people who have acted in defiance of the king's proclamations will be looked on as a confirmation of that independent spirit with which we are daily reproached."

Nothing daunted, Hogg pointed to a clause in the Proprietors' memorial disavowing any desire of throwing off their allegiance to the Crown. This, though, scarcely met the objection raised by the Adamses. Still Hogg persisted until, to be rid of him, they declared that, as Transylvania fell within the charter boundaries of Virginia, they could make no move in his favor without the consent of their colleagues from Virginia.

It was an unwelcome intimation, and with the gloomiest forebodings Hogg interviewed Jefferson and Wythe, two of Virginia's delegates to Congress. He was careful to say nothing whatever about the memorial, or about his pretensions to a seat in Congress, and simply explained that the Transylvania Company, fearing misrepresentations against it, had sent him to Philadelphia to let it be known that the Proprietors and people of Transylvania were heartily on the side of liberty. He hoped, therefore. that the gentlemen from Virginia would have no objection to his laying the views and desires of Transylvania before Congress.

In reply, as he had fully expected, Jefferson and Wythe hinted that it would be well first to determine the status of Transylvania, — that quite possibly Virginia might wish to exercise its charter rights, — and, until such determination were had, they would strongly oppose any "acknowledgment" of Transylvania by Congress. To be sure, Jefferson promised "that if his advice were followed, all the use they should make of their charter would be to prevent any arbitrary or oppressive government to be established within the boundaries of it"; and he further assured Hogg "that it was his wish to see a free government established at the back of theirs, properly united with them." [2] But he would by no means consent to Congressional recognition of Transylvania as a separate Colony, prior to the renunciation of Virginia's claim by the people of Virginia in convention assembled.

The thing for you to do, he bluntly told Hogg, is to send a representative to the next Convention and gain its approval — the matter is one for Virginia to decide, not Congress. Wythe was of the same opinion, and so was Richard Henry Lee, whom Hogg interviewed a few days later. Other delegates, including the North Carolinians Hooper and Hewes, who had been very friendly to him, warned him that Congress would do nothing, and that it would be unwise for him to press farther for recognition.

He had arrived at Philadelphia late in October; before the end of November he was homeward bound, reluctantly persuaded that his mission had proved a failure, at any rate on its diplomatic side; and, by the opening of the new year, the Transylvania partners were feverishly preparing for the bitter political fight which it was now certain they would have to wage in Virginia.

In the interval a storm had been brewing for them in quite another quarter — in Transylvania itself. All through the summer and autumn a constant, if as yet comparatively insignificant, stream of immigration had flowed across the mountains, through Cumberland Gap, and along the Wilderness Road to the mid-Kentucky wilderness. Among the newcomers were men destined to fill conspicuous roles in the dramatic and tragic struggle of the next few years. One of them was George Rogers Clark, the future conqueror of Kaskaskia and Vincennes and hero of the unforgettable mid-winter march across the drowned lands of the Wabash. Another was William Whitley, the celebrated hunter, scout, and Indian fighter.

Jesse Benton, the father of that great statesman of the West, Thomas Hart Benton, also came in about this time, as did the recklessly brave Hugh McGary, whom we shall find leading the Kentuckians to destruction at the battle of the Blue Lick. Still another arrival during the autumn of 1775, though not by the Wilderness Road, was Robert Patterson, a participant in the founding of three cities, Lexington in Kentucky, and Cincinnati and Dayton in Ohio.

All together, between two and three hundred home-seekers were added to the population of Transylvania before the close of 1775. They could not reasonably expect to take land under the terms offered by the Company to those who had opened up the country during the spring of that year, but they by no means anticipated the stiff advance in prices put into effect upon the arrival of the Company's agent, John Williams, about the beginning of December.

Formerly, land had been offered at twenty shillings per hundred acres; now the same acreage was to cost fifty shillings, with the expectation of a further advance after June 1, 1776. No single allotment was to include more than six hundred and forty acres, "except in particular cases," and on every hundred acres an annual quit-rent of two shillings would be exacted from old and new settlers alike. Every title-deed was to contain a clause requiring the purchaser to hand over to the Company one-half of all the gold, silver, copper, lead, or sulphur he might discover on his property. Moreover, certain fees had to be paid before a purchase would be considered complete — fees for entering a claim, for having a survey made, and for the drawing up of the deed — amounting in all to nearly two pounds. And, as Williams publicly advertised, every settler was required to pay these fees in full before April 1, 1776; otherwise his land would be adjudged open to settlement by any one making the necessary payments.

Nor was this all that exasperated the people of Transylvania and embittered them against the Company. The discovery was made that the Proprietors had reserved for themselves and a few favored friends nearly seventy thousand acres of choice land at the Falls of the Ohio, where it was almost certain the most important commercial centre of the Colony would ultimately be established. And the settlers found another, though minor, grievance in the opening of a Company's store at Boonesborough, with goods selling at exorbitant prices — how exorbitant may be judged from the fact that while the Company paid ordinary laborers less than a shilling and a half a day, and hunters and road-makers only two shillings, lead sold in the Company's store at nearly a shilling, and gunpowder at ten shillings per pound. Anger and dissatisfaction spread rapidly, and before long a determined movement was under way to break the power of the Proprietors.

This movement had its origin at Harrodstown and Boiling Spring, both of which places, it will be remembered, had been settled before the building of the Wilderness Road and the advent of Henderson, Hart, and Luttrell. Enraged at the thought that they were expected to pay tribute — in the way of quitrents and land-office fees — to men who had not even preceded them into Kentucky, James Harrod and other of the original settlers recalled with satisfaction the savagely denunciatory proclamations of the governors of Virginia and North Carolina. It should not be a difficult matter, they fancied, to pick flaws in the Company's title to Transylvania. They looked up the provisions of the Proclamation of 1763 and of the Treaty of 1768, by which the Six Nations had relinquished to the British Crown their pretensions to Kentucky. They also scrutinized more closely than heretofore the compact between the Proprietors and the people, and realized for the first time how cleverly Henderson had hoodwinked the members of the House of Delegates. In their anxiety, perplexity, and wrath they resolved that, come what might, they would disown the proprietary government and agitate for the recognition of Transylvania as a part of Virginia.

An incident which occurred two days before Christmas greatly advanced their "treasonable" project by affording an object-lesson in the need the settlers might have for outside aid against the Indians, and the advantage it would be to them if they were in a position to demand assistance from one of the older and more powerful colonies. The Indians had observed their treaty obligations so faithfully that the Transylvanians had almost come to believe that they would be quite free from molestation. But on December 23 two Boonesborough boys, McQuinney and Saunders, were surprised by a party of Shawnees. Four days afterwards McQuinney, killed and scalped, was found in a corn-field three miles north of the Kentucky. Saunders's fate was never learned.

Naturally there was much excitement until it developed that the raiders were not more than half a dozen in number, and that no organized attack was imminent. But even so, the affair drove home to the minds of the Transylvanians a vivid appreciation of their exposed situation, and inclined them all the more towards the views of the Harrodstown-Boiling Spring agitators, who made such progress that before the snows of winter had melted they were able to send to Virginia a largely signed memorial voicing their discontent and their aspirations.

For a backwoods production this was a remarkable document, devised with a shrewdness that would have done credit to Richard Henderson himself. It was addressed to the Virginia Convention, as a petition from "the inhabitants and some of the intended settlers of that part of North America now denominated Transylvania," and without any superfluous words plunged directly into an attack on the Company. "Whereas," the memorialists declared, "some of your petitioners became adventurers in that country from the advantageous reports of their friends who first explored it, and others since allured by the specious show of the easy terms on which the land was to be purchased from those who styled themselves Proprietors, have, at a great expense and many hardships, settled there, under the faith of holding the lands by an indefeasible title, which those gentlemen assured them they were capable of making. But your petitioners have been greatly alarmed at the late conduct of those gentlemen, in advancing the price of the purchase money from twenty shillings to fifty shillings, per hundred acres, and at the same time have increased the fees of entry and surveying to a most exorbitant rate; and, by the short period prefixed for taking up the lands, even on those extravagant terms, they plainly evince their intentions of rising in their demands as the settlers increase, or their insatiable avarice shall dictate.

"And your petitioners have been more justly alarmed at such unaccountable and arbitrary proceedings as they have lately learned from a copy of the deed made by the Six Nations with Sir William Johnson and the commissioners from this Colony [Virginia] at Fort Stanwix in the year 1768, that the said lands were included in the cession or grant of all that tract which lies on the south side of the river Ohio, beginning at the mouth of Cherokee or Hogohege River [the Tennessee] and extending up the said river to Kettaning [on the Allegheny River]. And, as in the preamble of the said deed, the said confederate Indians declare the Cherokee River to be their true boundary with the southard Indians, your petitioners may with great reason doubt the validity of the purchase that those Proprietors have made of the Cherokees — the only title they set up to the lands for which they demand such extravagant sums from your petitioners, without any other assurance for holding them than their own deed and warrant; a poor security, as your petitioners humbly apprehend, for the money that, among other new and unreasonable regulations, these Proprietors insist shall be paid down on the delivery of the deed.

"And, as we have the greatest reason to presume that His Majesty, to whom the lands were deeded by the Six Nations for a valuable consideration, will vindicate his title, and think himself at liberty to grant them to such persons and on such terms as he pleases, your petitioners would, in consequence thereof, be turned out of possession or obliged to purchase their lands and improvements on such terms as the new grantee or proprietor might think fit to impose; so that we cannot help regarding the demand of Mr. Henderson and his Company as highly unjust and impolitic, in the infant state of the settlement, as well as greatly injurious to your petitioners, who would cheerfully have paid the consideration at first stipulated by the Company, whenever their grant had been confirmed by the Crown, or otherwise authenticated by the supreme legislature.

"And, as we are anxious to concur in every respect with our brethren of the United Colonies, for our just rights and privileges, as far as our infant settlement and remote situation will admit of, we humbly expect and implore to be taken under the protection of the honorable Convention of the Colony of Virginia, of which we cannot help thinking ourselves still a part, and request your kind interposition in our behalf, that we may not suffer under the rigorous demands and impositions of the gentlemen styling themselves Proprietors, who, the better to effect their oppressive designs, have given them the color of a law, enacted by a score of men, artfully picked from the few adventurers who went to see the country last summer, overawed by the presence of Mr. Henderson.

"And that you would take such measures as your honors in your wisdom shall judge most expedient for restoring peace and harmony in our divided settlement; or, if your honors apprehend that our cause comes more properly before the honorable the General Congress, that you would in your goodness recommend the same to your worthy delegates to espouse it as the cause of the Colony. And your petitioners will ever, etc." [3]

The reference to the "score of men artfully picked" was hardly complimentary to the Transylvania House of Delegates, nor was it altogether candid, seeing that the foremost signer of the memorial, James Harrod, was himself a member of the House of Delegates. But it cannot be denied that the memorialists had good cause for grievance, and it is no less certain that in putting their names to their petition they signed the death warrant of Transylvania.

Henderson, hearing that they had appealed to the Convention, knew that the long-dreaded day of battle had dawned, and hastened to submit a counter-memorial in behalf of the Company. This was about the middle of June, 1776, and even while he was writing it the insurgent Transylvanians were taking a decisive step to repudiate their allegiance. Beginning June 6 an eight-day election was held at Harrodstown for the choosing of two delegates to the Virginia Convention from "West Fincastle," as Harrod and his associates now designated Transylvania. The choice fell on George Rogers Clark and John Gabriel Jones, who soon set out for Williamsburg, at that time the capital of the Old Dominion, bearing with them a second petition in which the Proprietors were attacked more bitterly than before, and the Convention was urged to organize "West Fincastle" as a county of Virginia.

Before Clark and Jones reached Williamsburg the Convention had adjourned after having appointed a commission to take evidence and report on the validity of the Company's title to Transylvania. Henderson, at bay, fought desperately for a favorable verdict, but all his efforts were unavailing. His last chance for success may be said to have been blotted out with the adoption, by the Continental Congress, of the Declaration of Independence. Under the new order of things there was no room whatever for a proprietary government on the soil of America. December, 1776, during the first session of the recently created State Legislature of Virginia, an act was passed organizing Kentucky County out of the domain destined at no distant day to blossom into the State of Kentucky, and including within the boundaries of the new county the delectable realm which Henderson had bought from the Cherokees. With this act Transylvania became only a memory, and the ambitious project of the Transylvania partners was ended forevermore.

Virginia, however, did not condemn them to suffer utter loss. Nov. 4, 1778, the House of Delegates resolved that "as the said Richard Henderson and Company have been at very great expense in making the said purchase and in settling the said lands — by which this Commonwealth is likely to receive great advantages, by increasing its inhabitants and establishing a barrier against the Indians — it is just and reasonable to allow the said Richard Henderson and Company a compensation for their trouble and expense." Acting on this resolution, the Virginia General Assembly voted the Proprietors a grant of two hundred thousand acres of land in Kentucky, and a similar grant was subsequently made to them by North Carolina, whose limits embraced a portion of the Cherokee cession. Strangely enough, while not spurning these donations Henderson refused to acknowledge defeat, and long nursed the vain hope that he would in some way regain the vast region thus wrested from him. We shall once more encounter him, somewhat chastened by his Transylvania experiences, but still aggressively keen for power and for wealth.

In Transylvania — or what had been Transylvania — there were few who felt any sympathy for the luckless Proprietors. But Daniel Boone was one of the few. He saw in Henderson not a grasping, law-defying land speculator, but the good angel who had enabled him to make his home in the land of his heart's desire. And however strongly he resented and deplored the avaricious policy of Henderson's Company, he was not ingrate enough to forget the generous gift its members had made to him in reward for his road-building.

At the moment, however, not even Boone could spare much thought to the misfortunes of the Transylvania Proprietors. For by the time the Blue Grass settlements learned of Virginia's decision, their people were in the midst of war's alarms.

[1] It is perhaps worth noting that the term "nerve" also found place in the slang of the border. But the pioneers used it to indicate a high and praiseworthy degree of courage, not in its modern implication of unblushing effrontery.
[2] From Hogg's report of the results of his "embassy," a curious and interesting document. It may be consulted in Peter Force's "American Archives," Vol. IV of the Sixth Series; or in Mr. Ranck's "Boonesborough."
[3] From the "Journal of the Virginia Convention."

Chapter Ten - War-Time in Kentucky

THE Struggle between the red man and the white for possession of Kentucky began in the summer of 1776, with a dramatic prelude. One July afternoon three girls — Jemima, the second daughter of Daniel Boone, and Elizabeth and Fanny, the daughters of Boone's old friend and fellow-roadmaker, Richard Callaway — left Boonesborough for a boat-ride on the Kentucky. It was a warm day, and the girls, whose ages ranged from fourteen to sixteen, after paddling a short distance from the fort, allowed their canoe to drift idly with the current, which gradually carried them towards the opposite bank. They had no thought of danger, for not an Indian had been seen near Boonesborough since the McQuinney-Saunders affair of the previous winter.

As ill luck would have it, however, a party of young warriors, refusing to abide longer by the treaty forced upon them at the conclusion of Lord Dunmore's War, had left the Shawnee towns only a few days before, and had crossed the Ohio into Kentucky, with the intention of dispersing through the settlements and inflicting what damage they could. Five of these Indians, bedecked in war-plumes and hideous in war-paint, had approached Boonesborough unobserved, and were in hiding near the river's edge at a point where the current carried the drifting canoe close to shore.

As it swept towards the bushes among which they lay concealed, one of them slipped noiselessly into the water, waded out, and, almost before the terrified girls realized his purpose, drew their frail craft within reach of his companions. Tradition has it that the oldest girl, Elizabeth Callaway, made a brave resistance, using her paddle as a weapon, and with it gashing an Indian's head to the bone. But she was quickly disarmed and dragged up the river-bank to where her sister and Jemima Boone, still shrieking with fear and horror, had already been carried.

By gestures more expressive than any words could have been, the Indians bade them cease their cries and save their strength for the long march to the Shawnee towns, threatening instant death to them if they faltered on the way. The girls knew that this was no idle threat, for they had often heard of the ruthlessness with which Indians when returning from a successful raid were wont to slaughter, without regard to sex or age, any captive unable to keep up with the swift pace they usually set. Stifling their sobs, they followed the Shawnees without a murmur through clover field and prairie meadow, cane-brake and maple grove, every step carrying them farther from home.

But, with a resourcefulness that proved them true daughters of pioneer fathers and mothers, they stealthily endeavored to leave a well-marked trail for those who they felt certain would soon be speeding to their rescue. Wherever the ground was at all soft, they trod heavily in it, and at every opportunity they secretly tore from their clothing little pieces of cloth which they fastened to the thorny bushes of the surrounding undergrowth.

It was late in the afternoon before they were missed and the cause of their disappearance made known to the people of Boonesborough through discovery of the empty canoe and the marks of the struggle on the river-bank. Two parties of settlers at once started in hot pursuit. One, consisting of a dozen or more mounted men under Richard Callaway, headed direct to the Licking River, hoping to intercept the Shawnees at the ford of the lower Blue Lick. The other party, smaller and on foot, followed their trail from the Kentucky. It was led by Boone and John Floyd, who had left St. Asaph and was then living at Boonesborough, and it included five other men, three of whom

— Richard Henderson's brother Samuel, Richard Callaway's son Flanders, and John Holder — were in love with the captured girls.

Darkness overtook them before they had gone more than five miles, but at dawn the pursuit was renewed. That day they covered thirty miles, noting with satisfaction the torn fragments of cloth, which told them that the girls were keeping up their strength and courage.

Early next morning, after travelling two miles more, which brought them within two or three miles of the upper Blue Lick, Boone and his companions noticed a thin line of smoke curling upwards through the air. Advancing cautiously, so that the Indians should not be aware of their presence in time to tomahawk the helpless captives, they soon came upon the Shawnees grouped about a fire at which they were cooking buffalo meat for breakfast. A little distance off sat Elizabeth Callaway, with her sister and Jemima Boone on the ground beside her, their heads resting in her lap.

It was evident that the Indians imagined they had thrown off all pursuit, and no less evident that the younger girls were thoroughly exhausted and could not possibly travel much farther. At a signal from Boone the pursuers closed in upon the encampment. But let one of them — John Floyd — tell the story of the rescue in his own words, as he afterwards described it in a letter to his friend. Colonel William Preston of Virginia.

"We discovered each other nearly at the same time," Floyd wrote to Preston, "four of us fired, and all rushed on them, which prevented them from carrying away anything except one shot-gun without ammunition. Mr. Boone and myself had a pretty fair shot just as they began to move off. I am well convinced I shot one through, and the one he shot dropped his gun; mine had none. The place was very thick with canes, and being so much elated on recovering the three broken-hearted little girls, prevented our making further search. We sent them off without their moccasins, and not one of them with so much as a knife or tomahawk." [1]

Whatever idea the settlers may have had that this was a solitary outrage similar to the December incident, was dispelled shortly after the rescuers returned to Boonesborough. Besides the original four settlements of Transylvania, the country to the north as well as to the south of the Kentucky had by this time become dotted with stations and single cabins put up by "improvers" from the frontiers of Pennsylvania, Maryland, Virginia, and North Carolina. McClelland's Station on the Elkhorn, Hinkson's Station on the Licking, and Huston's Station on the site of the present-day Paris were the most important settlements between the Kentucky and the Ohio.

South of the Kentucky the greatest activity was in the country about Harrodstown and Boiling Spring, and along Logan's Branch of the Wilderness Road. The Transylvanians themselves had spread out for many miles, some, like the McAfees, uniting to lay the foundations of new settlements, and others, among whom was Michael Stoner, the companion of Boone's memorable ride to the Falls of the Ohio, removing in little groups of three or four to spy out the land and build homes in particularly desirable locations.

Now, in July of 1776, fugitives came flying from every quarter to the larger settlements, bringing with them dismal tidings of Indian depredations. Men had been murdered, horses and cattle stolen, buildings burned. On the very day that Boone and Floyd arrived with the rescued girls, a party of fugitives from Hinkson's Station galloped into Boonesborough, stayed overnight, and in the morning started for Virginia by way of the Wilderness Road, taking with them ten of the inhabitants of Boonesborough, whom they had infected with their panic.

They were soon followed by others, despite the entreaties of Boone, Callaway, Harrod, Logan, and kindred fearless souls, who refused to flee, and labored day and night to strengthen their defences.

To add to the general alarm, word was received that the Cherokees had attacked the Watauga settlements and purposed, if successful, moving northward into Kentucky. This was the signal for a fresh panic and a still greater exodus across the mountains. But not all could go, and not all wished to go, and many of those who did wish themselves well out of Kentucky felt that duty constrained them to remain.

"I want to return as much as any man can do," Floyd candidly confessed to his friend Preston, "but if I leave the country now, there is scarcely one single man who will not follow the example. When I think of the deplorable condition a few helpless families are likely to be in, I conclude to sell my life as dearly as I can in their defence rather than make an ignominious escape." In the sad years that followed many a man and woman had occasion to bless John Floyd for this noble resolution. [2]

Had the Shawnees taken advantage of the demoralized condition into which the Kentuckians were thrown by their unexpected appearance, there is every reason to believe that they could have wiped out the settlements, and put a stop to westward expansion until after the War for Independence, besides clearing the way for the British, with whom they later became allied, to deliver deadly rear attacks against the insurgent colonists. But instead of concentrating their efforts in successive assaults upon the stations where those who remained had taken refuge, — Boonesborough, Harrodstown, and McClelland's, — they contented themselves throughout the summer and autumn in roaming about the country, destroying the deserted settlements and cabins, and slaying all who happened to fall into their hands. This gave the pioneers a breathing space, enabled them to mature plans for defence, lay in supplies, and despatch messengers to Williamsburg, imploring aid from Virginia.

Had it not been for the presence of George Rogers Clark in Williamsburg it seems altogether likely that these messengers would have found their journey fruitless, for the Virginians were so preoccupied with the urgent problems raised by the War for Independence that they at first paid scant attention to the frantic appeals of the men from the West. But when Clark heard of the danger threatening his fellow-Transylvanians, the situation rapidly changed.

Clark, it will be remembered, had been elected a delegate with John Gabriel Jones to state the case of the Transylvanians against Richard Henderson and Company. Imperious, impetuous, and forceful, he had all along taken the position that Transylvania should approach Virginia in an independent, not a suppliant, spirit, and when he discovered that the authorities were disposed to let the Westerners shift for themselves, he adopted a tone of haughty defiance. If Transylvania, he said in effect, were not worth saving, it was not worth claiming, and if it were compelled to save itself, it assuredly would not acknowledge Virginia's sovereignty.

The threat had the desired result. Late in the summer an initial supply of powder and lead was sent to Boone, — thus tacitly recognized as commander-in-chief of the defending forces, — and a further grant of five hundred pounds of powder was afterwards made, which Clark and Jones undertook to carry by flatboat down the Ohio.

Simon Kenton

Accompanied only by seven daredevil borderers, who readily engaged to serve as boatmen, notwithstanding that the Indians were known to be keeping a close watch on the river, they set out from Pittsburg and after many adventures landed their precious cargo on an island not far from the site of the modern Maysville, hiding it in the woods until they could get help in carrying it to the settlements.

On every side, as they struck cautiously across country, they found evidences of the blight that had fallen on Kentucky, and they frequently had proof — in the way of smouldering camp-fires and fresh trails — that war-parties were even then hovering about. But by dint of the woodcraft in which most of them were masters, they avoided detection and reached McClelland's Station, the only occupied settlement north of the Kentucky River. Here, perhaps for the first time, Clark met a man scarcely less famous than Daniel Boone in the camp-fire talk of the border.

This was Simon Kenton, only twenty-one years old, but already renowned as guide, scout, and Indian fighter — a fair-haired giant of six feet, with nerves of steel and the sunniest of dispositions. Like so many of the makers of the early West, Kenton was Virginia born, and of the restless, aggressive Scotch-Irish stock. He had fled from his native settlement when a lad of sixteen, in consequence of a hand-to-hand frontier duel in which he left for dead his successful rival in a youthful love affair.

From that time forward he had been an adventurous, danger-defying wanderer in the wilds of western Pennsylvania and Virginia, penetrating as far as the mouth of the Kentucky. During Lord Dunmore's War he acted as a spy for both Lord Dunmore and Andrew Lewis, the conqueror of Point Pleasant, and earned the venomous hatred of the Indians for the skill with which he gained information of their movements and intentions. After the war he definitely removed to Kentucky, clearing land and building a cabin near Maysville at about the time the foundations of Boonesborough were being laid in the Blue Grass country farther south. He is credited with having raised the first crop of corn planted and harvested by white men in northern Kentucky.

The winter of 1775-76 he passed at Hinkson's Station on the Licking, and when that settlement was abandoned, owing to the outbreak of Indian hostilities, he removed to McClelland's. As in Lord Dunmore's War he was now employed to spy on the Indians, and many pioneers owed their lives to the vigilance with which he tracked marauding parties of red men and brought timely warning of their approach.

Besides Kenton, Clark found at McClelland's only half a dozen fighting men, or too few to provide a sufficiently strong escort for the ammunition. It was arranged that Kenton should pilot him to Harrodstown for reenforcements, while Jones and the boatmen remained at McClelland's, pending their return. Had this programme been followed all would have been well. As it was, the departure of Clark and Kenton was the signal for a display of rashness that led to the first pitched battle and the first serious reverse of the Indian wars in Kentucky.

Possibly because he wished to enhance his reputation for courage, possibly because he underestimated the fighting qualities of the foe, Jones persuaded the boatmen and some of the people of McClelland's to join him in an immediate attempt to bring in the hidden powder. As was too often the case at that time, no precautions were taken to guard against a surprise; no scouts were sent ahead, no watch kept for unusual sights and sounds that might indicate the presence of an enemy. Yet from the moment Jones and his escort left the protecting palisades of the settlement their every step was dogged, and when they halted for the noonday meal, the lurking foe silently stole ahead to lie in ambush for them.

Jones was the first to perish, falling dead with a bullet in his heart; a second man was killed, and two others were taken prisoners to undergo the lingering tortures of death at the stake. The rest, cutting their way through the living wall that sought to bar them from safety, fled back to McClelland's, whence a messenger was soon speeding to Harrodstown, carrying the tale of folly and disaster and an urgent appeal for help.

In response, Clark, Kenton, and a number of volunteers hastened to the station on the Elkhorn, drove off the Indians after a fight in which several whites were killed, and in the opening days of the new year secured the powder which had been the cause of so much bloodshed, and distributed it among the defenders of Boonesborough and Harrodstown, McClelland's Station being abandoned because of its remote location from the Transylvania settlements.

Now the war entered into a new phase, and one of far more serious import to the brave men and women who were so desperately striving to maintain their foothold in Kentucky. Beginning with the early spring of 1777, not only the Shawnees, but many other tribes abandoned all pretence of neutrality in the conflict between the colonists and the mother country, and openly sided with the latter, being spurred to bloody aggression by the rich presents and glowing promises of Henry Hamilton, the British lieutenant-governor of the Northwestern region, whose headquarters were at Detroit.

It no longer was safe for even fairly strong parties of settlers to move about Kentucky, and all travel in and out of the country, whether along the Wilderness Road or by the Ohio River, came practically to an end. In the single year 1777 Harrodstown was besieged three times and Boonesborough twice, and when free from open attack, both places were so closely invested that, in the daytime at all events, it was next to impossible for the settlers to enter or leave the stockades. Thus besides severing the slender threads of communication which united the Kentucky settlements with the settlements of the East, hundreds of miles away, the Indians frequently succeeded in isolating Boonesborough and Harrodstown from each other, although they were less than fifty miles apart.

So serious did the situation become, owing to a shortage in the food supply, that hunters like Kenton and Boone were obliged to creep out after night-fall, travel long distances before venturing to seek game, and await the return of darkness in order to be able to smuggle in the food thus stealthily won. It was in very truth a starvation-time in Kentucky, Yet when the opportunity offered, as it did more than once, for the settlers to take their wives and children and follow those who had fled to safety the previous year, they stubbornly refused to leave.

"Brother," a chieftain had prophetically told Boone, at the signing of the Sycamore Shoals Treaty, "it is a fine land we sell to you, but I fear you will find it hard to hold." They were finding it hard to hold, but they had resolved to hold it at any cost.

Heroes and heroines all of them, this first year of systematic warfare was marked by many romantic episodes bringing out in clear relief the innate greatness of the men and women who faced the tawny allies of the British in the border battles of the Revolution. As striking an instance as any occurred during a siege of St. Asaph, which had been reoccupied in February by the courageous Benjamin Logan and was now better known as Logan's Fort than by the name it had borne when Transylvania was in its prime.

One morning, about the middle of May, the women of the station were milking outside the stockade, protected by a small detachment from the garrison, which did not number more than fifteen men all told. During the night a force of Shawnees had concealed themselves in a near-by cane-brake, and at the first favorable moment they fired upon the guard. One man was killed outright and two were wounded, one of whom succeeded in escaping to the stockade, where the women had instantly taken refuge, while the other, Burr Harrison, after running a few yards, fell to the ground completely disabled. From a cabin port-hole his wife beheld him lying helpless, and in a frenzy of grief begged that he be rescued before the Indians should rush up and despatch him.

For a moment no one answered her appeal. The Shawnees' first volley had reduced the effective force in the fort to twelve men, and it seemed madness to expose the survivors to further loss. But as she continued to lament and wring her hands, Logan, always chivalrous and devoid of fear, called for volunteers to aid him in an attempt to carry in the wounded man. One stepped forward, John Martin, and together they threw open the stockade gate and leaped towards the groaning Harrison.

Their appearance was the signal for a second volley from the Indians, who were still under cover. Appalled by the leaden hail, Martin turned and sprang back within the fort; but Logan, undaunted, dashed on alone, passed safely through the storm of bullets, lifted Harrison from the ground, threw him across his burly shoulders, and, scarcely slackening his speed beneath the heavy burden, beat a triumphant retreat to the stockade.

Nor was this all. Unable to carry the fort by storm, or to "smoke out" its inmates by setting fire to it, the Indians settled down to a patient siege. Before long the defenders found themselves short of ammunition, with apparently no means of replenishing their supply, as both Harrodstown and Boonesborough were too hard pressed to spare either powder or lead. Again Logan rose to the occasion. Saddling the best horse he possessed, he slipped undiscovered through the enemy's lines, and made for the distant settlements of the Watauga country.

It was impossible to travel by way of the Wilderness Road, so closely were the Indians guarding it; and the alternative was a hazardous journey through a network of Indian trails and buffalo traces, in which even the best-trained woodsman might lose his way and perish. But Logan did not pause to contemplate the difficulties he would have to overcome. Riding each day from dawn until dark, fording streams, guiding his horse up and down rocky heights, crashing recklessly through brushwood and cane-brake, he reached the hamlets on the Holston within a week, and within another week was back at his fort, bearing the glad assurance that an ammunition caravan was on the road and that a hundred militiamen from the Virginia frontier were hastening to the relief of the beleaguered Kentucky stations.

Simon Kenton was another who proved his sterling worth in that grim year 1777. Making his headquarters at Boonesborough he spent most of his time in the open, flitting like a will-o'-the-wisp from one Indian camp to another, eavesdropping near the council-fire, and keeping the settlers thoroughly informed of the enemy's plans. Once, when for some reason he had been detained at Boonesborough, the Indians contrived to approach and attack it before the defenders suspected their presence; but, as things turned out, this gave Kenton an opportunity of performing what was perhaps the most brilliant deed of his entire career.

There were only twenty-two riflemen in Boonesborough at the time, while the attacking force comprised from fifty to one hundred warriors. But, as was their custom, the Indians preferred to rely on strategy rather than on open assault, and most of them remained hidden in the weeds and long grass near the stockade, leaving a mere handful to act as a decoy in enticing the settlers to give chase to them. The trick was successful. Boone, Kenton, and a majority of the garrison rushed out in hot pursuit, and as soon as they were some little distance from the fort the Indians in hiding rose to cut off their retreat.

Realizing the nature of the trap into which they had fallen, Boone shouted to his men to wheel about and make a dash for the gate, firing as they ran. A minute more, and they were in deadly hand-to-hand conflict. Isaac Hite, John Todd, Michael Stoner, and other notables of the early Transylvania days fell, more or less seriously wounded; and with them fell Boone, his leg broken by a bullet.

Whooping in triumph at the thought that the noted "Captain Boone" was in his power, a tall, sinewy brave sprang at him with uplifted tomahawk. Kenton, who had been fighting valiantly, and had already killed two Indians, chanced to catch a glimpse of the impending tragedy — saw Boone half-prostrate on the ground, his arm raised above his head to ward off the death-stroke. With lightning-like rapidity Kenton turned, raised his rifle, pressed it against the warrior's breast, and discharged it. Then, stooping, he lifted Boone and bore him swiftly to the fort; afterwards returning to plunge into the fight once more.

When the battle was over, and the Indians had been driven off, Boone sent for Kenton and knighted him in backwoods fashion. "Well, Simon," said he, "you have behaved like a man — you are a fine fellow." Few words and simple words, but coming from such a source they amounted to a certificate of merit which would forever establish Kenton's reputation.

For Boone's preeminence in the defence of Kentucky was by this time universally recognized. His readiness to encounter danger, his resourcefulness in surmounting the greatest obstacles, — he even learned the art of making gunpowder, — and his constant cheerfulness endeared him to all and made him the inspiration of all. In the words of one well acquainted with his career, he was looked upon as an oracle, whose every utterance was to be obeyed.

It would be quite incorrect, though, to describe Boone as a great military genius. He was not that. His distinction lay in the fact that he was supremely equipped to conduct operations in the kind of warfare in which the Kentuckians were then engaged. He knew the red man and the red man's ways, and besides being a splendid fighter he was the peer of the most wily chieftain in cunning and dissimulation. Other things being equal, he could be depended on to beat the Indian at his own game as could no other borderer of his generation, with the possible exception of Simon Kenton.

But he was deficient in one quality without which no commander may hope to excel — the penetrating vision, almost equivalent to prescience, that impels to drastic, far-reaching action in a time of crisis. Superb in defensive fighting, he was less conspicuous when the occasion demanded a vigorous offence. For this reason he was eventually overshadowed, from the military point of view, by the man who had dragooned the authorities of Virginia into lending the Kentuckians a helping hand — George Rogers Clark.

[1] Samuel Henderson married his sweetheart, the plucky Elizabeth Callaway, three weeks later, this being the first marriage in Kentucky. Some interesting details have been preserved. The ceremony took place in a Boonesborough cabin, Daniel Boone officiating by virtue of having been commissioned a justice of the peace. There was dancing to fiddle music by the light of buffalo tallow candles, and the guests were treated to the first watermelons grown at Boonesborough. At a later date Flanders Callaway became the husband of Jemima Boone, and John Holder, who developed into a redoubtable Indian fighter, married Fanny Callaway.

[2] Floyd, however, was not in Kentucky throughout its seven years of almost perpetual warfare. He had been appointed official surveyor for the Transylvania Company, and in the autumn of 1776 Henderson summoned him to Williamsburg, where he remained until the Virginia Legislature passed the act absorbing Transylvania. He then fitted out a privateer to destroy British shipping, and did considerable damage before being made a prisoner of war. Escaping after a year's imprisonment, he was smuggled across the English Channel to France, where, it is said, Benjamin Franklin supplied him with means to reach Virginia. Once in America again, he hurried back to Kentucky, did splendid service under George Rogers Clark, and by his daring became known throughout the West. In April, 1783, while riding with his brother Charles, he was shot from ambush by an Indian and died a few hours afterwards, at the early age of thirty-three. He was a splendid specimen of the American pioneer, and should find a place in any gallery of portraits of heroes of the early West.

Chapter Eleven - The Campaigning of George Rogers Clark

WHILE Boone was battling with bull-dog tenacity at the settlement that bore his name, Clark was at Harrodstown, rendering magnificent assistance in the defence of that station and carefully maturing a plan whereby he hoped to put an end for all time to the Indian invasions. As yet it was not generally known that the continual struggle with the Indians had its origin in anything other than the natural wrath of the savages at the loss of their favorite hunting-grounds. But Clark, a man of the broadest imagination and the keenest insight, intuitively understood that the true source of hostilities was to be found in the adverse influence radiating from the Northwestern forts and trading-stations which had been established by the French as part of their scheme for New World empire, and now were British possessions.

He rightly suspected that all of them — and especially Detroit in western Canada, and Kaskaskia and Vincennes in the Illinois country — were hotbeds in which the seeds of Indian hatred for the American borderers were assiduously cultivated. Could these posts but be wrested from the British, the problem of persuading or compelling the Indians to maintain peace would be greatly simplified, for they would be deprived of the moral and material support of their white allies.

Moreover, as Clark saw it, the conquest of the country north of the Ohio was absolutely essential to the saving of Kentucky. Thus far the Kentuckians had held their ground, with practically no outside assistance; nor could they reasonably expect much aid, so great were the demands made upon the Eastern settlements by the exigencies of the protracted War for Independence. Yet without aid, or without a respite from the grinding pressure of the Indian onslaughts, the pioneers would in time be worn out, and would have to surrender or retreat. This would mean the complete abandonment of Kentucky, and its abandonment would mean the exposure of the entire Virginia frontier to the tomahawk, the scalping-knife, and the torch.

In this fact Clark saw his only chance for putting into execution an ambitious project that gradually took shape in his mind during the spring and summer of 1777. He would again visit Williamsburg, would depict to the men at the head of affairs the horrors certain to overwhelm border Virginia unless British activity among the Indians were checked, and would himself undertake to check it by the conquest of the Northwestern posts — which, as he would make it a point to remind the authorities, were situated in a region long claimed by Virginia under the terms of her all-embracing charter, and which would thus become doubly Virginia's by right of charter and by right of conquest. All that he should require would be official authorization for the organizing of an expedition, and money to finance it. Everything else, from the recruiting to the fighting, he would engage to carry through without Virginia's aid.

He would march first of all against Kaskaskia, as being most conveniently located for attack from Kentucky; when Kaskaskia had fallen, he would assail the more northerly Cahokia and Vincennes and afterwards, as circumstances permitted, faraway Detroit. It might be objected that the way to Kaskaskia, Cahokia, and Vincennes lay through trackless forests and tangled prairies, by quagmires and over rushing streams — a country, in fine, of the most difficult travel, and teeming with bitterly hostile tribesmen. Clark would airily wave his hand, and assure the sceptical Virginians that all this was of small importance — the men of his army would be men whom nothing could daunt and nothing defeat.

It was a dream such as could be conceived only by a rash, reckless adventurer, or by a man of true genius, certain of his ability to command success. Clark was no mere adventurer. When his vision of conquest first began to assume definite form, he calmly set about ascertaining its feasibility. He took no one into his confidence, — excepting possibly Simon Kenton and James Harrod, with both of whom he was on the most intimate terms, — but sent for two young frontiersmen and employed them to visit the Illinois country in the guise of hunters and traders, examine its resources and defences, and in particular discover the sentiments of the inhabitants of Kaskaskia, Cahokia, and Vincennes with respect to the contest between Great Britain and the American colonies. Most of the people of these three settlements were French or of French descent, and it was Clark's hope that they would at most prove lukewarm in their British allegiance, and would offer no very serious opposition if an American force were sent against them.

The report brought back by his spies confirmed this idea. The commandants and garrisons of the Illinois posts, they informed him, were loyal to the British interest, and took every opportunity of inciting the Indians to depredations in Kentucky. But most of the inhabitants — a care-free, easy-going Creole population, whose life was made up chiefly of feasting and dancing — viewed the struggle with entire indifference, heedless which side won as long as their butterfly existence was not disturbed. They had been taught, however, to regard the American backwoodsmen as devils in human form, far more cruel than any Indian; a piece of news that was not unwelcome to Clark, since he readily perceived how he might profit from it by working on the fears of the French and then gaining their affection by unexpected leniency.

Satisfied that he was not attempting the impossible, he left Harrodstown on October 1, 1777, and after a tedious journey over the Wilderness Road and across the mountains of southwestern Virginia, reached Williamsburg early in November. The fiery Patrick Henry — another Scotch-Irishman, and not unlike Clark in vigor, audacity, and sweep of imagination — was then governor of Virginia, and listened with rapt enthusiasm when the Kentuckian sought him out and unfolded the details of his daring plan. But, Henry declared, Virginia's means were exhausted, she could spare neither troops nor money for even so promising an enterprise.

With the persistence characteristic of the men of the West — and without which they could never have won the West — Clark plied him with new arguments, fervid entreaties. The ardent Henry, willingly persuaded but at a loss to know how he could further Clark's desires, turned for advice to some trusty counsellors — Thomas Jefferson, George Mason, and George Wythe. They, too, were won over by the Kentuckian's eloquence, his air of confidence, his tone of certitude.

Secrecy being indispensable for the success of the enterprise, — since, if an inkling of Clark's intentions got abroad, messengers would be hurried by the British to put the Illinois commandants on their guard, — it was arranged that the sum of twelve hundred pounds should be privately advanced to him, and that he should be given two sets of instructions by Governor Henry. One of these, intended to be made public, simply authorized him to raise three hundred and fifty militiamen for the defence of Kentucky; the other, contained in a private letter, directed him to march against the posts in the Northwest. He was also given the commission of colonel.

So much time had been consumed by these negotiations that it was not until the end of January, 1778, that Clark was able to begin the task of raising his little army. He knew that he could not look for many recruits from among his fellow-Kentuckians, because no matter how strongly they might desire to serve under him they would be obliged to stay at home and protect the settlements; and accordingly he sought for followers from among the people of the less exposed frontier region of the Alleghenies. Even there he found the greatest difficulty in securing volunteers, such was the dread of an Indian invasion, and in the end he was obliged to set out accompanied by a force of only one hundred and fifty — most of them, however, men like himself, strong-limbed, quick-witted, and of lion's courage and endurance.

Voyaging down the Ohio in flatboats, and maintaining a constant watch to prevent a surprise from the Indian-infested forest through which the noble river flowed, the expedition safely reached the Falls of the Ohio, May 27, 1778. Here Clark landed and built a fort, and here his following was strengthened by the arrival of Simon Kenton and several other Kentuckians, as well as a company of volunteers who had marched over the Wilderness Road from the settlements of southwestern Virginia.

Now, for the first time, the true purpose of the enterprise was disclosed to the backwoods army. There were a few who deserted rather than hazard their lives in what they regarded as a mad and suicidal business. But the great majority hailed it with enthusiasm, and swore to follow Clark wherever he might see fit to lead them. To increase their enthusiasm came news of the French Alliance, which they at once interpreted as rendering easier the task of pacifying the inhabitants of the old French posts. June 24, work on the fort having been completed, they once more embarked and voyaged swiftly down the Ohio to a point a few miles below the mouth of the Tennessee. The boats were now abandoned, and a march begun in a northwesterly direction.

Kaskaskia, which Clark intended attacking first, stood in the angle formed by the juncture of the river of that name with the Mississippi; and it would have been much easier to have made the entire journey by water. But Clark rightly feared discovery if he attempted to ascend the Mississippi; and, in fact, he learned from some American hunters, whom chance brought to his camp on the lower Ohio, that the French commandant at Kaskaskia had been warned that some hostile move was contemplated against that town, and had posted a number of sentinels on the banks of the Mississippi to sound an immediate alarm at the approach of any armed force. Besides giving him this valuable information, the hunters offered to guide Clark to Kaskaskia by the shortest possible overland route.

Scouts were sent ahead, both to kill game for provisions and to make sure that no wandering Frenchman or Indian should escape with tidings of the coming of the invaders. Not an ounce of superfluous baggage was taken along, and not a man lagged behind when once the command to start had been given, as every one realized that the only chance for success lay in arriving at their destination in time to catch the garrison unawares. Progress was slow, however, for forty or fifty miles, as the country was heavily timbered, with a dense undergrowth through which a trail had to be cut; and after entering the open prairies that stretched to the north of the forest, some delay was caused by the principal guide losing the way. But just at sunset of July 4 Clark and his weary but undaunted followers — they had marched the last two days "without sustenance" — found themselves on the bank of the Kaskaskia, about three miles above the town.

The mere fact that they had not been attacked was sufficient proof that their presence was still unknown to the garrison. Still, before giving battle, Clark wished to learn if possible the exact state of affairs. Leaving the main body to follow more leisurely, he pushed ahead with a small detachment until he reached a farm-house a mile or so from Kaskaskia. Its Creole occupants were at once made prisoners but treated kindly, and without much urging they told him what he was anxious to learn.

There were, it appeared, comparatively few Indians at Kaskaskia, but a great many French, most of whom had been well armed and drilled by the commandant, an officer named Philippe de Rocheblave. The defences of the fort had been strengthened, and repeated requests had been sent to Governor Hamilton at Detroit, begging him to reenforce the militia by a regiment of regulars. Thus far no reenforcements had arrived, and Rocheblave had latterly relaxed his vigilance, believing that the early rumors of an invasion must have been unfounded. It was quite possible that entrance might be gained not merely into the town, which stood to the north of the fort, but also into the fort itself, before any alarm would be given. Thus reassured, and guided by the Creoles, Clark marched his troops back to the river, where boats were found and a crossing effected. Night had set in, but the moon and stars gave light sufficient for a rapid advance. Just before reaching Kaskaskia, Clark again divided his "army," selecting twelve or fifteen to continue with him to the fort, and ordering the rest to disperse silently through the town in groups of four or five, ready to act as soon as they heard sounds of conflict. Both town and fort were in complete darkness, [1] and the absence of sentinels testified to the feeling of security with which the inhabitants had gone to rest. But, as Clark and his little band drew near the fort gate, which luckily was open, some keen-scented watchdogs set up a noisy howling.

Undeterred, the Americans rushed in, made direct for Rocheblave's house, broke through the door, and captured the commandant in an upper room. With whoops of triumph — which served both to terrorize the bewildered and already panic-stricken garrison, and as a signal to the force in the town — they brought Rocheblave downstairs, placed him under guard, and then overpowered and disarmed his subordinate officers. Meanwhile, yelling like demons, their fellow-Virginians came thundering through the streets, shouting to the people to keep indoors. In fifteen minutes they were masters of Kaskaskia without the firing of a gun.

That night there was no sleep for either the conquerors or the conquered. The frightened Creoles, huddled together in their homes, spent the hours until morning on their knees, praying that God would preserve them. At daybreak Clark's men made a house-to-house search for arms, a proceeding which naturally intensified the prevailing terror. Clark's attitude, when a deputation waited on him to learn his intentions, was even more alarming.

"Giving all for lost," he wrote to George Mason, one of the Virginia statesmen who had been so helpful to him at Williamsburg, "their lives were all they could dare beg for, which they did with the greatest servancy. They were willing to be slaves to save their families. I told them it did not suit me to give them an answer at that time, and they repaired to their houses, trembling as if they were led to execution." [2]

A little later, however, feeling that they had been sufficiently overawed, he called their leading men together, informed them of the alliance between France and the United States, and told them they would be free to come and go as they pleased, provided only that they took an oath of allegiance to the Republic.

All anxiety was at once forgotten in an ecstasy of rejoicing. Light-hearted — one might almost say irresponsible — creatures that they were, it mattered not one whit to the Kaskaskians under what flag they lived. They danced and sang, they decorated their cabins, and, in further token of their joy, erected in the streets curious little pavilions of leaves and flowers. Commandant Rocheblave alone remained irreconcilable, and lest he should stir up trouble Clark soon packed him off to Virginia as a prisoner of war.

But the crowning feature of Clark's policy of pacification was the assurance he gave the local priest, Father Pierre Gibault, that the people would be undisturbed in the practice of their religion. Devout Catholics all of them, the Creoles thenceforward rallied about him with greater enthusiasm than ever, while Father Gibault, overwhelmed with astonishment and gratitude, blossomed forthwith into a zealous promoter of Clark's plans for the extension of the conquest to the neighboring town of Cahokia and the more distant Vincennes.

Bidding some of his parishioners accompany a small party of Americans to Cahokia, and explain to the people of that place the great desirability of offering no resistance to the Americans, the worthy priest himself mounted a horse and rode to Vincennes, a journey of nearly two hundred miles. Early in August he was back with the welcome news that through his influence the American flag had been raised there, and Clark immediately sent one of his officers. Captain Leonard Helm, to take command of the Vincennes militia. In similar fashion he installed Captain Joseph Bowman as commandant at Cahokia, he himself remaining at Kaskaskia.

The problem of pacifying the Illinois Indians had still to be solved, but, by the aid of the Creoles and through a masterly exhibition of strength and tact on his own part, Clark was entirely successful in treating with them at a great council held at Cahokia.

More serious was the difficulty caused by the desire of most of his followers, whose term of service had expired, to return to their homes. He well knew that, pending the arrival of fresh troops from Virginia, he could not afford to lose a man, as it was certain the British would make an attempt to regain the conquered posts. But his expostulations, entreaties, and promises of rich rewards fell on unheeding ears, nearly one hundred of the self-willed backwoodsmen refusing to reenlist, and marching hastily away. To fill their places Clark enlisted an equal number of young Creole volunteers, whom he drilled into really efficient soldiers. This work helped the time pass swiftly and agreeably.

"Our troops," he wrote to Mason, "being all raw and undisciplined, you must be sensible of the pleasure I felt when haranguing them on parade, telling them my resolutions and the necessity of strict duty for our own preservation, etc., for them to return me for answer that it was their zeal for their country that induced them to engage in the service; that they were sensible of their situation and danger; that nothing could conduce more to their safety and happiness than good order, which they would try to adhere to, and hoped that no favor would be shown those that would neglect it. In a short time perhaps no garrison could boast of better order, or a more valuable set of men."

Every day was bringing nearer the moment when the mettle of this "most valuable set of men" would be put to one of the severest tests imposed on any body of troops in the history of warfare. As Clark had fully expected, Governor Hamilton, so soon as he learned the amazing news from the Illinois country, began to organize an expedition of reconquest. An entire month was devoted to fitting it out, and when it left Detroit, Oct. 7, it consisted of about one hundred and fifty whites, mostly French-Canadian volunteers, and one hundred Indians, or a total of two hundred and fifty men, led by Hamilton himself. Later accessions, both of whites and Indians, brought the total up to five hundred.

The shortest and most practicable route to Vincennes was chosen — across Lake Erie to the mouth of the Maumee, up that stream to a large Indian village, and thence by a nine-mile portage to a tributary of the Wabash, down which the expedition floated to its destination; but the weather turned unexpectedly cold, forming surface ice which impeded the progress of the boats to such an extent that Vincennes was not reached until Dec. 17, or seventy-one days after the start had been made from Detroit.

Besides Captain Helm there were only two Americans at the quaint old fort on the Wabash, and as the Creole militia immediately went over to the enemy there was nothing for Helm to do but surrender. An interesting, but quite incredible, tradition has it that when Hamilton approached Vincennes at the head of his motley army, he found Helm standing, match in hand, beside a loaded cannon, and that Helm refused to allow any one to enter until satisfactory terms of capitulation had been arranged.

What actually happened was that, instead of marching out with "the honors of war," as this tradition declares, the Americans were held prisoners and closely guarded to prevent their escaping to Clark with a warning of Hamilton's arrival. It was also decided by the British commander not to advance against Kaskaskia and Cahokia at that time, but to remain at Vincennes until the open weather of spring should render travel less difficult and hazardous. Feeling perfectly secure in his position, he permitted rather more than half his force to go home with orders to return to Vincennes in the early springy to bring reenforcements with them, and to come prepared for a campaign having as its object not simply the expulsion of the Americans from the Illinois region, but the blotting out of the settlements in Kentucky.

Had it been possible for him to execute this ambitious project, the whole course of American history would in all likelihood have been changed. But by lingering at Vincennes he gave Clark a chance to save himself and to save the West for his countrymen — and Clark was not the man to let slip any chance, no matter how slender it might be.

Having once learned of Hamilton's presence at Vincennes and his intended inaction until spring, he determined to march across country and endeavor to repeat his exploit of the previous July. As was immediately pointed out by his Kaskaskia volunteers, who had little relish for so daring a venture, a succession of thaws had caused such heavy floods that a great part of the intervening territory was under water, and even should the troops succeed in dragging themselves through the innumerable bogs and morasses they would scarcely be in a condition to make a winning fight at their journey's end. By way of reply Clark bluntly told them that they could accompany him or not as they chose — that he knew he could depend on his brave Americans, and that he had made up his mind to go to Vincennes if he had to swim every foot of the way.

His air of confidence was not without effect, nor was the attitude taken by the Creole girls of both Kaskaskia and Cahokia, who showed the greatest interest in his expedition and sought to shame their brothers and lovers into joining it. Largely as a result of their urging, the "principal young men of the Illinois" finally consented to undertake the perilous march, and early in February, 1779, Clark was able to set out for Kaskaskia at the head of a combined force of one hundred and seventy Americans and French.

For a week the journey, though slow and difficult, was not so arduous as had been expected. Its monotony was broken by several buffalo hunts, and in the evenings all fraternized together around huge camp-fires, feasting, singing, and telling stories. In this way the men contrived to keep up their spirits, even for some days after they entered the so-called "drowned lands" of the Wabash, a wide tract of flooded country extending from the Little Wabash almost to Vincennes.

Their first experience of the fearful hardships in store for them came when they struck the peninsula between the two branches of the Little Wabash. Here the opposite heights of land were five miles apart, and from one to the other stretched an unbroken sheet of flood-water, at no place less than three feet deep. "This would have been enough," as Clark picturesquely wrote, "to have stopped any set of men that was not in the same temper we was in." A large canoe was hurriedly built to ferry the troops and supplies across the deeper channels, the packhorses swimming behind to be reloaded from scaffolding set up in the shallow parts of the submerged plain. But for most of the way men and beasts alike dragged their weary limbs through the bush-strewn water.

Thenceforward not a mile of the journey was made on dry land, and Clark's desperate followers were frequently obliged to traverse broad expanses of swamp-land and meadow, where the water rose breast-high. Often, too, they were hard pressed to find a dry enough spot on which to camp; and as all game had been driven away by the floods, they began to suffer from hunger as well as from exposure and exhaustion. Under the circumstances it is not surprising that many talked of turning back, and that the Creole volunteers openly threatened to desert. But Clark, with the masterfulness that distinguished his entire career as a military commander, held them firmly to their purpose, and constantly set them an example of heroic boldness and endurance.

Once, it is said, when they refused to trust themselves to a water-filled depression that seemed unfordable, he blackened his face like an Indian, gave the war-whoop, and sprang into the ice-cold water; upon which, without another word, his men waded in after him, following his tall form until they reached in safety the point at which they had been aiming.

The last few miles were far and away the worst. On the fifteenth day from Kaskaskia the famished and worn soldiers crossed the Wabash in a pouring rain and turned north for the final stage of the heartbreaking march. All about them was a watery waste, broken only by some scattered hillocks that barely crested the flood. Many of the men were so weak that they had to be carried in canoes, while the rest staggered wearily forward, the water often up to their chins. That day they covered less than three miles, and, drenched to the bone, passed the night on a boggy island-knoll "within sound of the evening and morning guns from the fort." Next day the story was the same, and nightfall found them still some miles from Vincennes. Before morning it turned bitterly cold — so cold that their wet garments stiffened on them like so many coats of armor. Now came a renewal of the mutterings of discontent and mutiny, but Clark, unshakable as ever, grimly took his accustomed place at the head of the column, and bade his officers bring up the rear and shoot any one who refused to march.

A little while and they could plainly see the thick fringe of forest behind which Vincennes nestled. In between lay what was in the summer a verdant, smiling plain, but was then a shallow lake four miles wide and without one inch of ground showing above its smooth surface. All but the strongest began to slacken their pace when halfway across. Some, unable longer to maintain their footing, were saved from drowning only by the efforts of their sturdier comrades, who lifted them into the waiting canoes. As they approached the woods the water deepened until it was up to the shoulders of the tallest, but by the aid of the canoes and of floating logs all managed to reach shore without mishap. Not a few, however, were so exhausted that they fell forward the moment they set foot on land. Had Hamilton and his British garrison put in an appearance at that moment, Clark's ever memorable march across the "drowned lands" of the Wabash must have come to an inglorious end.

Fortunately, as Clark learned from a Vincennes Frenchman whom some of his Creoles captured, Hamilton had not the slightest suspicion that a hostile force was — or could be — within striking distance. The prisoner also gave Clark the pleasing assurance that the people of Vincennes were none too fond of the British governor, and would certainly not take up arms in his behalf if they could avoid doing so. This led the bold Kentuckian to map out a course of action which, even for him, was singularly audacious.

Waiting until his men had warmed themselves beside some blazing fires, had dried their clothes and rifles, and had refreshed themselves with a little buffalo meat, he sent the prisoner to Vincennes as the bearer of a "proclamation" in which he announced his intention of attacking the fort that night, promised generous treatment to all who proved themselves "true citizens," and advised all others to "repair to the fort, and join the Hair-Buyer General, and fight like men."

The town of Vincennes was some little distance from the fort, and although the invaders could be seen from the former they were hidden from the view of the garrison. In order to give the townspeople a false idea of his strength, Clark caused his men to parade up and down in such a way that they seemed to be three or four times as numerous as they really were. But he need not have resorted to this stratagem. The mere mention of his name, and his sudden and totally unexpected appearance out of the flood-swept meadows, so appalled the inhabitants of Vincennes that not one of them dared show sufficient friendliness to Hamilton to visit the fort and warn him. How unprepared Hamilton was, may be judged from the fact that, when the attack began, shortly after seven o'clock, he supposed that the first shots were fired by some drunken Indians.

Looking out, however, and perceiving in the bright moonlight that the fort was surrounded by white men, he instantly grasped the situation and made hurried preparations for defence. As in most structures of the kind, there was a blockhouse at each of the four corners of the high stockade surrounding the garrison's quarters, and all four blockhouses were equipped with cannon. These were at once discharged against the assailants, who scattered in every direction to renew their attack from whatever would give them cover.

George Rogers Clark

Although without artillery himself, Clark realized that it was imperative to silence the enemy's guns in some way, and he quickly passed the word to concentrate the rifle-fire on the batteries of the blockhouses. All of his Americans, and many of the Creoles were crack shots; and so deadly accurate was their aim that before many minutes none of the garrison dared attempt to operate the cannon. But they kept up a brave defence until one o'clock in the morning, when the moon set and darkness compelled a suspension of hostilities.

Before sunrise Clark gained a decided advantage by throwing up a strong intrenchment near the fort, thus enabling his sharpshooters to harass its defenders with comparatively little danger to themselves. The absence of any attempt at a sortie, and the silencing of the guns, convinced him that unless aid came from outside, Hamilton must in the end surrender. To guard against possible interference he detached fifty men to watch the approaches to the town; and it was well that he did so, for early in the morning a party of Indians rode into Vincennes, fresh from a successful foray against the frontier.

Maddened by the sight of the scalps which the savages ostentatiously displayed, Clark's men fell upon them, killed and wounded a number and made six of them prisoners. By Clark's orders these captives were ruthlessly tomahawked and thrown into the Wabash in full view of the garrison — an act which had the double effect of terrorizing the people of Vincennes into continued neutrality, and of creating a panic among the French-Canadians in the fort.

An hour or two earlier Clark had sent a messenger to Hamilton inviting him to save himself from "the impending storm," but Hamilton had angrily declined "to be awed into an action unworthy of a British subject." Now, convinced by the attitude of his French-Canadian militia that it was impossible to hope to hold out much longer, he requested a truce for three days.

"Colonel Clark's compliments to Mr. Hamilton," came the stern reply, "and begs leave to inform him that Colonel Clark will not agree to any other terms than that of Mr. Hamilton's surrendering himself and garrison prisoners at discretion. If Mr. Hamilton is desirous of a conference with Colonel Clark, he will meet him at the church, with Mr. Helm."

To the little French church in Vincennes, at a late hour in the afternoon, came the helpless "Mr. Hamilton," ablaze with impotent wrath at the thought of being obliged to yield his fort to "a set of uncivilized Virginia woodsmen armed with rifles."

It was not a pleasant meeting. Clark, in his rugged, outright way, and unsparing in his use of epithets, denounced Hamilton to his face as the one man responsible for the atrocities of the Indian allies of the British. Defending himself on the plea that he had but been carrying out the orders of his superiors, hot and angry words flew fast. Ultimately, though only after much disputing, terms of capitulation were arranged, Hamilton agreeing to surrender the fort at ten o'clock the following morning, Feb. 25, together with its garrison of seventy-nine men. Promptly at the hour appointed, the victorious Clark marched in, hoisted the American colors, and gave to the fort the new name of "Patrick Henry," in honor of the man without whose aid his dream of conquest would never have come true.

That it had come true, and that it was pregnant with the most far-reaching consequences to posterity, not even Clark realized as he stood in the battle-scarred stockade amid the brave fellows who had followed him through flood and forest. Yet, with the fall of Vincennes a new era opened in the history of the isolated region where, so many years before, the Frenchman had planted his forts and trading stations in the vain hope of checking the irresistible advance of his English rival.

Gone forever was the day of French dominion — gone, too, the day of British supremacy. Henceforth it was to be the American — bold, hardy, enterprising, and progressive — who should hold and open up and develop the prairies and valleys of the great Northwest. With fewer than two hundred ragged, starving, and enfeebled soldiers, George Rogers Clark had won for the United States an inland kingdom of magnificent possibilities, had dealt a giant's blow in behalf of his fellow-Kentuckians and of the larger cause of independence, and had earned for himself an imperishable renown in his country's history.

Not that the conquest of Kaskaskia, Cahokia, and Vincennes, and the capture of Hamilton — who was sent in irons to Virginia — brought immediate peace to the men of Kentucky. They still had to fight long and manfully and desperately to defend their homes against the raiding savage. But without the respite afforded by Clark's campaigning, which had the effect both of weakening the enemy and of encouraging immigration to the West, the Kentuckians must in time have acknowledged defeat. The marvel is that they did not succumb during his absence, when they experienced many severe losses, not the least of which was the dragging away of their leader, Daniel Boone, into a prolonged Indian captivity.

[1] Modern historical research seems to have completely demolished the romantic and well-known tradition in which Clark is represented as having arrived at Kaskaskia during the progress of a ball given by the officers of the fort and as having made his way unnoticed to the ball-room, where he grimly bade the revellers continue their dancing, "but to remember that they now danced under Virginia and not Great Britain." For a criticism of this legendary version, see Dr. Thwaites's "How George Rogers Clark won the Northwest."

[2] Clark's letter to Mason (dated Louisville, Nov. 19, 1779) is an invaluable document for the study of the conquest of the Northwest. It is printed in full, together with the public and private instructions given to Clark by Governor Henry, in No. 3 of the "Ohio Valley Historical Series." Copious extracts are quoted from it in Dr. Thwaites's "How George Rogers Clark won the Northwest." For a detailed account of Clark's campaign, see also Consul Wilshire Butterfield's "George Rogers Clark's Conquest of the Illinois and the Wabash Towns, 1778 and 1779."

Chapter Twelve - Boone among the Indians

IT was while attempting to render an important and necessary service to his fellow-settlers at Boonesborough that the famous explorer and road-maker for the second time became an Indian captive.

Travel along the Wilderness Road, as has been said, had almost completely ceased as a result of the war, and the Kentuckians had consequently been unable to obtain the supplies they had formerly imported from the manufacturing centres of Virginia. Among these was that indispensable article of food — salt. During the fall of 1777, however, they had received from the Virginia government a number of boiling kettles which it was hoped would enable them to make salt for themselves at the various buffalo licks.

Early in January, 1778, a party of thirty settlers, headed by Boone, left Boonesborough for the lower Blue Lick for the purpose of securing at least a year's supply of salt, so that they should have an ample quantity on hand in case the activity of the Indians prevented them from resuming its manufacture. For some weeks the savages had given comparatively little trouble, and it was confidently hoped that the salt-makers would be able to carry out their undertaking without molestation. Nevertheless a sharp watch was kept, and while half the party worked at the boiling, the others ranged cautiously through the woods, ready to run in and give the alarm at the least sign of Indians.

Several weeks passed uneventfully. A considerable amount of salt was made, and shipped to Boonesborough in charge of three or four men, and in a few more days the entire party intended returning to the fort. But, by an unlucky chance, just as they were about to depart, a war-band of Shawnees surprised and captured Boone and compelled him to lead them to the camp, where all were made prisoners.

At the time of his capture Boone was scouting about ten miles from the Blue Lick, in the midst of a blinding snowstorm. It was late in the afternoon and he was homeward bound, leading a pack-horse laden with buffalo meat which he had shot during the day. Suddenly, out of the whirl of the snow, four burly Indians confronted him. Dropping the horse's halter he turned and ran, dodging in and out among the trees, with the Shawnees in hot pursuit. Fleet of foot though he was, the Indians were faster, and in a few minutes he was in their grasp and securely bound.

They took him some miles to an encampment where he found more than a hundred warriors, commanded by a Shawnee chieftain, Black Fish, and accompanied by two Canadians and two American renegades from Pittsburg, James and George Girty, brothers of a notorious "white Indian," Simon Girty. [1] Among the Indians, by a singular coincidence, were several of the party who had captured him eight years before, and these at once recognized him, and, with mock politeness, introduced him to their mates.

He learned, to his dismay, that the Indians were en route to attack Boonesborough. But first, they told him, he must conduct them to the camp of the salt-makers and induce the latter to surrender. His decision was quickly reached. He knew the Indian character well enough to be aware that if they did succeed in capturing the salt-makers, they would abandon all idea of attacking Boonesborough, and would instead return in triumph to their villages, perfectly content with having taken a few prisoners. For the sake of the settlement he felt that he ought to acquiesce in the Shawnees' demands, even though they might afterwards fail to live up to their promise to treat the salt-makers kindly. Accordingly, the following day he guided the Indians to the camp at the lower Blue Lick, and, pointing out to his luckless companions that resistance to such an overwhelming force would be useless, persuaded them to lay down their arms.

For this he was later court-martialed, but justly acquitted. Things fell out exactly as he had hoped they would. In spite of the angry protests of the Girty brothers and the two Canadians, the Shawnees refused to proceed another step, and began their homeward march, which turned out to be a terrible journey for captors and prisoners alike. The weather was intensely cold, there was a heavy snowfall, and before reaching the Shawnee town of Chillicothe — situated on the Little Miami, about three miles north of the present town of Xenia, Ohio — the Indians, in order to obtain food, were forced to kill some of their horses and dogs. Whatever provision they had they shared liberally with the salt-makers, not out of any kindly feeling but because they wished to take them to Detroit and receive the liberal rewards offered by the British governor, Hamilton, for all prisoners brought in.

Even so, there was a strong minority that would have preferred torturing them to death. At a council held immediately after their capture a vote was taken on the question of burning them at the stake or of reserving them for the governor's rewards, and fifty-nine voted for the stake as against sixty-one for the money, the majority in favor of keeping faith and sparing their lives being thus only two.

There was one prisoner, indeed, who they soon determined not to release for any consideration. This was Boone. Appreciating keenly the responsibility he had taken upon himself by delivering his friends into their power, he spared no effort to placate the Indians and keep them in good humor. As a result they became sincerely fond of him, and announced their intention of making him one of themselves.

It was all in vain that, as soon as he learned this, Boone exerted himself to win the good-will of Governor Hamilton, assuring him, with pardonable mendacity, of his entire willingness to turn Tory and desert the American cause. Hamilton, believing him, and regarding him, on account of his knowledge of forest life and skill with the rifle, as a most desirable acquisition, offered as high as one hundred pounds sterling for his release. The Indians merely shook their heads, while their chieftain, Black Fish, declared that not only would he take Boone back with him from Detroit to Chillicothe, but that he would adopt him into the tribe as his own son.

The ceremony of adoption was no perfunctory affair. "The hair of the candidate's head," says one well acquainted with Indian customs, "is plucked out by a tedious and painful operation, leaving a tuft, some three or four inches in diameter, on the crown, for the scalp-lock, which is cut and dressed up with ribbons and feathers. The candidate is then taken to a river and there thoroughly washed and rubbed, 'to take all his white blood out.' He is then taken to the council-house, where the chief makes a speech in which he expatiates upon the distinguished honors conferred on him and the line of conduct expected from him. His head and face are painted in the most approved and fashionable style, and the ceremony is concluded with a grand feast and smoking."

How far the details of this programme were executed in Boone's case it is impossible to say, but it may safely be hazarded that by the time the Indians had finished painting and decorating him not even his mother would have recognized him. Still, he was careful to keep them from suspecting that he considered his transformation into a full-fledged Shawnee brave anything but a high honor. Not the least valuable of the many accomplishments he had gained through his constant contact with the wilderness, was the art of concealing not merely his person but his feelings. He entered with well-simulated enthusiasm into the life of the Indians, smoked with them, hunted with them, ate with them, and seemingly enjoyed it all, although, as he afterwards naively said, the food and lodging were "not so good as I could desire, but necessity made everything agreeable." In a short time Big Turtle, as he had been named, was one of the most popular warriors in the village.

All the while he was patiently planning a way of escape, and resorting to the most ingenious devices to thwart the vigilance with which the Indians, notwithstanding their liking for him, watched his every movement. It was their custom, whenever they permitted him to leave Chillicothe on a hunting expedition, to count the bullets he took with him, and he was required to return all excepting those spent in shooting game. By dividing a number of bullets into halves, and using light charges of powder, just sufficient to kill turkeys, squirrels, and other small game, he managed to save several charges for his own use if a chance to escape presented itself.

Early in June, having then been a prisoner of the Shawnees for more than four months, he was sent with a small detachment of Indians to make salt at a lick on the Scioto. Upon his return, ten days later, he was astonished to find that during his absence Indians from other towns and tribes had been pouring into Chillicothe, until nearly five hundred warriors were assembled there, decked in all the panoply of a war-party. He had picked up a smattering of the Shawnee tongue, and by unobtrusively mingling with the throng he learned that within a week it was planned to send a strong expedition into Kentucky, having for its special object nothing less than the destruction of Boonesborough.

Now indeed Boone felt that the time had come when, at all hazards, he must attempt to escape. He spent a day in making secret preparations, gathering together his little stock of powder and bullets, cleaning his rifle, sharpening his hunting knife, and mending his moccasins. Then, early in the morning of June 16, having obtained permission to go hunting, he struck off from Chillicothe in a direct line for the Ohio. He would have at least ten hours' start, but pursuit was certain to be fast and furious the moment his flight was discovered, and knowing this, he raced through the forest at top speed in the effort to put as many miles as possible between him and Chillicothe before nightfall.

Perhaps no other incident in Boone's long and remarkable career brings out so clearly the noble characteristics that have made his memory so dear to Americans as does this flight through the Ohio wilderness. He was fleeing, not to gain freedom for himself, but to save the lives of others. Like a father ready to make any sacrifice for the sake of his children, Boone was deliberately taking his life in his hands that he might carry a warning to the settlers who had so often looked to him in the past for protection and guidance. Were he captured his fate was sealed — a terrible doom awaited him. His flight would seem to the Shawnees the basest ingratitude, punishable by death in its most horrid form and after excruciating tortures. But he thought not of himself — he thought only of the brave men, the helpless women and children, who would inevitably fall victims to the ferocity of the savages were he overtaken.

Doubling on his tracks, setting blind trails, wading down the beds of streams, using every artifice of the skilled woodsman to baffle his pursuers, he finally reached the Ohio. He was not a good swimmer, and he anticipated great difficulty in crossing that river, which had been swollen by heavy rains and was running with a strong current. But he was lucky enough to find an abandoned canoe caught among some bushes growing along the bank, and although the frail craft was badly damaged, he contrived to mend it sufficiently to bear him in safety to the other side.

He was still many miles from Boonesborough, and by no means out of danger, for at any moment he might stumble into the camp of some wandering party of Indians. Renewing his precautions, sleeping in hollow logs and dense thickets, preferring to go hungry rather than fire his gun, and setting blind trails as before, he journeyed painfully on, his clothing in tatters, his body bleeding from the wounds of thorn and bramble, his feet bruised and aching. Not until the third day after his departure did he have a real meal, when at one of the Blue Licks he ventured to shoot a buffalo. The evening of the fourth day, or the morning of the fifth, the exact time being uncertain, he staggered into Boonesborough, where he was welcomed as one risen from the dead.

While he was in captivity many of the settlers, despairing of receiving aid from Virginia, and losing all confidence in their ability to hold Kentucky unaided, had returned to the settlements east of the mountains. Among these was Mrs. Boone, who had given him up for lost, and taking their family with her, had gone to her father's home on the Yadkin, travelling by pack-horses over the Wilderness Road. Of all Boone's kinsfolk there were only two to greet him, his brother Squire and his daughter Jemima, who had, as we know, become the wife of Flanders Callaway. The latter was still at Boonesborough, together with his father Richard Callaway, John Kennedy, John Holder, and others of the original settlers. But the entire population of that station was less than a hundred, of whom barely a third were men of "fighting age"; and the defences were in great need of strengthening and repair.

Boone, exhausted though he was by the hardships of his flight, promptly took upon himself the task of preparing to meet the expected attack. He despatched an express rider to the Holston settlements in southwestern Virginia, with an urgent appeal for reenforcements; set men to work on the fortifications; and sent out scouts to report the coming of the foe. To his great relief it soon became evident that, having failed to recapture him, the Indians had either entirely abandoned their project or had postponed it to a later day, when they might again hope to take the settlers unawares.

The arrival of his trusted comrade-at-arms, Simon Kenton, with news of the taking of the Northwest posts made his heart still lighter, and aroused a lively hope that the settlers' days of tribulation would soon be at an end. But this hope was dissipated almost immediately when Stephen Hancock, one of the salt-makers who had been taken prisoner with Boone, escaped to Boonesborough and reported that, in response to the insistent demands of Governor Hamilton, Black Fish was once more assembling his warriors for a blow against the "rebels of Kentuck."

In order to obtain confirmation of Hancock's story, and if possible alarm Black Fish into again desisting from an attack, Boone determined to carry the war into the enemy's country. About the middle of August he marched from the fort at the head of a scouting party of nineteen sharpshooters, — including Kenton, Hancock, and Holder, — crossed the Ohio, and penetrated to within a short distance of Chillicothe. Near Paint Creek, a branch of the Scioto, he fell in with a war-party of thirty Shawnees, marching to join the main body which, as Boone had already learned, was even then on its way to Kentucky. Although outnumbered he promptly ordered his men to charge, and, after a brief skirmish, put the Indians to flight and captured their horses and baggage.

Wisely enough, however, instead of attempting to follow up his victory, he began a rapid march back to Boonesborough, evaded the Indian army, and reached the fort barely two hours before the enemy encamped opposite it on the north bank of the Kentucky. It was, as his biographer. Dr. Peck, has said, an exceedingly "gallant and heroic affair for twenty men to march one hundred and fifty miles into the heart of the Indian country, surprise and defeat thirty warriors, and then effect a successful retreat in the face of a foe twenty times more numerous than their own force."

Had he not got back to Boonesborough in safety there could have been no hope for that place. As it was, even the stout-hearted Boone acknowledged that the outlook was of the gloomiest. There were but fifty men and boys in the fort fit to bear arms, and even counting the women, who rendered noble assistance in the defence, the total fighting force did not exceed seventy-five. Against this. Black Fish brought the largest army that had yet threatened the Kentucky settlements.

It included upwards of four hundred Indians, mostly of the war-loving Shawnee tribe, and a company of Canadians, commanded by Lieutenant De

Quindre, of the Detroit militia. Without exception the minor chieftains were, like Black Fish, veterans of many fights. One was Black Bird, called by Governor Henry of Virginia "the great chief of the Chippewas," who shortly afterwards changed his allegiance from the British to the American side. Another was Black Hoof, who had been conspicuous in Braddock's defeat. A third was Moluntha, known to the Kentuckians as one of their most implacable enemies. None, it is true, was of the caliber of a King Philip, a Pontiac, or a Tecumseh, but all were warriors to be dreaded.

It was just before sunset of Sept. 6 that Boone and his scouts galloped hastily through the gate of the Boonesborough stockade, and in the ensuing dusk of twilight the defenders could see the plumed and painted forms of the Indians moving through the trees and bushes on the opposite side of the river. We may feel sure that there was little sleep for any one in the fort that night. But morning dawned without the expected attack, revealing the Indians, however, among a thick covert of undergrowth only a few hundred feet from Boonesborough. They had marched down the Kentucky, crossed it at a point still called "Black Fish Ford," climbed the steep southern bank, and drawn near to the fort under cover of the darkness.

It soon became evident that they hoped to gain a bloodless victory. A Canadian carrying a flag of truce advanced into the open space in front of Boonesborough, announced himself the bearer of a letter from Governor Hamilton, and called on the garrison to send commissioners to discuss its contents with delegates from the invading army. Delighted at the prospect of gaining time which might permit the arrival of the reenforcements expected from Virginia, the settlers readily consented, naming Boone, the elder Callaway, and William Bailey Smith as their commissioners. For the enemy, De Quindre, Black Fish, and Moluntha advanced to meet them, bringing as a token of good faith a present of some roasted buffalo tongues.

Now began a series of negotiations without parallel in border warfare. Hamilton's letter, it appeared, demanded the surrender of Boonesborough on terms which both the governor and the Indian chieftains evidently thought too tempting to be rejected, for Black Fish informed Boone that "he had come to take the people away comfortably, and had brought along forty horses for the old folks, the women, and the children to ride." With great gravity Boone replied that he would have to consult the settlers before returning a reply, and asked for a two days' truce, which was readily granted.

The two days were spent by the garrison not in debating Hamilton's offer, but in preparing for a vigorous resistance. While the Indians smoked, chatted, and lolled about in full view of the fort, the whites brought in their cattle, which had been grazing near the stockade, put their rifles in perfect condition, and laid in a large supply of water from a near-by spring. [2] Then, on the expiration of the truce, they defiantly announced through Boone that they had "determined to defend the fort while a man was living."

Still the invading army refrained from hostilities. De Quindre, acting as their spokesman, replied that they were under instructions from Hamilton to avoid bloodshed, and declared that if the settlers would only sign a treaty swearing allegiance to the British cause, the Indians would be withdrawn and they be left in peaceable possession of their fort.

"Send out nine representatives," said he, "with full powers to act for the whole, and things can be speedily adjusted."

It was a proposal that smacked of treachery, but the settlers, still anxious to gain time, accepted it. Early the next morning, under the great elm that had witnessed the signing of the Transylvania Compact, Boone, Richard and Flanders Callaway, and six other settlers met De Quindre, Black Fish, Black Bird, Black Hoof, and Moluntha to consider the terms of the proposed treaty.

Around them, although at a considerable distance, the Indian army squatted on the ground, smoking and impassively watching the proceedings. In the fort, under strict orders from Boone, sharpshooters peered through the portholes, ready, should they receive a prearranged signal, to pour a volley into the Indians. As a further precaution every woman and child in Boonesborough made a showing at the pickets to deceive the enemy as to the garrison's strength.

The whole day was spent in "pow-wowing" and feasting, and by nightfall the nine commissioners had promised to sign next morning a treaty which would result in raising the British flag above the backwoods fort. Again every precaution was taken to prevent a surprise. At Boone's demand the commissioners of both parties went to the meeting-place unarmed. But there was no indication that the Indians really meditated treachery until, after the treaty had been formally signed, Black Fish took his pipe from his mouth, and quietly observed: —

"Brothers, to confirm this treaty we must have a hand-shake all round, two braves to each white brother."

At his words eighteen stalwart young Indians strode towards the nine commissioners, extended their hands in a friendly manner, and then, getting a firm grasp, attempted to drag the whites away. But the latter were too quick for them, each freeing himself by a dexterous movement and springing aside, while Boone gave the signal to the sharpshooters, who answered with a leaden hail that for a moment checked pursuit.

Running at utmost speed, the settlers made for the fort, bullets whistling after them as they fled. Only two were struck, neither being fatally wounded, and before the Indians could rally from the sharpshooters' attack eight of the nine were out of harm's way behind the stockade, which the ninth also managed to reach at night-fall after having lain concealed in the underbrush all day.

There followed a siege, bitter, vindictive, and prosecuted by the Indians with a pertinacity vastly different from their customary method of making war. But, as usual, they first resorted to strategy to gain a victory. Throughout the afternoon the settlers could plainly hear sounds that indicated they were breaking camp, and the next morning, while it was still dark, the splashing and clattering of horses as the crossed the river. Bugle calls by the Canadians resounded through the neighboring hills, growing fainter and fainter until they could no more be heard. But all the time, stealthily and noiselessly, the Indians were recrossing the Kentucky and hiding themselves along the trail that led from the stockade gate.

It was a well-laid plan, but quite futile, for the Kentuckians had expected that some such scheme would be hatched by their crafty foe, and not one of them ventured forth. By noon, realizing that the stratagem had failed, the Indians once more drew near Boonesborough, and raked it with a fire which did little damage because the covert in which they kept hidden was almost out of rifle-range. Creeping still nearer, protecting themselves behind trees, stumps, logs, and hillocks, they directed their bullets against every port-hole and crevice in the stockade; while the settlers, of necessity sparing of their ammunition, held their fire until they were sure of making every bullet count.

Among the Indians was a runaway negro, an expert shot, who climbed a tree overlooking the stockade with the intention of picking off any settler that might chance to pass within range of his rifle. But he had fired only two or three shots when his position was detected, and a well-aimed bullet, said to have been discharged by Boone himself, brought the negro crashing to the ground, from which he rose no more. As was always the case, the Kentuckians were far better marksmen than the Indians, but the latter were so adept in concealment that it was extremely difficult to get a good shot at them.

Victory for the invaders could not have been long delayed had De Quindre been able to spur his tawny army to make a charge. Finding this impossible, he set a squad at work digging a mine which would enable them either to blow up the fort or force an entrance into it. Meantime an incessant firing was kept up to mask this movement. But an eagle-eyed settler, noticing a broad, muddy streak in the Kentucky, jumped to the conclusion that it was caused by dirt being thrown from an excavation beneath the river-bank; and Boone, who was in full charge of the defence, at once started a countermine that would cut into and expose the enemy's tunnel.

More than once an attempt was made to burn the garrison out by hurling fire-brands on the cabin roofs, but the flames were quickly extinguished by brave volunteers, and drenching rains soon rendered this device useless. Still, there was imminent danger that the defenders would be overcome by sheer hunger and fatigue. For ten weary days and nights the Indians encircled the fort, while night and day the surrounding hills echoed with their taunting cries and the spiteful cracking of their rifles. Within its smoke-choked enclosure, their eyes reddened, their faces drawn and powder-grimed, the settlers stood doggedly at their posts, the women as well as the men constantly on the alert to repel a charge or detect any new stratagem. As Ranck, the historian of Boonesborough, has well said: —

"Even in this, the season of their greatest extremity, there was no thought of surrender. Encompassed overwhelmingly by the savage power of England, cut off from the world in the depths of a solitude vast and obscure, forgotten by the overburdened Continental Congress, unaided by hard-pressed Virginia, worn out by privations and sorely tempted, the feeble little handful of 'rebels' at Boonesborough were true to the last to the principles of the Revolution and suffered as nobly for freedom and for country as did the men of Bunker Hill or the shivering heroes of Valley Forge."

September 18, after a night of constant rain, day dawned without a renewal of the gun-fire that had for so long a time heralded sunrise. Not a sound came from the besiegers' camp. To Boone and his comrades the silence seemed ominous, and hastily snatching a slender breakfast, they redoubled their precautions to meet some unexpected move. But as the hours passed and the silence remained unbroken, the hope began to grow in their hearts that the Indians had raised the siege. One after another, wary scouts slipped out of the stockade, to hurry back at noon with the joyful news that the enemy had actually departed and were well on their way to the Ohio.

The cause of their retreat was then ascertained. During the night, or the previous day, the big tunnel which they had been so laboriously constructing had caved in; and, never liking manual labor, it was evident that the Indians had refused to begin work on it anew, and, disgusted with their repeated failures to take the fort, had determined to return home. Had it not been for the presence of De Quindre and the Canadians, the red men would in all probability have reached this decision long before, for persistency in attack has never been an Indian characteristic. But that, on this occasion, they had exerted themselves to the utmost to beat down the stubborn defence they encountered, is shown by the fact that after their departure Boone and his men picked up a hundred and twenty-five pounds of flattened bullets which had been fired at the stockade; while it was estimated that a hundred pounds more had been lodged in the stout walls of a single blockhouse.

Despite this extravagant expenditure of ammunition the casualties within the fort had been amazingly small — only two men killed and four wounded. The Indian loss was far heavier, owing to the superior marksmanship of the whites, and included, according to an estimate by Boone, thirty-seven killed and probably twice as many wounded. It had been a signal victory, the more memorable because it marked the last attempt of the savages to capture Boonesborough.

[1] The Girtys were borderers who, joining the British, participated in numerous Indian raids against the frontier settlements. Simon was especially dreaded and hated by the backwoods people, and was credited with many acts of diabolical cruelty which, as recent historical research has made certain, he did not commit. Still, when everything that can be said in his favor is said, he remains a thorough-

ly despicable figure. For an excellent account of Simon and his brothers, see Consul Wilshire Butterfield's "History of the Girtys."

[2] Prudent in most things, the early settlers of Kentucky were inexplicably careless with respect to the important matter of having a protected source of drinking water. With few exceptions they sank no wells within their stockades, but were dependent on springs in the open. During the Indian wars this resulted in disaster on more than one occasion. Once, as we shall see, it gave opportunity for an almost incredible act of heroism by pioneer women.

Chapter Thirteen - The Last Years of the War

ONE week after the departure of the Indians, a company of militiamen arrived from Virginia, the reenforcement whose tardy coming had placed the settlers in such great peril. Boone, feeling that the fort was now in no immediate danger of attack, was anxious to start east at once for the purpose of bringing back his family. But ere he could do so, he was called upon to answer, before a court martial at Logan's Fort, a series of sensational and most unjust charges.

His accuser was none other than his old friend Richard Callaway, who had been steadily opposed to the policy of negotiating with the invaders. In his charges Callaway specifically asserted: —

First, that Boone had unnecessarily surrendered the salt-makers at the Blue Lick.

Second, that when a prisoner he engaged with Governor Hamilton to surrender the people of Boonesborough, who were to be removed to Detroit and live under British protection and jurisdiction.

Third, that having returned from captivity he encouraged a party of settlers to accompany him on an expedition into the Indian country, thereby weakening the garrison at a time when the arrival of an Indian army was daily expected.

Fourth, that preceding the attack on Boonesborough, he was willing to take the officers of the fort, on pretence of making peace, to the Indian camp, beyond the protection of the guns of the garrison.

In effect, Callaway practically accused Boone of treason, an accusation which the vast majority of the settlers knew to be ridiculous, and it is not surprising that, after having heard his spirited defence, the court martial not only honorably acquitted him, but advanced him to the rank of major. A few weeks later he was journeying rapidly along the Wilderness Road, — his own road, as he might proudly have boasted, — eager to carry to his wife the glad assurance that he was still among the living.

More than a year passed before he returned to Kentucky, which in the meanwhile, thanks to the confidence inspired by George Rogers Clark's victories, began to increase rapidly in population. New stations and forts were established in the country around Boonesborough, and on tributary streams both north and south of the Kentucky, among the most prominent being Bryan's Station, on the North Fork of the Elkhorn; Bowman's, six miles east of Harrodstown; Estill's, on Muddy Creek; Ruddle's, on the South Licking; Martin's, five miles from Ruddle's; Hart's, or White Oak Spring Station, on the Kentucky, a mile north of Boonesborough; Hoy's and Irvine's, to the south of Boonesborough; Grant's, five miles northeast of Bryan's; Harlan's, on Salt River; and Dutch Station, on Beargrass Creek. During the same period (1779-81) the foundations were laid of Lexington, while Boonesborough, by an act of the Virginia Legislature, was elevated to the dignity of a town, and Kentucky was divided into three counties — Jefferson, Lincoln, and Fayette — each with its own administrative officials.

All this activity in the way of settlement was bitterly if ineffectively opposed by the Indians. There were frequent raids and counter-raids, in which the settlers suffered severely. In 1779, after Boone's departure for the Yadkin, Bowman and Logan headed an expedition against Chillicothe, but were outfought by the Shawnees and compelled to retreat with a loss of nine killed and many more wounded. The following year, as an act of reprisal, a British officer. Colonel Byrd, brought a mixed force of Canadians and Indians into Kentucky, supported by six pieces of artillery, captured Ruddle's and Martin's stations, and returned to Detroit with three hundred prisoners, many of whom were cruelly tortured by the savages. George Rogers Clark, then commander-in-chief of the Western forces, in return promptly organized an expedition against the Indian town of Pickaway, which he destroyed after a severe engagement that cost him the lives of seventeen men.

It was, however, through the marauding of individual Indians, or small war-parties of ten to twenty, that the American loss was heaviest, and the difficulties of settlement were most keenly felt. At any moment, returning from his day's labors in the field, the settler might be laid low by a bullet fired from ambush; or, if he reached home in safety, might find his cabin in ashes, with the mutilated corpses of his wife and children among the ruins. Many stories are told illustrative of the dangers that daily threatened the bold pioneers, the sufferings they endured, and the sacrifices they were obliged to make. Others afford a vivid idea of the unfailing courage, hardihood, and resourcefulness they displayed, no matter how great their peril. I quote one from John A. McClungs "Sketches of Western Adventure," an old work which, although not entirely trustworthy, is invaluable for the light it throws on the conditions attending the settlement and conquest of the early West.

"In the spring of 1780," writes McClung, "Alexander McConnel, of Lexington, went into the woods on foot, to hunt deer. He soon killed a large buck, and returned home for a horse, in order to bring it in. During his absence a party of five Indians, on one of their usual skulking expeditions, accidentally stumbled on the body of the deer, and perceiving that it had been recently killed, they naturally supposed that the hunter would speedily return to secure the flesh.

"Three of them, therefore, took their stations within close rifle-shot of the deer, while the other two followed the trail of the hunter and waylaid the path by which he was expected to return. McConnel, expecting no danger, rode carelessly along the path, which the two scouts were watching, until he had come within view of the deer, when he was fired upon by the whole party and his horse killed. While laboring to extricate himself from the dying animal, he was seized by his enemies, instantly overpowered, and borne off^ a prisoner.

"His captors, however, seemed to be a merry, good-natured set of fellows, and permitted him to accompany them unbound; and, what was rather extraordinary, allowed him to retain his gun and hunting accoutrements. He accompanied them with great apparent cheerfulness during the day, and displayed his dexterity in shooting deer for the use of the company, until they began to regard him with great partiality.

"Having travelled with them in this manner for several days, they at length reached the banks of the Ohio River. Heretofore the Indians had taken the precaution to bind him at night, although not very securely; but on that evening he remonstrated with them, and complained so strongly of the pain which the cords gave him that they merely wrapped the buffalo tug loosely around his wrists, and having tied it in an easy knot and attached the extremities of the rope to their own bodies, in order to prevent his moving without awakening them, they very composedly went to sleep, leaving the prisoner to follow their example or not as he pleased.

"McConnel determined to effect his escape that night if possible, as on the following night they would cross the river, which would make it much more difficult. He therefore lay quietly until near midnight, anxiously ruminating upon the best means of effecting his escape. Accidentally casting his eyes in the direction of his feet, they fell upon the glittering blade of a knife which had escaped its sheath and was now lying near the feet of one of the Indians.

"To reach it with his hands without disturbing the two Indians to whom he was fastened was impossible, and it was very hazardous to attempt to draw it up with his feet. This, however, he attempted. With much difficulty he grasped the blade between his toes, and after repeated and long-continued efforts, succeeded in bringing it within reach of his hands.

"To cut his cords was then but the work of a moment, and gradually and silently extricating his person from the arms of the Indians he walked to the fire and sat down. He saw that his work was but half done; that if he should attempt to return home without destroying his enemies, he would assuredly be pursued and probably overtaken, when his fate would be certain. On the other hand, it seemed almost impossible for a single man to succeed in a conflict with five Indians. He could not hope to deal a blow with his knife so silently and fatally as to destroy each one of his enemies in turn without awakening the rest. Their slumbers were proverbially light and restless; and if he failed with a single one, he must instantly be overpowered by the survivors. The knife, therefore, was out of the question.

"After anxious reflection for a few minutes, he formed his plan. The guns of the Indians were stacked near the fire; their knives and tomahawks were in sheaths by their sides. The latter he dared not touch for fear of awakening their owners; but the former he carefully removed, with the exception of two, and hid them in the woods, where he knew the Indians would not readily find them. He then returned to the spot where the Indians were still sleeping, perfectly ignorant of the fate preparing for them, and taking a gun in each hand he rested the muzzles upon a log within six feet of his victims, and having taken deliberate aim at the head of one and the heart of another, pulled both triggers at the same moment.

"Both shots were fatal. At the report of the guns the others sprang to their feet and stared wildly around them. McConnel who had run instantly to the spot where the other rifles were hid, hastily seized one of them and fired at two of his enemies, who happened to stand in a line with each other. The nearest fell dead, being shot through the body; the second fell also, bellowing loudly, but quickly recovering, limped off into the woods as fast as possible. The fifth, and only one who remained unhurt, darted off like a deer, with a yell which announced equal terror and astonishment. McConnel, not wishing to fight any more such battles, selected his own rifle from the stack and made the best of his way to Lexington, where he arrived safely within, two days.

"Shortly afterwards, Mrs. Dunlap, of Fayette County, who had been several months a prisoner amongst the Indians on Mad River, made her escape and returned to Lexington. She reported that the survivor returned to his tribe with a lamentable tale. He related that they had taken a young hunter near Lexington, and had brought him safely as far as the Ohio; that while encamped upon the bank of the river, a large party of white men had fallen upon them in the night, and killed all his companions, together with the poor defenceless prisoner, who lay bound hand and foot, unable either to escape or resist."

The feat of shooting two Indians with a single bullet was, it seems, duplicated by our hero, Daniel Boone. According to the story, Boone, soon after his return to Kentucky with his wife and children, was making a solitary journey to the upper Blue Lick when, on the brow of a little hill descending to a broad creek, a rifle-ball whistled past his ear and scaled a piece of bark from a tree against which he had been leaning.

Quick as thought he bounded down the hill, leaped into the creek, waded across, and, taking advantage of the cover afforded by a thick cane-brake, crept noiselessly through it, along the bank of the creek, until he had gone about a hundred yards downstream. Then he stealthily parted the cane and peered out, to behold two Indians cautiously approaching the opposite bank.

Aiming his rifle at the foremost, he was astonished and delighted to see the other also come within range. As he did so, Boone fired, his bullet passing through the head of the first and lodging in the second's shoulder. The Indian who had been struck in the head fell dead without a groan; while the second, with a howl of pain and terror, dropped his gun and fled through the forest, leaving Boone to continue his journey undisturbed.

In those dread times not only the men but also the women, and even young girls, were inspired to deeds of the greatest courage and heroism. Here is a story told by McClung, which may not be altogether accurate in detail, but which graphically and forcefully depicts the spirit displayed by the mothers of the early West in the perilous days of its first settlement:

"One summer the house of John Merril, of Nelson County, was attacked by the Indians, and defended with singular address and good fortune. Merril was alarmed by the barking of a dog about midnight, and upon opening the door in order to ascertain the cause of the disturbance, he received the fire of six or seven Indians, by which his arm and thigh were both broken. He instantly sank upon the floor and called upon his wife to close the door.

"This had scarcely been done, when it was violently assailed by the tomahawks of the enemy and a large breach soon effected. Mrs. Merril, however, being a perfect Amazon both in strength and courage, guarded it with an axe, and successively killed or badly wounded four of the enemy as they attempted to force their way into the cabin.

"The Indians then ascended the roof and attempted to enter by way of the chimney, but here again they were met by the same determined enemy. Mrs. Merril seized the only feather-bed which the cabin afforded, and hastily ripping it open, poured its contents upon the fire. A furious blaze and stifling smoke instantly ascended the chimney, and brought down two of the enemy, who lay for a few moments at her mercy.

"Seizing the axe, she quickly despatched them, and was instantly afterwards summoned to the door, where the only remaining savage now appeared endeavoring to effect an entrance while Mrs. Merril was engaged at the chimney. He soon received a gash in the cheek, which compelled him, with a loud yell, to relinquish his purpose and return hastily to Chillicothe, where, from the report of a prisoner, he gave an exaggerated account of the fierceness, strength, and courage of the 'long-knife squaw.'"

But the dauntless bravery of the women of the West was never manifested more impressively than at the siege of Bryan's Station, a siege the more memorable because of its disastrous sequel at the lower Blue Lick, when the settlers of Kentucky, in a battle with the Indians, sustained the severest loss in all their stormy history.

Bryan's Station was founded in 1779 by four brothers of that name from North Carolina, the oldest of whom, William Bryan, had married a sister of Daniel Boone's. It stood, as was said above, on the North Fork of the Elkhorn, and was most advantageously situated on the sloping southern bank, about five miles northeast of Lexington. Like all of the early settlements of any importance, it consisted of a group of log-cabins arranged in a hollow square, connected with one another by a high stockade, and further protected by overhanging blockhouses at the corners of the stockade. It was the largest station in Kentucky and considered one of the strongest.

The Bryans, however, did not occupy it long. Early in 1780 it was decided by a land-court that the land on which they had built their station was within the limits of a survey made in 1774 for William Preston, a Virginian, who had already traded it off to Joseph Rogers, also a resident of Virginia. With a carelessness common to the first settlers, the Bryans had failed to make sure that the site they selected had not been preempted, and although neither Preston nor Rogers had done anything to improve the land, they were ordered to vacate.

Stubborn and strong-willed men that they were, they might have chosen to defy the decision of the court, had it not been for Byrd's expedition and the death of William Bryan, who was slain by the Indians in May of 1780. The ease with which Byrd captured Ruddle's and Martin's stations, the cruelties practised on the prisoners, and the killing of their brother, convinced them that it was scarcely worthwhile to attempt to hold a home which was not legally theirs and from which, even if they fought off the Indians, they were certain to be ousted as soon as peace was established. During the summer, therefore, they journeyed back to North Carolina over the Wilderness Road, never to return to the station they had founded and with which their name became permanently associated.

In their stead now came a company of settlers from Virginia, whose numbers were increased by later immigration until, by midsummer of 1782, there were twelve families at the station, besides twenty-five or thirty men — scouts, hunters, and surveyors — who made it their headquarters. Thus far it had been little troubled by the Indians, who, indeed, had been comparatively quiet since Clark's successful invasion of their country two years before. But, at sunset of Aug. 15, a messenger galloped up with news that the men of Holder's Station had been surprised and defeated by a large force of Indians at the upper Blue Lick, and that aid was needed from all the stations to hunt down the savages. The plan was, the messenger said, to rendezvous at Hoy's next day and thence march in search of the Indians.

No one suspected the true strength or immediate object of this latest army of invasion. It was part of a large expedition organized in the spring by a British officer, Captain William Caldwell, for the purpose of destroying the West Virginia settlement of Wheeling. When near Wheeling, runners brought word to Caldwell that Clark was collecting an army for another raid on the Indian towns, and the contemplated attack on Wheeling was at once abandoned, the Indians hurrying back to defend their homes, which they found were in no danger whatever, as Clark had not crossed the Ohio and had no intention of doing so. It was then too late to hope to surprise Wheeling, but Caldwell, rather than return to Detroit without striking a blow, proposed to his allies to march with him into Kentucky. More than half of them refused, but the remainder — some five or six hundred, and including three hundred Wyandots, a tribe fiercer even than the Shawnees — gave their consent.

A tradition, long accepted by Kentucky historians and still repeated by many writers, although with more or less hesitancy, declares that Caldwell would have failed to induce the Indians to take up his Kentucky enterprise, had it not been for a fiery speech by Simon Girty, who urged them to rise "in the majesty of their might" and destroy the whites whom Girty himself had so basely deserted. However this may be, there is good reason to believe that it was to Girty rather than to Caldwell that the Indians looked for leadership, and that his mind rather than Caldwell's conceived the plan of campaign which, while partially defeated, ultimately brought the savages a greater victory than they could possibly have anticipated.

Boonesborough had by that time become too thickly surrounded by other settlements to be easily captured, but Bryan's Station, being somewhat isolated, offered a tempting prey. To make assurance doubly sure, some of the Indians were sent to Hoy's Station, with the idea both of concealing their real destination and, if possible, of enticing the different garrisons to a point remote from that at which they intended to strike. It was these Indians whom Holder's men had encountered, and in pursuit of whom the settlers were to start next day. Meantime, while the men of Bryan's were making hurried preparations for departure, Caldwell and Girty and their blood-thirsty followers were silently closing in on them.

Sunrise of Aug. 16 found the station completely hemmed in by the Indians, not one of whom, however, was visible from the stockade. Girty, of course, was unaware that the garrison intended leaving for Hoy's. Had he known this, he need only have awaited their going in order to have made certain of an easy victory. As it was, he devised a cunning scheme that promised almost equally well.

At his orders the main body of the Indians remained concealed in the weeds, long grass, and growing corn between the rear of the station and the river, while a small company was posted among the trees along the broad trail that led to the front gate of the stockade, the intention being that they should keep hidden until daylight when they were boldly to show themselves. It was expected that the settlers would immediately rush out to attack them, upon which they were to retreat rapidly along the trail, shouting and firing as they ran to drown the noise made by their comrades, who would at the same time leap from their hiding-places and storm the station from the rear.

A few years earlier this plan would undoubtedly have been effective. But the Kentuckians had learned much from bitter experience, and among the inhabitants of Bryan's Station were veterans who instantly penetrated the crafty device. Instead of sallying forth in response to the Indians' demonstration, the gate of the stockade was firmly barred, and orders were given for every man to arm himself and prepare to repel any attack that might be made from behind.

More than this, a counter-plot was formed, calculated to inflict tremendous damage on the Indians. Ten or twelve volunteers were to be sent out to attack the company on the trail, while the rest, posted at the port-holes, were to reserve their fire until the Indians among the undergrowth hurled themselves against the stockade, when they were to be given a volley that would greatly thin their ranks and send the survivors scurrying back to cover.

Now, however, an alarming discovery was made — the station was without a drop of water. Its sole source of supply was a spring at the foot of the slope leading down to the river, and located among the trees and grass where the Indians were in ambush. Yet without water it would be impossible to endure the siege which the invaders were certain to establish in case they failed to carry the day by a single blow.

It was at this juncture that the women of Bryan's Station proved themselves the bravest and noblest of heroines. While all was confusion and anxiety; while, in excited whispers, the men were consulting together, Mrs. Jemima Sugget Johnson, the wife of Colonel Robert Johnson and mother of Colonel Richard M. Johnson, — afterwards a hero of the battle of the Thames and Vice-president of the United States, but then a tiny infant slumbering in a rough-hewed cradle, — quietly stepped forward and offered to conduct a party of women and girls to the Indian-surrounded spring.

Every morning, she reminded her astonished hearers, it was the custom of the women to go to the spring and procure the day's supply of drinking water. There was just a chance that the Indians in their eagerness to surprise the garrison, would not molest them if they went out as usual. At any rate she was ready to go, and she was sure that her daughter Betsey, a little girl often, would accompany her, even if nobody else would.

There was a moment's hesitation while the women gazed inquiringly into one another's faces. Then, one after the other, they announced their willingness to make the desperate attempt. The men would have dissuaded them had they not realized that this was the only possible means by which the all-essential water could be obtained. Buckets, piggins, noggins, [1] gourds, — every utensil capable of holding water, — were hastily brought together, the rear gate of the stockade was thrown open, and the women and girls, twenty-eight in all, set out on their perilous journey.

Along the narrow trail that wound down the hill to the spring, they leisurely made their way, laughing and chatting as though in entire ignorance of the danger threatening them. As they approached the undergrowth they could distinctly see, gleaming in the light of the morning sun, the glint of the Indians' rifle-barrels; and, here and there, a waving plume, a lithe, brown arm, and the glare of a savage eye. Not for an instant did they falter, but, advancing with apparent unconcern, dipped their buckets and gourds, their piggins and noggins, into the spring, and returned to the station at the same leisurely gait. It was a consummate piece of acting, a marvellous exhibition of self-control, and it completely deceived the Indians, who, intent on executing their original plan, permitted them to go and come unharmed.

Memorial Wall to Heroines of Bryan's Station
Erected by the Lexington Chapter, Daughters of the American Revolution

With their safe return the defenders of Bryan's Station hastened into action. While most of them stationed themselves at the port-holes overlooking the hill in the rear, the volunteers who were to engage the Indians on the trail dashed out, firing and shouting; making, in fact, such a tremendous noise that Girty felt certain his scheme had succeeded and that the entire garrison had left the station. Delaying no longer, he signalled to his followers to charge.

Out of the cornfield, out of the weeds and the grass, sprang the Indians, leaping like panthers up the long hill, whooping and hallooing, and bearing in their midst the flaming torch, dread instrument of the destruction that would ensue if they broke through the stockade. At their head raced Moluntha, supreme in the leadership of the Shawnees since the death of Black Fish, who had fallen in battle not long after his futile siege of Boonesborough; close behind Moluntha came a stalwart Wyandot chieftain, weirdly streaked with war-paint. Nor was Girty outdistanced in the wild dash up the hill. Nearing the station, the entire mass of Indians converged towards the stockade gate. On they came, rapidly on, while the settlers, silent as death, grimly set their lips and waited. Still nearer they came. Then, at a hoarse word of command, a deadly volley flashed from every port-hole. Casting their rifles aside, and snatching others from the hands of their wives and daughters, the settlers fired again. Through the smoke could be heard howls of amazement, wrath, and pain; and when the air had cleared, not an Indian was to be seen save those who had been laid low by the garrison's bullets.

Still, even before they broke and fled, some had contrived to toss their torches over the stockade, and the crackling of flames from half a dozen cabins warned the settlers that they were menaced by a new peril. To the women and boys was given the task of quenching the blaze, while the men, now reenforced by the volunteers from the trail, who had successfully regained the station, reloaded and awaited a second charge.

But there was no second charge, the Indians choosing rather to adopt their usual tactics of assailing the settlement with bullets and fire-arrows launched from cover. More than once a cabin-roof was set on fire, but the flames were quickly beaten out. Thus the morning passed. Early in the afternoon, to the chagrin of the savages, a small party of horsemen, summoned from Lexington by a messenger who had left Bryan's Station before the engagement began, forced their way through the Indians' lines and entered the station without the loss of a single man. Their arrival not merely strengthened the garrison, but brought the siege to a sudden end; for, realizing that the entire countryside would soon be aroused, the Indians, after continuing their attack until nightfall, started in full retreat to the Ohio.

Next day three different relief parties, each about fifty strong, arrived from Boonesborough, Lexington, and Harrodstown. Among them were many of the best-known men in Kentucky. Foremost of all, of course, was Boone, burning to avenge the death of his brother Edward, who had been killed during an earlier Indian invasion. With Boone came his oldest living son, Israel, grown to be a fine, stalwart young fellow of twenty-three. John Todd, who will be remembered as one of the first settlers and a member of the short-lived Transylvania House of Delegates, commanded the troops from Lexington, and associated with him was his brother Levi. The Harrodstown contingent was led by Stephen Trigg, who, although a resident of Kentucky for only three years, had won an enviable reputation for daring and courage; and it also included the fiery Hugh McGary, Silas Harlan, a tried leader of men, and William McBride, a redoubtable Indian fighter.

In addition to these three companies, it was known that Benjamin Logan was raising troops in the neighborhood of Logan's Fort. But, at a council of war held in Bryan's Station, it was decided not to wait for Logan, as, in case he should be delayed, the enemy would be sure to escape scot-free. There were some who pointed out that, even including the garrison of Bryan's, the total force then available was far less than that of the Indians; but the majority were in favor of hastening after them, and, on Aug. 18, the pursuit was begun, the Kentuckians marching in three divisions commanded respectively by Boone, Trigg, and Levi Todd, while John Todd, as the senior militia officer present, acted as commander-in-chief.

The route taken by the Indians was soon ascertained, and, pressing forward with great rapidity, the settlers by noon came to the place where the enemy had encamped the previous night. This was on the bank of Hinkston Creek, near the site of Millersburg. Thence the trail led to the lower Blue Lick, which was reached early in the morning of the nineteenth. All along the way, however, were signs indicating to the experienced veterans in the little army that the Indians were courting rather than evading pursuit; and before fording the Licking another council of war was called, at which Boone declared that it would be madness to proceed without Logan's reenforcements, as the enemy were almost certainly setting a trap. This wise counsel might have been heeded had not McGary, with a taunting cry, spurred his horse into the river, swinging his rifle above his head, and exclaiming:—

"Delay is dastardly! Let all who are not cowards follow me!"

With excited shouts the Kentuckians plunged in, helter skelter, and it was with difficulty that their officers reformed them into companies on the opposite bank.

Here the trail ran up a broad ridge, rocky and barren, but with timber-filled ravines extending down from both sides of the ridge. Among the trees of these ravines the Indians lay in perfect concealment until the pursuers had reached a point where they were completely exposed to a cross-fire. Then, at a prearranged signal, a few scattering shots rang out, followed by a furious fusillade.

Flinging their rifles away, the Wyandots, with a fury that appalled even the stout-hearted Kentuckians, charged into the open, tomahawk in hand, to grapple like demons with those who had survived the carnage of the first attack. For a few minutes, fighting shoulder to shoulder, the settlers stood their ground. But, raked by a galling fire from the Shawnees, who now advanced at the double, they gradually gave way, and then, pressed still harder, broke into a mad flight.

It could scarcely be called a battle, so quickly was it at an end. Rather it was a massacre, a butchery, a pitiless hewing down. All who, escaping the tomahawk, plunged headlong to the river and sought safety by swimming, found themselves assailed by a hail of bullets. Among the first to fall, after the retreat became general, was young Israel Boone, fatally wounded. His father, fighting manfully up to that moment, hurled his rifle aside with a groan of despair, lifted his son from the ground, and, staggering under the burden, leaped down the rocky slope. But ere he reached the other side of the river the boy was beyond human aid, and Boone himself with difficulty escaped the vengeful Indians scouring the forest in quest of fugitives.

Of the army that had so gallantly, though recklessly, responded to McGary's challenging appeal, nearly seventy were left dead on the field, while four were carried off to the Indian towns and tortured to death. The commander-in-chief, John Todd, was among the slain, as were Trigg, Harlan, and McBride. The mortality among the officers was, indeed, remarkably high, only seven escaping, and these with more or less severe wounds. To add to the bitterness of the defeat, as the survivors approached Bryan's Station they were met by Logan with an army of almost five hundred men, a force which, in conjunction with their own, would have overwhelmed the enemy had they only heeded Boone's warning.

It was then too late to do anything but bury the dead, as, on advancing rapidly, Logan found that the Indians had crossed the Ohio immediately after the battle, and were secure in the tangled fastnesses of their own country. But from all over Kentucky rose a loud and insistent demand for vengeance. The Indians must be punished as they had never been before. Late in October, therefore, in response to a call from George Rogers Clark, a thousand mounted riflemen came together at the mouth of the Licking, and from the site of Cincinnati marched through the Ohio forests to the Indian towns on the Little Miami.

The red men, taken wholly by surprise, fled without offering the slightest resistance, leaving the Kentuckians free to ravage and destroy at will. No fewer than five towns in the region where Girty's army had assembled in August were put to the torch, and immense stores of grain and dried meats were destroyed, thus entailing great suffering among the Shawnees throughout the approaching winter.

It was, however, the one and only sure means of protecting Kentucky. Overcome by the severity of the blow, and further weakened by the withdrawal of British support as a result of the ending of the Revolution, the Indians never again invaded Kentucky in force. They did, it is true, for some years maintain an irregular warfare, small parties making incursions among the settlements or waylaying travellers down the Ohio River and along the Wilderness Road. But no longer were they the constant menace they had been ever since that fateful day, more than six years before, when Boonesborough was first besieged.

[1] A piggin was a small wooden bucket with one upright stave for a handle; a noggin was a small wooden bucket with two upright staves for handles.

Chapter Fourteen - Pioneering in Watauga

THRILLING events had meanwhile been in progress at the other end of the Wilderness Road, in the Watauga country, where, as we have seen, James Robertson and John Sevier had laid the foundations of the present State of Tennessee some half-dozen years before Kentucky was opened up to civilization. For more than a decade the Watauga settlers were exposed to a succession of Indian wars almost as severe as those in Kentucky; throughout the Revolution they were harassed not only by Indians, but even by men of their own blood, Americans who refused to adhere to the movement for Independence and fought bitterly to reestablish British domination; and towards the close of the great struggle they were called on to take part in one of its most memorable battles, the battle of King's Mountain. Yet through all this they more than held their own; progressing, in fact, so remarkably that before the close of the Revolution they were able to undertake, by way of the Wilderness Road, a colonization movement that extended the southwest frontier far into the inland wilds, and had as an immediate result the founding of what is now the political centre of Tennessee, the city of Nashville.

At the beginning of the Revolution the Watauga settlements had a total population of about six hundred, but up to that time had been leading an absolutely independent existence as a self-governing community organized according to the Articles of Association described in our fifth chapter. In 1776 they determined, both as a measure of self-defence and as a means of testifying their loyalty to the Revolutionary cause, to throw in their fortunes definitely with the people of North Carolina, and they therefore petitioned the Provincial Council to annex Watauga to North Carolina "in such manner as will enable us to share in the glorious cause of Liberty, enforce our laws under authority, and in every respect become the best members of society." The petition was granted, and Watauga was formally annexed under the name of Washington District, being afterwards subdivided into three counties, Washington, Sullivan, and Greene.

The change of government, however, affected the life of the settlers but little. Beyond forming county organizations and enacting a few special laws — such as a pension law for the benefit of the widows and orphans of Wataugans slain in the service of the Revolution — North Carolina left its new citizens pretty much to their own devices. They still had to rely almost entirely on themselves, they were virtually as independent as before, and the management of affairs remained in the hands of those who had won public confidence during the Association period.

Preeminent in this respect were Robertson, Sevier, and Evan and Isaac Shelby, each of whom might not ineptly be compared to a Highland chieftain surrounded by a band of intensely loyal clansmen. Each of them, too, had many of the characteristics of the traditional Highland chieftain — the fiery temper, the hot, fighting blood, the restless spirit, the great muscular strength, the marvellous power of endurance. With the exception of Sevier, who had inherited from his Huguenot ancestors a rich fund of tact and courtesy, they were, like the ancient Highlanders, rough and uncouth. But they were precisely the kind of leaders best qualified to inspire and sustain their followers through the dread years of merciless carnage that marked the struggle for independence as fought beyond the mountains.

Long before the Indians were actually upon them they made their preparations for defence. It was known that an agent of the British was actively intriguing among the Cherokees, and that the war-belt had been carried to them by emissaries from the Shawnees, Delawares, and other of the Northern tribes already ruthlessly endeavoring to exterminate the pioneers of Kentucky. But even so, the first blow struck against the Wataugans almost caught them unawares. July 7, 1776, an Indian woman, who had always been friendly to the whites, visited a settler named Thomas and warned him that a large expedition was about to start northward with the intention of destroying all the settlements up to and beyond the Virginia line, thus opening a way for later expeditions to penetrate into the western counties of Virginia and co-operate with the British in their attempt to subjugate the Southern States. Thomas, as may be imagined, was soon on his way north, spreading this dire news.

In a few days every outlying cabin was deserted, the inhabitants fleeing for protection to the nearest forts. Chief among these were Fort Watauga, where Robertson and Sevier were in command, and Fort Eaton, erected at the suggestion of William Cocke, who, it will be remembered, had played a gallant role in the founding of Kentucky, but had returned east shortly after Boonesborough was built. It was expected that Fort Eaton would be the first attacked, and in fact a strong force of Cherokees soon marched against it, led by a greatly dreaded chieftain, Dragging Canoe — the same chieftain, by the way, who had prophesied to Boone, at the time of the Sycamore Shoals Treaty in 1775, that the Kentuckians would find it hard to hold the land they bought from the Cherokees.

Dragging Canoe, not without reason, believed that Fort Eaton was almost defenceless. But in the ten days that had passed since the settlers received their warning, five companies of militiamen had been rushed to that fort from the border counties of Virginia, bringing the total strength of the garrison close to two hundred. Scouts were sent out daily to watch for the enemy's approach, and when, on July 20, it was learned that the Indian army was drawing near the fort, the entire garrison marched out to give battle.

They had not gone far when they fell in with a party of twenty Cherokees, whom they easily put to flight. But, while giving instant pursuit, they now advanced with the greatest caution, fearing that this vanguard of the enemy might be merely a decoy detachment sent forward to lure them into an ambuscade. Late in the afternoon, having seen no further signs of the Indians, and believing that they now planned a night attack on the fort, orders were given to hurry back. Only a few minutes more, however, and their rear was unexpectedly assailed by the whole of Dragging Canoe's force. Evidently a trap had actually been set, and though the garrison had failed to walk into it the Cherokees were still hopeful of overwhelming them. And at first it looked, in truth, as though the tragedy at the Blue Lick would be repeated.

Emptying their rifles in one withering volley, the Indians did not wait to reload, but leaped upon the rear-guard with a swiftness that gave them no time either to seek cover or form for battle. Driven irresistibly forward, they brought confusion into the ranks of those ahead. But, rallying, the settlers quickly spread out in two long, narrow lines, so that they could not be outflanked, and, taking sure aim at the oncoming horde of savages, instantly checked their rush. [1] A fight of the usual backwoods type followed, both sides firing at each other from behind trees; and in the end, after Dragging Canoe had fallen, severely wounded, the Indians fled, leaving thirteen of their dead to be scalped by the victors.

That night, according to ever doubtful tradition, an express rider was sent to carry the glad tidings to Robertson and Sevier at Fort Watauga. "A great day's work in the woods!" was Sevier's reported comment when the news reached him.

But it was out of the question for him to attempt to duplicate the achievement of the men from Fort Eaton. He had only forty men to oppose to the far greater force hurled against Fort Watauga by another powerful chieftain, Oconostota. His only hope lay in exhausting the patience of the savages by maintaining a stubborn defence behind the stout palisades, and this he did to such good effect that for nearly three weeks the Cherokees were held at bay. Then, learning that Dragging Canoe had abandoned the siege of Fort Eaton, and that reenforcements were coming to Sevier's aid, Oconostota, baffled and dispirited, hurried his warriors back to their wigwam homes. The first attempt to cleave open a path to Virginia had ended in disastrous failure.

Very different was the outcome of a retaliatory expedition undertaken a few weeks later by a combined force of Virginians and Wataugans. Its commander was Colonel William Christian, a Virginian, while Robertson marched at the head of the Watauga troops and Sevier led the advance with a picked company of scouts. Nearly two thousand men took part in this expedition. From the starting-point on the Holston there was incessant skirmishing in which Sevier and his scouts acquitted themselves with the greatest credit. Not once, however, did the Indians venture to give open battle, and finally, appalled by the danger that threatened them, they sent a messenger with a flag of truce to sue for peace.

The backwoods army had by that time reached the border of the Cherokee country, and was encamped on the bank of the French Broad, one of the upper tributaries of the Tennessee River. Christian's reply to the Cherokee envoy was curt and to the point. He had come, he said, to destroy the Cherokee towns, and after he had done that, not before, he would talk of peace. That night, leaving half his followers in camp, he forded the French Broad and made a rapid march to surprise the Indians in their encampment. But they had expected some such move, and had already fled to their doomed villages.

Thenceforward no opposition whatever was offered to the advance of the whites. For two weeks Christian moved from village to village, burning their cabins and destroying the stores of grain and potatoes which the Indians had laid in to carry them through the winter. Not until the Cherokees had surrendered every prisoner they had taken, and every horse they had stolen from the settlements, and had agreed to pay a heavy indemnity in land, did he accede to their frantic appeals for peace.

There were many warriors, however, who took no part in the peace negotiations. Headed by the implacable Dragging Canoe, they fled westward, to form, with adventurous members of the Creek, Chickasaw, and other Southwestern tribes, a rude confederacy banded together to make war on the white man. For the next few years the Watauga settlements frequently suffered from raids by these red outlaws, and as frequently there were retaliatory raids that resulted in a constant weakening of the Indians' power. In this work no one was more conspicuous than Sevier, who, putting himself at the head of a body of mounted riflemen, repeatedly harried the Cherokees, the swiftness of his movements rendering it possible for him to take them by surprise and escape to Watauga before a strong enough force could be gathered to cut him off.

On one occasion, in the winter of 1780-81, he entered the Indian country with fewer than three hundred men, laid a successful ambuscade for a Cherokee war-party, and, after routing it, laid waste several towns, burning a thousand cabins and destroying fifty thousand bushels of grain. Two months afterwards he led a still smaller force one hundred and fifty miles through a wilderness hitherto untrodden by the white man, to burst like a thunderbolt upon a cluster of Indian villages in the hollows of the Great Smoky Mountains, burn five of these villages, kill thirty warriors, and return unscathed to his home on the Nolichucky. To Sevier's daring forays, more than to any other single cause, must be attributed the final subjugation of the Cherokees and the establishment of permanent peace in east Tennessee.

John Sevier

Yet he was not a mere "fighting man," like so many of the border notables. He was a born leader of men in peace as well as in war, and to the day of his death, which occurred in 1815, he remained the foremost figure in his section of the country. When, after the Revolution, east Tennessee, exasperated at its treatment by North Carolina, attempted to embark on its own account as the independent State of Franklin, he was the man chosen by its people to direct the destinies of this short-lived commonwealth. When Tennessee became a State, it was to Sevier that the Tennesseeans turned for their first governor, and he is recognized by Tennessee historians as one of the best governors that State has had. The last years of his life found him still serving Tennessee, as one of its representatives in Congress. Valiant, courteous, masterful, and true, his was assuredly a career of brilliant achievement.

But, in the days with which we are concerned, Sevier's chief claim to fame was based on his exploits as a soldier. It was a time of almost constant warfare, not only with the Indian but also, as was said, with those of the same blood as the Wataugans, for there was a numerous Tory element in the border settlements that had to be repressed with a stern hand. There was, moreover, always the danger that, in the event of British success in the Southern States, Watauga and the neighboring settlements of transmontane Virginia would be overrun by invasion. So imminent did this danger at one time become that, to avert it, the borderers organized an expedition that took them far from their homes and culminated in a victory as glorious as it was astonishing.

As is well known, the year 1780 was, from the American point of view, the most disastrous of the entire Revolution. Even Washington "almost ceased to hope." It was marked by a succession of British victories, particularly in Georgia and the Carolinas, where Cornwallis and his able lieutenants, Rawdon, Tarleton, and Ferguson, proved more than a match for the American commanders sent against them. After the conquest of the seaboard cities, Cornwallis despatched Tarleton and Ferguson with orders to subdue the "back counties" and organize regiments of loyal inhabitants — the hated Tories — to assist the British in their further operations. Both officers executed their orders with alacrity, thoroughness, and unfailing success, until, early in the autumn, Ferguson found his westward progress opposed by the mountain wall.

He then learned, perhaps for the first time, that beyond the mountains were a few scattered settlements of strong "rebel" tendencies, and, through a prisoner whom he released on parole, he immediately sent word that if the mountaineers did not "desist from their opposition to the British arms," he would march his army over the mountains, hang the leaders, and lay waste the country.

So far from alarming the Wataugans, his threat aroused an instant determination to strike him before he could strike them. Within a few days more than a thousand men were assembled at the Sycamore Shoals of the Watauga. They included a contingent of five hundred from the Virginia settlements, under William Campbell, a famous Indian fighter and implacable in his hatred of the British and their Tory supporters; two hundred and forty under Sevier; a like number under Isaac Shelby, and nearly two hundred refugees who had fled across the mountains after a vain effort to check Ferguson's triumphant march.

Nearly all were well mounted, and all were armed in regulation backwoods style — that is to say, with rifle, tomahawk, and hunting-knife. A few, though very few, of the officers carried swords. Only the lightest baggage was taken along, the hope being to make a rapid passage of the mountains and give Ferguson no time to prepare a strong defence.

It is worthy of remark that before setting out, on September 26, 1780, this rude, rough, undisciplined army gathered in an open grove to listen to a sermon preached by the first clergyman to settle in that region, the Rev. Samuel Doak, who, in words of burning zeal, exhorted them to go forth and smite their enemies with the sword of the Lord and of Gideon.

Three days later, after a terrible journey over what Shelby afterwards described as "the worst route ever followed by an army of horsemen," they descended the eastern slope of the Blue Ridge, not far from the North Fork of the Catawba in North Carolina, and began their search for Ferguson, who, they were told, was encamped near Gilbert Town. En route they elected William Campbell commander-in-chief, and received reenforcements that brought their total strength up to about fifteen hundred.

This was more than Ferguson could muster, for, not expecting to be attacked, he had allowed many of his Tory recruits to go home on furlough. Wisely, therefore, he broke camp and fled, turning and twisting among the mountains in the hope of baffling pursuit. But he soon found that the backwoodsmen were not to be shaken off", and when, on the evening of October 6, he crossed into South Carolina, he halted his army on the stony slope of King's Mountain, just south of the North Carolina line, and made ready to give battle, confident that he had taken a position from which "all the rebels outside of hell," as he defiantly put it, could not dislodge him.

It was noon of the next day before the mountaineers were informed of his exact location by two Tories whom they captured. By that time their number had dwindled to less than a thousand, — or about as many as Ferguson had with him, — those who had become too exhausted to continue the pursuit having been weeded out a couple of days before. According to all the rules of warfare it was madness to attack a numerically equal force situated to such great advantage as Ferguson's men were, and having the further advantage of being armed with bayonets, while not a backwoodsman possessed this exceedingly useful weapon. But the men in buckskin knew nothing of, and cared less for, the rules of warfare, and boldly decided to push ahead, surround Ferguson, and storm his position.

As they marched they formed their army for the coming battle. The right centre was composed of Campbell's troops, the left centre of Shelby's; Sevier took command of the right wing; the left was under the command of Benjamin Cleveland, a patriotic North Carolinian who had joined with three hundred and fifty men. When close to King's Mountain, all dismounted and advanced on foot, the wings spreading out so as to approach the British camp from opposite sides. The orders given to all were to stand their ground as long as possible, but, if attacked by the bayonet, to give way and then rally for another charge. So swift were their movements that they were almost upon the British commander before he knew of their presence.

As the Americans swarmed up the hill, Ferguson, who was to prove himself a second Braddock for bull-dog grit, ordered his troops to fix bayonets and charge down upon them. For nearly ten minutes the whole burden of the battle fell on Campbell's and Shelby's men, Sevier and Cleveland being delayed in getting into position. Each man, in backwoods fashion, fought for himself, making use of every inch of cover. So incessant was the rifle-fire that, tradition says, "the mountain was covered with smoke and flame, and seemed to thunder." Ferguson's advancing column, massed in close formation, suffered fearfully. Still they kept on, and before the resistless pressure of the bayonets the American centre was shattered and driven back.

Now, from points higher up the mountain, the two wings attacked the British. Ferguson, undaunted, turned his bayonets against these new foes. As he did so, Campbell and Shelby again brought their men into action. Bewildered, the bayonet men charged to and fro, the Americans invariably fleeing before them, but returning to the assault the instant pursuit ceased.

Every moment the defenders' ranks became thinner, while the agile and hardy backwoodsmen, quick of foot and skilled in the tactics of forest warfare, sustained comparatively little loss. Ferguson, realizing that the battle was going against him, hurled his men forward again and again, in a vain effort to turn the tide and snatch victory from defeat. With reckless bravery he rode along the lines, waving a sword and imploring his followers not to let the "rebels" rout them. Two horses were killed under him, but with the same desperate valor he continued to lead the bayonet charges until at last, as he galloped full speed against Sevier's Wataugans, their fire was concentrated upon him, and he fell to the ground pierced by half a dozen bullets.

Ten minutes afterwards the Americans gained the crest of the ridge where the British camp stood. The end could not be long delayed. Huddled in a confused mass among their tents and baggage-wagons the broken remnants of Ferguson's army despairingly hoisted the white flag. Many of the backwoodsmen did not know what it meant; others deliberately disregarded it, until Campbell, rushing among them with his sword pointed to the ground, called upon them in God's name to cease firing.

Ignored or slighted by many historians, this was in reality one of the decisive battles of the Revolution. On the one hand, it ruined the Southern campaign of the British, compelling Cornwallis to abandon his plan for the conquest of North Carolina, and spurring the patriots of the South to a renewed activity that bore abundant fruit the following year. On the other hand, it insured the safety not simply of the Watauga settlements, but of the settlements planted by Boone and his comrades in faraway Kentucky.

Had Ferguson been able to cross the mountains and carry out his threat of ravaging Watauga, the one obstacle to Indian invasion of Kentucky from the south would have been removed; the Cherokee and the Creek, sweeping westward along the Wilderness Road, could have united with the northern tribes to hem in the Blue Grass settlers; cut off completely from reenforcements and supplies, the people of Kentucky must inevitably have perished, Clark would have been obliged to relinquish his grip of the Illinois country, and the whole West would have once more become a British possession.

Not without reason have the men who fought and won the battle of King's Mountain been called the "Rear-guard of the Revolution."

[1] Tradition has been exceedingly busy with this battle in the Tennessee wilderness, and has woven about it many romantic but highly improbable tales. According to one often-repeated story, the prowess of Isaac Shelby and four other backwoodsmen, who held the Indians in check while their comrades were forming a line of battle, alone averted a terrible disaster. But Shelby was on a visit to Kentucky at this time.

Chapter Fifteen - From Watauga to the Cumberland

THERE were few prominent Wataugans who did not take part in the battle of King's Mountain, but there was one conspicuous absentee — the founder of the little settlements from which the victors came. It was not cowardice, however, that held James Robertson back. While Shelby and Sevier were marching across the mountains to strike so valiantly for home and country, Robertson was engaged on a mission no less hazardous than theirs and fraught with equally important consequences. Far out in the West with a company of loyal followers, he was establishing another American community and thereby laying deeper the foundations of the present State of Tennessee. The record of Robertson's achievements in the valley of the Cumberland forms one of the most interesting passages in the history of the early West and of the Wilderness Road.

Just when or why Robertson decided to leave Watauga and seek a new home on the bank of the westward-flowing Cumberland, it is impossible to say with absolute certitude. But it is known that he acted largely under the influence of Richard Henderson, the ambitious land-speculator and colonizer of Transylvania fame. Although, by the joint action of the Transylvanians and the Virginia Assembly, Henderson had been compelled to relinquish his hold of Kentucky, North Carolina had not as yet proceeded against him, and he promptly went to work to dispose of the western lands within its borders purchased by him from the Cherokees. The terms he offered were so extremely liberal that many were tempted by them, and among others James Robertson.

Now history began to repeat itself. Precisely as he had done in the case of Transylvania, Henderson organized a company of pioneers to spy out the land and select sites for settlement. Robertson willingly agreed to take charge of this work, and, in the spring of 1779, started west with eight companions, the understanding being that after they had found a suitable location they were to sow corn, build cabins, and erect stockades; and were then to return to Watauga for their families and any other settlers who might wish to join them. This was the course that had been followed in the founding of Boonesborough, and, like the builders of Boonesborough, Robertson and his party struck off for the West by way of Cumberland Gap and Boone's Wilderness Road.

But, unlike Boone and his road-makers, they had no Felix Walker to chronicle the adventures that befell them on their journey. Not even the route they took can be accurately described. All that is known is that they continued along the Wilderness Road to the Cumberland River, crossed the Cumberland, and turned to the southwest, threading their way through the wilderness by Indian trail and buffalo trace until they reached the Great Bend of the Cumberland, where Nashville now stands. This seemed to them an ideal spot for settlement, and they at once began felling trees and shaping logs for the building of their future homes.

There was some doubt in their minds, however, whether the site they had chosen came within the limits of Kentucky or North Carolina the boundary line not having as yet been run so far west. Accordingly, while four of the men returned to bring out the settlers, and three remained "to keep the buffaloes out of the corn," Robertson journeyed north to distant Kaskaskia to visit George Rogers Clark, who was understood to have authority to sell cabin-rights to intending settlers in Kentucky. He might have spared himself this long and hazardous trip, for the boundary was soon afterwards officially determined, and it was found that the Cumberland settlements were on North Carolina soil.

On his way back Robertson met a large party of homeseekers bound for western Kentucky, and without much urging persuaded them to change their destination and accompany him to the Cumberland. Meantime other settlers had arrived at the Bend, from Virginia and South Carolina, and were scattered in small groups for several miles up and down the river. So steady was the stream of immigration that within a twelvemonth eight stations were established, the largest of which was named Nashborough, — afterwards Nashville, — while the others were called Gasper's, Eaton's, Bledsoe's, Stone's River, Asher's, Freeland's, and Fort Union. Nashborough was so named in honor of Governor Nash of North Carolina, [1] while the others were in most cases named after their principal settlers.

Thus far comparatively few families had come out, owing to the difficulty of transporting household goods along the Wilderness Road and the still narrower Indian trails from the Wilderness Road to Nashborough. But in the winter of 1779-80 a large expedition was organized, under the command of John Donelson, father of the Rachel Donelson who became the wife of Andrew Jackson, and, had she lived, would have been mistress of the White House. Robertson's family accompanied this expedition, which went by water down the Tennessee and up the Ohio and Cumberland, and was so large and well equipped as to fill a flotilla of about thirty "flatboats, dug-outs, and canoes." The story of its adventures en route to Nashborough, as told in a journal [2] kept by Donelson himself, reads, as some one has said, like a chapter out of one of Mayne Reid's novels.

The *Adventure* was the "flag-ship" of the flotilla, and was a large flat-boat in which were more than thirty men and their families. Although a start was made December 22, 1779, low water and heavy frosts so delayed progress that the voyage did not really begin until February 27, of the following year, when the flotilla left Cloud Creek, a tributary of the Holston. Except for occasionally running aground all went well until the Tennessee was reached. March 7 the adventurers passed a deserted Chickamauga village, and the following day arrived at another that was not deserted.

"The inhabitants," writes Donelson, "invited us to come ashore, called us brothers, and showed other signs of friendship, insomuch that Mr. John Caffrey and my son, then on board, took a canoe which I had in tow, and were crossing over to them, the rest of the fleet having landed on the opposite shore. After they had gone some distance, a half-breed, who called himself Archy Coody, with several other Indians, jumped into a canoe, met them, and advised them to return to the boat, which they did, together with Coody, and several canoes, which left the shore and followed directly after him.

"After distributing some presents among them, with which they seemed much pleased, we observed a number of Indians on the other side embarking in their canoes, armed and painted with red and black. Coody immediately made signs to his companions, ordering them to quit the boat, which they did, himself and another Indian remaining with us, and telling us to move off instantly. We had not gone far before we discovered a number of Indians, armed and painted, proceeding down the river, as it were to intercept us. Coody, the half-breed, and his companion sailed with us for some time, and, telling us we had passed all the towns and were out of danger, left us."

They were soon undeceived. Before nightfall they came to another Indian village, where, after vainly endeavoring to lure them ashore, a war-party launched canoes and started in pursuit. It happened that a few days earlier smallpox had broken out among the occupants of a flat-boat containing twenty-eight persons who, as a safeguard for the health of the rest, had been ordered to keep at a good distance in the rear of the flotilla. The Chickamaugans naturally singled out this boat for attack, boarded it, butchered all the men, and carried the women and children into captivity. In so doing they brought upon themselves a fearful retribution, for they became infected with the disease of their victims and, the infection spreading to other villages and tribes, hundreds of Indians perished — a fact which helps to account for the comparative immunity of the Cumberland settlements from Indian raids until they were strong enough to defeat all attempts to drive them back to the mountain settlements.

In another boat a man was killed by a shot fired from ambush by a party of savages hiding on the opposite bank; and an hour or so later, when passing through the so-called "Whirl" of the Tennessee, where the river courses swiftly between lofty overhanging cliffs, the expedition was again attacked, the Indians firing down from the heights and wounding four people.

During the mad rush to escape a boat ran ashore, and its occupants, a family named Jennings, had to be left to their fate. Donelson took it for granted that they would unfailingly be slaughtered, but two days afterwards, under date of March 30, his "Journal" records: —

"This morning, about four o'clock, we were surprise by cries of 'Help poor Jennings!' at some distance in the rear. He had discovered us by our fires, and came up in the most wretched condition. He states that as soon as the Indians had discovered his situation, they turned their whole attention to him, and kept up a most galling fire on his boat. He ordered his wife, a son nearly grown, a young man who accompanied them, and his two negroes, to throw all his goods into the river, to lighten their boat for the purpose of getting her off; himself returning their fire as well as he could, being a good soldier and an excellent marksman. But before they had accomplished their object, his son, the young man, and the negro man jumped out of the boat and left them: he thinks the young man and the negro were wounded.

"Before they left the boat, Mrs. Jennings, however, and the negro woman succeeded in unloading the boat, but chiefly by the exertions of Mrs. Jennings, who got out of the boat and shoved her off; but was near falling a victim to her own intrepidity, on account of the boat starting so suddenly as soon as loosened from the rocks. Upon examination he appears to have made a wonderful escape, for his boat is pierced in numberless places with bullets."

Two days later the expedition was again attacked as it floated past another Indian village. On this occasion no injury was done, but on March 14, when almost out of the Chickamauga country, five men were wounded, their boats "approaching too near the shore," where the savages had laid an ambuscade. For the remainder of the voyage, to the relief of all, no Indians were seen. March 20 the travellers entered the Ohio, and on the 24th turned from the Ohio into the Cumberland, not completing their journey, however, until exactly a month later, for it was April 24 before they caught their first glimpse of the palisades of Nashborough.

They had been five months on the way, had been repeatedly forced to run a gauntlet of bullets, more than once had narrowly escaped shipwreck and death by drowning, and were utterly exhausted. Well might Donelson congratulate himself on having succeeded in bringing them safely to their goal.

"This day," he writes, in closing his unpolished yet, to modern Tennesseens, inestimably precious narrative, "we arrived at our journey's end at the Big Salt Lick, where we have the pleasure of finding Captain Robertson and his company. It is a source of satisfaction to us to be enabled to restore to him and others their families and friends who were intrusted to our care, and who, some time since, perhaps despaired of ever meeting again. Though our prospects at present are dreary, we have found a few log-cabins which have been built on a cedar bluff above the Lick by Captain Robertson and his company."

Mark well that last sentence. Seldom has the true spirit of America been given more eloquent expression than in those few simple words. Separated from even the small settlements of the border by hundreds of miles of black, tangled forest; surrounded by cruel foes who might fall upon them at any moment in overwhelming strength, John Donelson and his mates found sufficient cause for gratitude and hopefulness in the fact that they had a few log cabins to give them shelter. Dreary, in truth, was the prospect, yet there was no thought of surrender, no thought of turning back. This was the spirit of the early West, this is the spirit of the West to-day, it is the true American spirit.

To do, to dare, to conquer; always manfully confident, pressing on from achievement to achievement, beaten at moments, perhaps, but never acknowledging defeat, and doggedly returning to wrest triumph from disaster, — it was this spirit that enabled the pioneers under Boone and Clark, Sevier and Robertson, to win and hold for the United States the vast expanse of wild but fertile country between the Alleghenies and the Mississippi; it was this spirit that enabled their descendants and successors to carry the American flag beyond the Mississippi, until the Republic spanned the continent from sea to sea.

In a thousand ways the dauntless courage, the masterful independence, the bold self-reliance of the men of the early West were manifested, and not least in the measures they took to insure order and tranquillity in their isolated communities. We have already seen how the Watauga settlers, men without experience in state-craft, devised a form of government based on mutual confidence and esteem, and proving eminently workable; and we have also seen how the Transylvanians similarly established a government of their own, less satisfactory than that of Watauga, but still containing admirable features and testifying to the inherent capacity of the pioneers for the management of affairs. Now the settlers on the Cumberland in their turn proceeded to effect a governmental organization, based on a written constitution which, for its pure democracy, deserves to be carefully examined by all students of political science.

It was on May 1, 1780, — another historic American May-day, — that the people of the different stations, in answer to a call issued by Robertson, met in convention at Nashborough and signed articles of association drawn up, in all probability, by Robertson, with some assistance from Richard Henderson, who had come out to survey the boundary-line between the western lands of Virginia and North Carolina, and to arrange terms of payment with all who settled in the territory to which he laid claim.

An attempt, indeed, has been made to credit Henderson rather than Robertson with the authorship of the Cumberland Compact, but the internal evidence of that document itself would seem to disprove this. There is a complete absence of the proprietary characteristics of the Transylvania Constitution, and while Henderson by this time doubtless appreciated the absurdity and impossibility of attempting to establish a proprietary government on American soil, there are many clauses in the Cumberland Compact so extremely democratic that it is hard to see how he could possibly have penned them.

The "Articles of Agreement, or Compact of Government, entered into by settlers on the Cumberland River, 1st May, 1780," as the Cumberland Constitution is formally styled, provided, first of all, that until the laws of North Carolina were extended to the Cumberland settlements they were to be governed by a Court, or Assembly, of twelve Triers, Judges, or General Arbitrators, as they were variously called, elected from the different settlements on the basis of manhood suffrage and representation according to population.

There were to be three Triers from Nashborough, two from Gasper's and Eaton's, and one from each of the other five stations. They were to meet at Nashborough and have full jurisdiction in the settlement of all disputes, any three of them being competent to sit as a trial court. No appeal was allowed in cases where the "debt or damages or demand" did not exceed one hundred dollars. If the sum in dispute were larger, appeal could be taken to nine of the Triers sitting as an appellate court, their decision to be binding if seven of the nine agreed. As to criminal cases, the Compact declared: —

"And it is further agreed that a majority of the said Judges, Triers, or General Arbitrators, shall have power to punish in their discretion, having respect to the laws of our country, all offences against the peace, misdemeanors, and those criminal, or of a capital nature, provided such Court does not proceed with execution so far as to affect life or member; and in case any should be brought before them whose crime is or shall be dangerous to the State, or for which the benefit of clergy is taken away by law, and sufficient evidence or proof of the fact or facts can probably be made, such Court, or a majority of the members, shall and may order and direct him, her, or them to be safely bound and sent under a strong guard to the place where the offence was or shall be committed, or where legal trial of such offence can be had, which shall accordingly be done and the reasonable expense attending the discharge of this duty ascertained by the Court and paid by the inhabitants in such proportion as shall be hereafter agreed on for that purpose."

Provision was made for the establishment of a Land Office, and for the payment of Henderson and his associates at the rate of "twenty-six pounds, thirteen shillings, and four pence, current money, per hundred acres," after they could give the settlers "a satisfactory and indisputable title" — a clause which resulted in perpetual non-payment, owing to the action of the North Carolina Legislature in annulling Henderson's claims on the Cumberland, while voting him two hundred thousand acres in another part of the State as a compensation for the services he unquestionably had rendered in promoting the settlement of the West.

It was also agreed by the Cumberland Compact that Henderson should have the power of appointing the Entry Taker of the Land Office. On the other hand, if the Entry Taker neglected his duties, or was found "by the said Judges, or a majority of them, to have acted fraudulently, to the prejudice of any person whatsoever, such Entry Taker shall be immediately removed from his office, and the book taken out of his possession by the said Judges, until another shall be appointed to act in his room." The Judges themselves were made subject to removal, by one of the most noteworthy clauses in this backwoods constitution: —

"As often as the people in general are dissatisfied with the doings of the Judges or Triers so to be chosen, they may call a new election in any of the said stations, and elect others in their stead, having due respect to the number now agreed to be elected at each station, which persons so to be chosen shall have the same power with those in whose room or place they shall or may be chosen to act."

Thus, with a political wisdom and forethought lacking in many more enlightened communities, the cabin dwellers of the Cumberland kept in their hands the power of immediate recall — that strongest of agencies to insure a truly democratic government. Theirs was to be emphatically a government of the people by the people and for the people, as they made unmistakably clear in the closing clause of their compact; —

"The well-being of this country entirely depends, under Divine Providence, on unanimity of sentiment and concurrence in measures, and as clashing interests and opinions, without being under some restraint, will most certainly produce confusion, discord, and almost certain ruin, so we think it our duty to associate, and hereby form ourselves into one society for the benefit of present and future settlers, and until the full and proper exercise of the laws of our country can be in use, and the powers of government extended among us; we do most solemnly and sacredly declare and promise each other, that we will faithfully and punctually adhere to, perform, and abide by this our Association, and at all times, if need be, compel by our united force a due obedience to these our rules and regulations. In testimony whereof we have hereunto subscribed our names in token of our entire approbation of the measures adopted." [3]

The election of the Triers followed, Robertson being chosen to preside over their deliberations, and also being elected commander-in-chief of the military forces of the united settlements. After which the signers of the compact — to which two hundred and fifty-six names were attached — dispersed to their respective stations to resume the daily task of clearing the wilderness, and, erelong, to take up in addition the burden of defending their homes from the pitiless attacks of the American settler's deadliest foe.

From their forest-girt strongholds, in little war-parties of ten to twenty-five, the Cherokee and the Creek, the Chickamauga and the Chickasaw, set forth in the early summer of 1780 to carry death and destruction to the hardy adventurers who had taken possession of their choice hunting-grounds. But they had delayed their attack too long, and when they made it, did not carry on the steady, vigorous campaign that alone could have brought success. Despite frequent raids, despite occasional victories and the inflicting of some heavy losses, they signally failed to break the spirit or loosen the grasp of the iron-willed men of the Cumberland, who, under the inspiring leadership of Robertson, struck back as savagely as they. Two years of guerilla warfare ended in their complete discomfiture, and by the opening of the year 1783 there was no longer doubt as to who would henceforth be masters of the Cumberland Valley.

It was in that same year that peace with Great Britain was declared, and before its close the peopling of the West had begun in earnest — a great migration setting in, to occupy and hold and develop the glorious region won for the United States by the prowess of the buck-skinned heroes of Watauga, Kentucky, and the Cumberland.

[1] Also said, however, to have been named in honor of General Francis Nash, who was fatally wounded at the battle of Germantown, October 4, 1777.
[2] The full title is "Journal of a Voyage intended by God's Permission, in the good Boat Adventure, from Fort Patrick Henry, on Holston River, to the French Salt Springs on the Cumberland River, kept by John Donelson." It is printed in full in A. W. Putnam's "History of Middle Tennessee."
[3] The full text of the Cumberland Articles of Agreement, so far as that document has been preserved, may be studied in A. W. Putnam's "History of Middle Tennessee."

Chapter Sixteen - Annals of the Wilderness Road

At the close of the Revolution there were scarcely ten thousand American settlers in all the broad region between the Alleghenies and the Mississippi. When the first Federal census was taken, less than ten years later, it was found that the ten thousand had become more than one hundred thousand, nearly three-fourths of whom were located in Kentucky. In another ten years, or at the beginning of the nineteenth century, the population of the same transmontane region had increased to upwards of four hundred thousand, including two hundred and twenty thousand in Kentucky alone. Thus, for fully a quarter of a century after the time it was opened up to civilization by the Transylvania pioneers, Kentucky remained the premier Western State, and received the bulk of the enormous army of home-seekers who, immediately after the cessation of hostilities, hastened to take possession of the virgin lands of the West.

There were many reasons why the incoming stream of humanity flowed chiefly to Kentucky. For one thing, the marvellous fertility of its soil had been made known throughout the East by returned travellers and by speculators who had secured extensive holdings at a trifling outlay and were not overscrupulous as to the means they employed for disposing of them. To such lengths did some of these land-jobbers go that, as the French traveller, F. A. Michaux, indignantly noted, "even forged plans were fabricated, on which rivers were laid down, calculated for the establishment of mills and other uses." Nor did they hesitate on occasion to sell lands to which they were well aware they could not give a valid title.

Moreover, it was understood that only in Kentucky or Tennessee could any degree of security be had against attack by the Indians. As has been said, after Clark's punitive expedition against the Shawnee towns in 1782, the Shawnees and their allies, although continuing to make desultory raids, never again invaded Kentucky in force. But, even after the ending of the Revolution had deprived them of British support, they maintained a bitterly hostile attitude towards all Americans, and for years prevented occupation of the country north of the Ohio, except at such border points as Cincinnati and Marietta, both of which cities were founded in 1788. In fact, it was not until 1795, following Anthony Wayne's victory at the battle of Fallen Timber, and the subsequent Treaty of Greenville, that the settlement of the Old Northwest really began.

The hostility of the Indians had the further consequence of indirectly promoting the development of Kentucky and Tennessee by influencing many of the early home-seekers to enter the West by way of Cumberland Gap and the Wilderness Road; since, as long as Ohio remained in the possession of the savages, travel by the much easier Ohio River route was extremely hazardous. How hazardous may best be shown by relating one of the numerous tales that have been handed down in proof of the malignity and cunning with which the Indians, ever watchfully alert on the northern bank of the Ohio, entrapped unwary voyagers. The victims on this occasion were a party of six — four men named May, Johnston, Stiles, and Flinn, and two sisters named Fleming — who had set out, in the spring of 1790, to journey down the Ohio to Limestone, now Maysville.

"When near the mouth of the Scioto," continues the historian Collins, from whom I quote with some condensation, "they were awakened at daylight by Flinn, whose turn it was to watch, and informed that danger was at hand. All sprang to their feet, and hastened upon deck without removing their nightcaps or completing their dress. The cause of Flinn's alarm was quickly evident. Far down the river a smoke was seen, ascending in thick wreaths above the trees. No one doubted that Indians were in front. As the boat drifted on, it became evident that the fire was upon the Ohio shore, and it was instantly determined to put over to the opposite side of the river. Before this could be done, two white men ran down upon the bank, and clasping their hands in the most earnest manner, implored the crew to take them on board.

"They declared that they had been taken by a party of Indians a few days before, had been conducted across the Ohio, and had just effected their escape. They added that the enemy was in close pursuit of them, and that their death was certain unless admitted on board. Resolute in their purpose on no account to leave the middle of the stream, and strongly suspecting the supplicants of treachery, the party paid no attention to their entreaties, but steadily pressed their course down the river, and were soon considerably ahead of them.

"The two white men ran along the bank, and their entreaties were changed into the most piercing cries and lamentations upon perceiving the obstinacy with which their request was disregarded. Instantly the obduracy of the crew began to relax. Flinn and the two females earnestly insisted upon going ashore and relieving the white men, and even the incredulity of May began to yield to the persevering importunity of the supplicants. A warm controversy began, and daring its progress the boat drifted so far below the men that they appeared to relinquish their pursuit in despair.

"At this time Flinn made a proposal which, according to his method of reasoning, could be carried into effect without the slightest risk to any one but himself. They were now more than a mile below the pursuers. Flinn proposed that May should only touch the shore long enough to permit him to jump out. That it was impossible for Indians (even admitting that they were at hand) to arrive in time to arrest the boat, and even should any appear they could immediately put off from the shore and abandon him to his fate. That he was confident of being able to outrun the red devils if they saw him first, and was equally confident of being able to see them as soon as they could see him. May remonstrated upon so unnecessary an exposure; but Flinn was inflexible, and in an evil hour the boat was directed to the shore.

"They quickly discovered, what ought to have been known before, that they could not float as swiftly after leaving the current as while borne along by it, and they were nearly double the time in making the shore that they had calculated upon. When within reach, Flinn leaped fearlessly upon the bank, and the boat grated upon the sand. At that moment, five or six savages ran up, out of breath, from the adjoining wood, and seizing Flinn, began to fire upon the boat's crew. Johnston and Stiles sprang to their arms, in order to return the fire, while May, seizing an axe, attempted to regain the current. Fresh Indians arrived, however, in such rapid succession that the beach was quickly crowded by them, and May called out to his companions to cease firing and come to the oars. This was instantly done, but it was too late.

"Seeing it impossible to extricate themselves, they awaited in passive helplessness the approach of the conquerors. The enemy, however, still declined boarding, and contented themselves with pouring in an incessant fire. One of the females received a ball in her mouth, and almost instantly expired. Stiles immediately afterwards was severely wounded in both shoulders, the ball striking the right shoulder blade and ranging transversely along his back. May then rose and waved his night-cap above his head as a signal of surrender. He instantly received a ball in the middle of the forehead, and fell dead by the side of Johnston, covering him with his blood.

"Now the enemy ventured to board. Throwing themselves into the water, with their tomahawks in their hands, a dozen or twenty swam to the boat and began to climb the sides. Johnston stood ready to do the honors. Nothing could appear more cordial than the greeting. Each Indian shook him by the hand, with the usual salutation of "how de do" in passable English, while Johnston met every Indian with a forced smile, in which terror struggled with civility. The Indians then passed on to Stiles and the surviving Miss Fleming, where the demonstrations of mutual joy were not quite so lively. Stiles was writhing under his painful wound, and the girl was sitting by the body of her sister.

"Having shaken hands with all of their captives, the Indians proceeded to scalp the dead, which was done with great coolness, and the reeking scalps were stretched and prepared upon hoops for the usual process of drying, immediately before the eyes of the survivors. The boat was then drawn ashore, and its contents examined with great greediness. At length the Indians stumbled upon a keg of whiskey. This prize was eagerly seized, and everything else abandoned.

"On the next morning the Indians rose early and prepared for another encounter, expecting that boats would be passing as usual. It happened that Captain Thomas Marshall, of the Virginia artillery, was descending the Ohio in company with several other gentlemen. About twelve o'clock on the second day after May's disaster, the little flotilla appeared about a mile above the point where the Indians stood. Instantly all was bustle and activity. The oars were fixed to May's boat, the savages sprang on board, and the prisoners were compelled to station themselves at the oars, and were threatened with instant death unless they used their utmost exertions. Captain Marshall's three boats came down the river very rapidly, and were soon immediately opposite the enemy's. The Indians opened a heavy fire upon them, and stimulated their rowers to the greatest effort.

"But they lost ground from two circumstances. In their eagerness to overtake the whites they left the current and attempted to cut across the river from point to point, in order to shorten the distance. In doing so, however, they lost the force of the current, and soon found themselves dropping astern. In addition to this, the whites conducted themselves with equal coolness and dexterity. The second boat waited for the hindmost and received her crew on board, abandoning the goods and horses to the enemy. Being now more strongly manned, she shot rapidly ahead, and quickly overtook the foremost boat, which, in like manner, received the crew on board, abandoning the cargo as before; and, having six pairs of oars, and being powerfully manned, she was soon beyond the reach of the enemy's shot.

"The chase lasted more than an hour. For the first half hour the fate of the foremost boat hung in mournful suspense. The prisoners were compelled to labor hard at the oars, but they took care never to pull together, and by every means in their power endeavored to favor the escape of their friends. At length the Indians abandoned the pursuit, and turned their whole attention to the boats which had been deserted.

"Flinn was subsequently burnt by his fiendish captors at the stake, with all the aggravated tortures that savage cruelty could devise. Stiles, after running the gauntlet and having been condemned to death, made his escape and reached the white settlements in safety. Miss Fleming was rescued by an Indian chief, at the very time her captors had bound her to a stake and were making preparations to burn her alive, and was conducted to Pittsburg. Johnston was ransomed by a Frenchman at Sandusky, at the price of six hundred silver brooches, and returned in safety to his family."

Menaced by such a peril as this, it is small wonder that, throughout the decade between the close of the Revolution and Wayne's successful campaign against the Ohio Indians, many emigrants, even from points as far north as Philadelphia and New York, preferred to reach the West by the roundabout, difficult route over the Wilderness Road. Not that they thereby entirely avoided attack by the savages, who long made petty incursions that in the aggregate resulted in the shedding of much blood and the inflicting of heavy property losses. They were particularly active along the line of the Wilderness Road, and consequently it became the custom for travellers to wait at some designated meeting-place until a numerous enough company had been assembled to enable them to proceed without fear of being attacked.

Inward bound, the usual rendezvous was at a blockhouse on the Holston, at the very beginning of Boone's historic road; outward bound, it was at Crab Orchard, a Lincoln County pioneer station, so named because of the quantity of wild apple trees which the first settlers found growing there. After the establishment of *The Kentucky Gazette* — founded in 1787, and the first newspaper published in the Mississippi Valley — advertisements frequently appeared, setting dates for intending travellers to assemble at Crab Orchard. "A large company," runs one announcement, in 1788, "will meet at the Crab Orchard the 19th of November in order to start the next day through the Wilderness. As it is very dangerous on account of the Indians, it is hoped each person will go well armed." Another of the many similar advertisements that might be quoted, warned all travellers to arm themselves and "not to depend on others to defend them."

The newspapers of the day, too, bear striking testimony to the fact that these precautionary measures were amply justified, even long after Kentucky had become comparatively thickly settled. *The Virginia Gazette*, of November 5, 1791, under date of October 22, from Winchester, reported that: "A person arrived here on Wednesday last from Kentucky, who informs us that he started from the Crab Orchards in company with several other persons; that, as they passed through the wilderness, they discovered two human bodies which had been killed and scalped by some Indians, and that he and his companions stopped and buried them.

"Another party, who recently came in through the wilderness were attacked by a small number of Indians; but they all escaped, saving one woman, who fell into the hands of the savages. She, however, was fortunate enough to liberate herself afterwards, in the following manner: The night after she was taken, the Indians made a large fire, and placed her between themselves and it; they then fell asleep, and, apparently, the woman did the same; but, watching her opportunity, she stole away from them unperceived, and wandered in the woods until she came to a run of water, whose course she kept for a considerable number of miles, and at length arrived safe in a settlement of white inhabitants."

Cumberland Gap and the Wilderness Road

In the same year a band of Wilderness Road marauders penetrated as far east as the Watauga country, as we find from an item in *Dunlap's American Daily Advertiser*, a correspondent writing, in the issue for October 12, 1791, that "About the 1st of September a party of Indians came to a place called Moccassen Gap, in Clinch Mountain, within seven miles of Ross's furnace, and killed four persons. A party of men followed them immediately, but through some mismanagement returned without coming up with them. It is not known to what nation they belonged, but, from several circumstances, it is thought they were northern Indians."

So far as the Indian peril was concerned, however, the Wilderness Road was never so dangerous as the journey down the Ohio. But the home-seekers who thronged its path invariably discovered that it had disadvantages from which the water route was altogether free. Even to-day, after nearly a century and a half of use, it remains, as that genial Kentucky writer, Mr. James Lane Allen, has wittily declared, "as it was in the beginning, with all its sloughs and sands, its mud and holes, and jutting ledges of rock and loose boulders, and twists and turns, and general total depravity." In the time of the first great immigration — the ten years following the Revolution — it was a road of unending tribulations. Indeed, it could only by courtesy be called a road, for it was still merely the narrow, miry, forest-encompassed trail chopped out by Boone and his comrades in 1775.

For twenty years, or until it was widened in 1796 by order of the Kentucky Legislature, no wagon could traverse it. The men and women, the little children, who toiled wearily up the long ascent to Cumberland Gap, and thence pressed forward to the Blue Grass region or the settlements on the Ohio, had to make the entire journey on foot or on horseback, just as the Boones and the Harrods and the Logans of earlier days had been obliged to do; and everything they brought with them had to be carried on the backs of patient pack-horses. There were few if any roadhouses. All had to sleep in the open, huddled near the camp-fire. Often there was great suffering from storm and cold and want of food. Yet, such was the eagerness to occupy and hold the West that, at a conservative estimate, no fewer than seventy-five thousand persons passed through Cumberland Gap and along the Wilderness Road in the years before it was open to wagon travel.

Of all these thousands, though, scarcely one has left any record of the adventures that befell him on his journey. The sturdy folk who crossed the mountains, while by no means illiterate, were not a writing people; and when they reached their destination, they had much else to think of than the chronicling of the incidents of their long pilgrimage. Consequently the historian who would describe the Wilderness Road when it was at the height of its importance must fall back on inference and imagination, piecing out his narrative from such meagre sources of information as occasional references in contemporary newspapers, and brief statements in private letters and papers, the most detailed of which — a journal kept by William Brown, who visited Kentucky in 1782 — is painfully deficient in the way of affording a view of life on Boone's famous thoroughfare. But it has the merit of indicating plainly the difficulties of travel, and the hardships and dangers to which all wayfarers over the old road were exposed.

Brown, who was a Virginian and the father of Judge Alfred M. Brown, of Elizabethtown, Kentucky, set out on horseback from Hanover, Virginia, May 27, 1782. Thence he rode to Richmond, and in a direct line westward through Powhatan, Cumberland, Buckingham, and Amherst counties to the Blue Ridge, which he crossed into Botetourt County. His route then lay to the southwest, between a long succession of mountain ridges, to the blockhouse on the Holston, where the Wilderness Road began. "The road from Hanover to this place," he records, "is generally very good; crossing the Blue Ridge is not bad; there is not more than a small hill with some winding to go over. Neither is the Alleghany Mountain by any means difficult at this gap. There are one or two high hills about New River and Fort Chiswell. The ford of New River is rather bad. Therefore we thought it advisable to cross in the ferry-boat. This is generally a good-watered road as far as the blockhouse.

"We waited hereabouts near two weeks for company and then set out for the wilderness with twelve men and ten guns, this being Thursday, 18th July. The road from this until you get over Walden's Ridge generally is bad, some part very much so, particularly about Stock Creek and Stock Creek Ridge. It is a very mountainous country hereabout, but there is some fine land in the bottoms, near the watercourses, in narrow strips. It will be but a thin-settled country whenever it is settled. The fords of Holstein and Clinch are both good in dry weather, but in a rainy season you are often obliged to raft over.

"From there along down Powell's Valley until you get to Cumberland Gap is pretty good; this valley is formed by Cumberland Mountain on the northwest and Powell Mountain on the southeast, and appears to bear from northeast southwestwardly, and is, I suppose, almost one hundred miles in length, and from ten to twelve miles in breadth. The land generally is good, and is an exceeding well-watered country, as well as the country on Holstein River, abounding with fine springs and little brooks. For about fifty miles, as you travel along the valley, Cumberland Mountain appears to be a very high ridge of white rocks, inaccessible in most places to either man or beast, and affords a wild, romantic prospect.

"The way through the gap is not very difficult, but from its situation travellers may be attacked in some places, crossing the mountain, by the enemy to a very great disadvantage. From thence until you pass Rockcastle River there is very little good road; this tract of country is very mountainous, and badly watered along the trace, especially for springs. There is some good land on the watercourses, and just on this side Cumberland River appears to be a good tract, and within a few years I expect to have a settlement on it. Some parts of the road are very miry in rainy weather. The fords of Cumberland and Rockcastle are both good unless the waters be too high; after you cross Rockcastle there are a few high hills, and the rest of the way tolerable good; the land appears to be rather weak, chiefly timbered with oak, etc.

"The first of the Kentucky waters you touch upon is the head of Dick's River, just eight miles from English's. Here we arrived Thursday, 25th inst., which is just seven days since we started from the blockhouse. Monday, 29th inst., I got to Harrodsburg...

"I travelled but little about the country. From English's to Harrodsburg was the farthest west, and from Logan's Fort to the Blue Lick the farthest north. Thus far the land was generally good — except near and about the Lick it was very poor and badly timbered — generally badly watered, but pretty well timbered. At Richmond Ford, on the Kentucky River, the bank a little below the ford appears to be largely upward of a hundred feet perpendicular of rock.

"On my return to Hanover I set off from John Craig's Monday, 23d September, 1782; left English's Tuesday, 1 o'clock, arrived at the blockhouse the Monday evening following, and kept on the same route downward chiefly that I travelled out. Nothing untoward occurred to me. Got to Hanover sometime about the last of October the same year." [1]

From this matter-of-fact, but historically important, record of travel, it appears that the westwardbound emigrant from New York, New Jersey, Pennsylvania, Maryland, and Virginia had a fairly easy journey through the Valley of Virginia until he reached the blockhouse on the Holston. But, if only on account of the tremendous natural obstacles which he thenceforward had to overcome, it is not surprising that travel over the Wilderness Road fell off rapidly as soon as the pacification of the Ohio Indians rendered it possible to utilize less difficult and more direct routes.

From New York and New England the emigrant then found ready access to the West through the Mohawk and Genesee valleys to Lake Erie, or, crossing the Hudson at Albany, passed westward through the Catskill Mountains to the headwaters of the Allegheny River. Several roads led through Pennsylvania to the Ohio, on which, after 1800, the home-seeker could embark with his family and float to the Mississippi in perfect security from Indian attack. The opening of other more southerly routes hastened the decline of Boone's road as a main-travelled way, and its complete downfall may be said to have been accomplished with the building of the celebrated national turnpike, the Cumberland Road, which led from Baltimore through Cumberland, Maryland, — where unhappy Braddock had marshalled his troops, — to Wheeling, in West Virginia, being ultimately extended into Ohio.

Still, though its glory has long since vanished, the important part once played by the Wilderness Road in the development of the United States can never be forgotten. As one writer, Professor A. B. Hulbert, has well said: —

"The footsteps of the tens of thousands who have passed over it, exhausted though each pilgrim may have been, have left a trace that a thousand years cannot eradicate. And so long as the print of these many feet can be seen in dark Powell's Valley, on Cumberland Gap, and beside Yellow and Rockcastle creeks, so long will there be a memorial left to perpetuate the heroism of the first Kentuckians — and the memory of what the Middle West owes to Virginia and her neighbors. For when all is said, this track from tide-water through Cumberland Gap must remain a monument to the courage and patriotism of the people of old Virginia and North Carolina."

Aye, and a monument to its great maker, Daniel Boone, who, even when far advanced in years, displayed a lively interest in the highway he had opened for the nation. In 1796, as was stated, the Wilderness Road was for the first time made fit for wagon travel, by order of the Kentucky Legislature. The announcement of the projected improvement drew from Boone the following curious, but pathetic, letter addressed to Governor Shelby.

"Sir," Boone wrote, "after my best Respts to your Excelancy and famyly I wish to inform you that I have sum intention of undertaking this New Rode that is to be cut through the Wilderness and I think my Self intitled to the ofer of the Bisness as I first Marked out that Rode in March 1775 and Never rec'd anything for my trubel and Sepose I am no Statesman I am a Woodsman and think My Self as Capable of Marking and Cutting that Rode as any other man Sir if you think with Me I would thank you to Wright me a Line by the post the first oportuneaty and he Will Lodge it at Mr. John Milers on hinkston fork as I wish to know Where and When it is to be Laat [let] So that I may atend at the time I am Deer Sir your very omble sarvent Daniel Boone."

But others were to get the contract which should deservedly have gone to him. The Boone of 1796 was not the Boone of 1782 in point of influence and prestige in Kentucky. He was no longer one of its recognized leaders. Rather, he had been swept to one side, and into an unmerited obscurity, taking nc part whatever in the upbuilding of the great commonwealth whose very existence was so largely owing to his brave endeavor.

[1] Brown's "itinerary" is printed in full in Mr. Thomas Speed's Filson Club monograph on "The Wilderness Road," from which I have taken the extracts quoted.

Chapter Seventeen - Kentucky after the Revolution

THROUGHOUT the Indian wars, as we have seen, Daniel Boone was rivalled only by George Rogers Clark as the foremost figure in Kentucky, his daring deeds in defence of the infant settlements winning for him a renown that time has not faded nor can ever fade. But, after the crucial period of conflict was at an end, after the power of the red man to invade and ravage Kentucky had been broken, Boone's leadership rapidly waned. More than this, partly through his own fault and partly through the selfish scheming of others, a day came when he was stripped not only of influence but even of possession of a single acre of land. Homeless, burdened with debts, despairing of ever seeing justice done him, he finally was impelled to depart from the glorious domain with which his name will always be associated.

Still, even had misfortunes not crowded thick and fast upon him, it is altogether unlikely that Boone would have spent the remainder of his days in Kentucky. He was, as he had told Governor Shelby in the letter quoted in the preceding chapter, not a "statesman" but a "woodsman," with all of the true woodsman's distaste for the hurried and complex life of civilization. And Kentucky, with its influx of seventy thousand settlers within less than eight years after the battle of the Blue Lick, was no longer the Kentucky in which Boone as a woodsman had felt at home. The buffalo and the deer and all other fur-bearing animals on which he depended so largely for his livelihood were driven to far-distant parts; new customs and manners irksome to the simple-hearted first settlers, of whom Boone was so conspicuous a type, were fast introduced; almost everywhere there was bustle and change, the old palisaded stations giving place to thriving villages and towns, or being entirely deserted, their war-worn timbers left to stand as grim reminders of the years of desperate struggle.

Boonesborough itself, it is true, gave slight evidence of the new order of things in Kentucky. After the spring of 1783, when a mounted messenger rode into the stockade with the word *Peace* displayed on his coonskin cap, in token of the signing of the treaty with Great Britain, there was a temporary expansion. But for some reason immigration did not trend Boonesborough-wards, and as late as 1810 it was still a tiny hamlet. To-day it is not even a hamlet, its abandoned site being only a part of a lonely river farm. Mr. Ranck, in his "Boonesborough," argues that it was at one time a town of considerable size, basing this claim apparently on a British document which credits Boonesborough with having had, in 1789, "upwards of one hundred and twenty houses." But since the census of 1790 does not even mention it in the enumeration of the towns of Kentucky, it seems safe to conclude that Boonesborough's importance ended with the termination of the Indian wars.

As to its modern aspect, Mr. Ranck is well worth quoting. "One and only one institution survives," he writes, "that was established by the settlers of the place, and that figured familiarly in their lives. It is the picturesque old ferry, the oldest in Kentucky, and consecrated by the blood of its founders. The ferry-boat is fashioned still exactly like its quaint and simple predecessors of the Revolution, and is poled across the river in the same primitive style as in the fighting days of Boone.

"No remnant of the battle-scarred old fort remains. For nearly a century the plough has been busy where it stood, and year after year the tall corn has rustled and ripened above its site. Elevated as the fort ground is, it has not always, it is said, escaped the obliterating effects of great overflows of the Kentucky River, and now the graves of such of the founders and defenders of the old stronghold as were buried within or near its wooden walls have long been levelled and lost to sight.

"The famous 'hollow,' owing to successive deposits from river floods, is not nearly as deep as it was in the days of the pioneers, and, long undisturbed, it is thick with sycamores that have sprung up since the settlement died out, and once again the ancient haunt of the buffalo and the elk is a romantic and luxuriant wild. The mighty elm, whose majestic dome sheltered the first legislature and the first worshipping assembly of a wilderness empire, and which witnessed one of the strangest episodes of the American Revolution [the signing of the sham treaty at the last siege of Boonesborough], fell under the axe in 1828, and fell in all its stateliness and splendor. It was the most unique and precious historical monument in the whole domain of Kentucky, and was invested with a charm that the loftiest sculptured column could not possess.

"But hedged about and obscured as it has been by deposits from river floods, the sulphur water is there round which the wild animals of the wilderness gathered for unnumbered generations; the Lick Spring still exists which refreshed alike the Indian and the pioneer, and near it stands the last of the great sycamores that were there when the white man first invaded the vast solitude in which they grew."

Site of Boonsborough
As seen from the opposite bank of the Kentucky

If Boonesborough failed to profit from the flow of immigration, elsewhere the work of settlement and development went on apace, particularly north and east of the Kentucky, and along Logan's Branch of the Wilderness Road, where a number of promising little towns sprang up, of which at first the most important, historically speaking, was Danville. Situated near Crab Orchard, and between Logan's Fort and Harrodstown, Danville was virtually the capital of Kentucky until its admission as a State of the Union in 1792. [1] Farther west, along Logan's Branch, another prominent centre of settlement was at Bardstown, while, at the terminal of this branch, Louisville early began to give indications of the importance it was ultimately to attain.

On the Kentucky the foundations of the present capital of the State, Frankfort, were laid. Almost in a straight line east from Frankfort, Lebanontown (now Georgetown) and Paris were established, the latter being at first known as Hopewell and, for a time, as Bourbontown. In the extreme northeast, four miles south of Maysville and convenient of access from the Ohio, the town of Washington was laid out, with a population by 1790 of nearly five hundred. But the largest and most rapidly growing town of that day, the proudly styled "Metropolis of the West," was Lexington, south of, and midway between, Paris and Frankfort.

When the Revolution ended, Lexington was still merely a palisaded settlement like Boonesborough, Harrodstown, and all other of the pioneer stations of Kentucky. At the time of the taking of the first Federal census it was a town with more than eight hundred inhabitants; and within the next ten years, or by the beginning of the nineteenth century, its population had increased to upwards of two thousand. Its growth was favored both by its location in the heart of the rich Blue Grass region and by the ease with which it could be approached from the Ohio and from both branches of the Wilderness Road. As early as 1784, or only two years after the battle of the Blue Lick, a "dry-goods" store was opened in Lexington by the always enterprising, if notorious, James Wilkinson, who did so much to entangle the Kentuckians with their Spanish neighbors, and to create dissension between the East and the West. [2] The following year a grist-mill was put in operation, and an inn established for the accommodation of travellers. Two years later, in 1787, John Bradford hauled a printing-press to Lexington, by pack-horse over the mountains, and founded Kentucky's first newspaper. *The Kentucky Gazette.*

From the files of this old paper it is possible to gain a good idea of the rapidity with which Kentucky was transformed from a country of isolated and crude cabin settlements into a commonwealth with all the institutions, desirable and otherwise, of an advanced society. The news columns of *The Kentucky Gazette*, it must regretfully be said, furnish comparatively meagre information; for Bradford, like most of the editors of his time, ruthlessly subordinated local news to "general intelligence" — largely of happenings abroad. But the advertisements, with their unconscious mirroring of changing social conditions, amply compensate for the absence of any direct account of the life of the people of Lexington and the country round about it.

For one thing, the advertisements in the *Gazette* afford impressive proof of the earnest desire on the part of the settlers, at the cost of considerable sacrifice to themselves, to provide educational facilities for their children. Reference has already been made to the passion for education, if only of an elementary sort, found among the Scotch-Irish of the Virginia and Carolina border, the first winners of the West. Even before Bradford began the publication of his newspaper there were several schools in Kentucky. In 1779, while the struggle with the Indians was at its height, Joseph Doniphan, a young immigrant from Virginia, opened a school at Boonesborough. The following year another was opened at Lexington by John McKinney. John Filson, to whom we are indebted for Boone's "autobiography," also taught school at Lexington before the end of the Indian wars; and, in 1785, in a large cabin near Danville, a beginning was made of the "Transylvania Seminary," founded a couple of years earlier by act of the Virginia Legislature as an institution for higher education.

Not even the Transylvania Seminary, as then conducted, could compare favorably, however, with the "little red schoolhouse" of the country districts of to-day. But with the coming of the second generation of settlers, many of whom were people of some means, schools of a better order were soon established. In 1787 Isaac Wilson, a graduate of the University of Pennsylvania, opened the "Lexington Grammar School" to teach "Latin, Greek, and the different branches of science." A still more ambitious project was set on foot at Lebanontown, as appears from the following quaintly elaborate advertisement, inserted in the *Gazette* under date of December 27, 1787: —

"Notice is hereby given that on Monday, the 28th of January next, a school will be opened by Messrs. Jones and Worley at the royal spring at Lebanontown, Fayette County, where a commodious house, sufficient to contain fifty or sixty scholars, will be prepared. They will teach the Latin and Greek languages, together with such branches of the sciences as are usually taught in public seminaries, at twenty-five shillings a quarter for each scholar, one half to be paid in cash, the other in produce at cash price. There will be a vacation of a month in the spring and another in the fall, at the close of each of which it is expected that such payments as are due in cash will be made. For diet, washing, and house-room for a year, each scholar pays three pounds in cash, or five hundred weight of pork, on entrance, and three pounds each on the beginning of the third quarter. It is desired that as many as can would furnish themselves with beds; such as cannot may be provided for here to the number of eight or ten boys, at twenty-five shillings a year for each bed.

"N.B. It would be proper for each boy to have his sheets, shirts, stockings, etc., marked, to prevent mistakes."

In the same year (1788) that Messrs. Jones and Worley opened their academy, Transylvania Seminary was moved from Danville to Lexington, where it was located in "a plain, two-story brick building" instead of the rough log structure in which it had hitherto been housed. In its new home it seems to have prospered from the outset, and to have met to a large extent the need it was intended to supply. "Friday the 10th inst.," one reads in an April, 1790, issue of the *Gazette*, "was appointed for the examination of the students of the Transylvania Seminary by the trustees. In the presence of a very respectable audience, several elegant speeches were delivered by the boys, and in the evening a tragedy acted, and the whole concluded with a farce. The several masterly strokes of eloquence, throughout the performance, obtained general applause, and were acknowledged by a universal clap from all present. The good order and decorum observed throughout the whole, together with the rapid progress of the school in literature, reflects very great honor on the president."

This in Lexington in April, 1790, not eight years after the fateful day when John Todd and his men in buckskin galloped out of its stockade gate to the relief of Bryan's Station and the disastrous battle of the Blue Lick! Truly Kentucky was making marvellous progress. [3]

Nor was the activity of the settlers along educational lines confined to the establishing of schools. Towards the close of 1787, the "Kentucky Society for Promoting Useful Knowledge" was organized by the joint efforts of a number of public-spirited citizens of Lexington, Louisville, Danville, and other towns; and in 1795 a public library was opened in Lexington. Books, it would seem, and of a most varied character, were widely read. At all events, *The Kentucky Gazette* and *The Rights of Man,* or *Kentucky Mercury*, a newspaper founded at Paris in 1797, contain advertisements of books for sale by local merchants, who, in view of the great difficulties of transportation, would assuredly not have imported them had there not been considerable demand.

In the November 17, 1797, issue of the *Mercury,* for instance, Oba S. Timberlake offered to the public an extensive assortment of books, including Cook's "Voyages," Enfield's "Sermons," Price's "Sermons," Paley's "Evidences of Christianity," Milton's "Works," Carver's "Travels," Goldsmith's "History of England," Harrison's "Natural History," Franklin's "Works," "Gil Bias," "Irish Jests," and "Rosina, or Love in a Cottage."

Even more miscellaneous and more clearly indicative of an appreciation among eighteenth-century Kentuckians of the best in literature are the items in an advertisement inserted by a Lexington merchant in the *Gazette* of May 23, 1799, listing such works as Plutarch's "Lives," Homer's "Iliad," Milton's "Paradise Lost" and "Paradise Regained," Bunyan's "Pilgrim's Progress" and "The Holy War," Locke's "Essay on the Human Understanding," "The Spectator," Johnson's "Lives," Butler's "Analogy," "Robinson Crusoe," and "Evelina."

The newspaper advertisements also leave no doubt that, besides expanding intellectually, the people of Kentucky rapidly outgrew the primitive simplicity of costume, food, recreations, household furnishings, etc., that had prevailed throughout the period of first settlement. By 1789 they were beginning to build brick houses in their larger towns. The same year Kentucky's classic sport, horse racing, was instituted at Lexington, and in 1797 a jockey club was organized, as is shown by an advertisement in the *Gazette* calling on the subscribers to the Newmarket Jockey Club to meet for the purpose of establishing rules and regulations. Also in 1797 a theatre was opened in Lexington. Articles of comfort and luxury were imported in constantly increasing quantity and variety. In 1796 Benjamin Cox, a Lexington tradesman, announced through the *Gazette* that he was prepared to supply his patrons with —

"A handsome assortment of dry goods and hardware — amongst which are a few sets of saddler's and shoemaker's tools complete. A most elegant assortment of milliner's work, such as bonnets, hats, caps, feathers, and a number of other handsome pieces of ornament for ladies. Together with a few lady's watch chains and gold ear-rings, all of the newest fashion. Also a large and general assortment of medicine, amongst which is the following patent medicine — to wit, castor, sweet, and British oil, Godfrey's cordial, Bateman's drops, Turlington's balsam of life, Anderson's pills. Also madder, alum, whiting, ink powder, and a quantity of excellent sponge; together with a number of other things too tedious to mention."

Three years later, to quote a second advertisement illustrative of the rapidity with which the Kentuckians progressed out of the era of cabin homes, linsey and buckskin clothes, and plain viands, another Lexington merchant listed in the *Gazette:* —

"Young Hyson tea, pepper, nutmegs, copperas, alum, indigo, arnotto, iron, lead, glass bottles, window glass, slates, pins and needles, teakettles, bell-metal skillets for preserving, padlocks, muslins, writing-paper, pocket-books, spelling-books. Bibles and testaments, Watson's Apology for the Bible, black silk mode, black satin, wool and fur hats, an elegant horseman's sword, whips, casimirs, flannels, Scotch snuff, and tobacco."

Other advertisements of earlier date show that there was a lively demand for artisans of all sorts. Immigration societies were organized in Lexington, Louisville, Washington, and elsewhere, to make known the opportunities open in Kentucky to skilled mechanics as well as to agriculturalists. The price-lists published by these societies reveal even more clearly than the ordinary business announcements the far-reaching change in social conditions that developed with the coming of the army of home-seekers who took possession of Kentucky in the years immediately following the Revolution.

By 1797, it appears, carpenters and house-painters were assured of constant and remunerative occupation; shoemakers could find steady employment manufacturing "boots and bootees"; hat-makers were needed to provide the Kentuckians with "beaver, castor, smooth, rabbit, and wool" hats; tailors to garb them in "great coats, strait coats, coatees, surtouts, waistcoats, and breeches," and cabinet-makers to install in their homes "dining tables, breakfast tables, card-tables, buffets, sideboards, bookcases, bureaus, cases of drawers, clock-cases, and bedsteads."

At first, of course, it was only in and about the towns that the new and more elaborate mode of living was in evidence. There were plenty of thinly settled districts — just as, for that matter, there are in Kentucky to-day — where the inhabitants still lived in the most primitive fashion imaginable. But, speaking generally, in the more desirable sections of the State the old order of things had vanished before 1800, never to return. And, as may be imagined, there were many of the original settlers who bitterly deplored and resented the innovations forced upon them. In 1797, when money was particularly scarce in Kentucky, a series of articles appeared in *The Kentucky*

Herald, charging that the "hard times" were due to nothing so much as the "change in the manners" of the people.

"During the first period of its settlement," the writer declared, "the inhabitants expected and wished for nothing but what was the produce of the country. Men and women exerted themselves to the utmost to bring to perfection such necessary articles as the climate and soil were capable of producing...The table was entirely furnished with the produce of the country; and very few articles of clothing, or of woollen or linen for domestic use, were brought from any other country...But as soon as great sums of money were introduced, by the markets caused by the Indian war, [4] a change took place in our manners; a change which, although not very great at first, has been gradually increasing, until we now no longer resemble the people we were during the first period.

"The money which was then received for the cattle and horses which had been raised by the joint care of the whole family was to be expended in the way which would give most pleasure to all. Pride then commenced its operations and induced them to prove the superiority of their wealth by the purchasing to the greatest amount of those articles of foreign luxury which had before been equally unused by all. These articles when purchased would not have answered the purpose for which they were intended unless they had been exhibited to public view; this established an universal desire to show the greatest value in these articles. By this means home manufactures became disreputable. Those were considered as poor or mean who appeared in them, and it soon became as uncommon a sight to see a coat or a gown made of them as it formerly had been to see those articles made of imported materials...

"Home manufactures were not only discarded from our dress but were also laid aside in our diet; none but imported cheese was fit to be served upon a genteel table; country sugar did not agree with their stomachs; and home-made spirits were so little used that even a small quantity of them could not be procured but after a diligent search, when wine and imported spirits were used as freely as if they flowed spontaneously from our springs. Not satisfied with these alterations they turned day into night, and night into day, and every expensive and ridiculous fashion which was in use in any of the old countries was introduced here...The degree of extravagance caused by these changes in our manners has been witnessed by all, and felt by many. During the short time that money was flowing in upon us from all quarters, the imprudence of such conduct was great; but to continue it now, after all the channels are stopped through which we were supplied with the means of supporting that extravagance, would be folly in the extreme."

Scant attention was paid to censure like this. The old settlers were made to feel that either they must accommodate themselves to the altered conditions of their environment, or seek elsewhere the kind of life to which they had always been accustomed. As a result, many of them, by temperament and training fitted only for the free and simple existence of the frontier, departed from Kentucky as soon as it began to be, from their point of view, uncomfortably populous. Among those thus migrating. partly from necessity and partly from choice, was Daniel Boone.

The story of his life in Kentucky after it had been definitely won from the red man need not take long in the telling. Some time before the battle of the Blue Lick he left Boonesborough with his family, his pack-horses, and his dogs, and took up his residence on a small farm on the other side of the Kentucky, about five miles from his first settlement. Here he built a palisaded log-house, known on old maps of Kentucky as Boone's Station, and made his home until 1785, supporting himself by raising tobacco, surveying, and hunting. It was while he was living on this farm that he gave Filson the material for his singular "autobiography," the publication of which, in 1784, had the effect of making Boone's name known in every part of the United States, and even in foreign lands.

But, brilliant as his reputation was, it could not save him from the worries and troubles that he now began to experience in rapidly increasing number. In the course of the twenty years that had elapsed since the opening of the Wilderness Road and the building of Boonesborough he had acquired extensive holdings of land in various parts of Kentucky. Two thousand acres, the reader may remember, had been given to him by the Transylvania Company as a reward for his road-building services. In 1780, this grant having lapsed with the failure of Henderson and his partners to sustain their claim to Kentucky, the Virginia Legislature had voted Boone a compensatory grant of a thousand acres in what is now Bourbon County; and he had preempted many thousands of acres more, believing, in the words of his biographer. Dr. Thwaites, that no one would question his right to as much land as he cared to hold in a wilderness which he had done so much to bring to the attention of the world.

Unfortunately, he entirely neglected to perfect his claims in accordance with legal requirements, an omission that was soon discovered by hawk-eyed "claim-jumpers," who did not scruple to make entry of Boone's choice preemptions in their own names. Suit after suit for ejectment was filed against him, and, the courts having no alternative but to uphold those who had taken title in the proper way, the final outcome was to leave the brave old hero without an acre of land in his beloved Kentucky.

Meanwhile, in 1786, he made another removal, this time to Maysville, where he opened a small tavern and store, the merchandise for which he and his sons brought from Maryland by pack-horse. Often, too, he went on hunting and trapping expeditions, or traded up and down the Ohio, bartering his goods for furs, skins, tobacco, ginseng, and other Kentucky products, which he carried across the mountains and exchanged for more merchandise. Besides this, he was frequently employed as a scout and guide for parties of immigrants. Once, in 1788, he took his wife and son Nathan, then a little fellow of eight, on a horseback trip to Pennsylvania, where they remained a month visiting their relatives in Berks County. On his return, learning that the courts were still deciding against him in the matter of the lawsuits, and that he had been rendered almost entirely landless, Boone left Maysville, vowing never more to live in Kentucky, and established himself in the western Virginia settlement of Point Pleasant, at the juncture of the Ohio and the Kanawha rivers.

Here he was once more in a typical frontier community, and was received with an enthusiasm that must have been most pleasing to him. He had not been in his new home more than a year, when, as the result of a popular petition, he was appointed lieutenant-colonel of Kanawha County. In 1791, as a further mark of the esteem in which the Kanawha Valley people held him, he was elected to the Virginia Assembly, an honor which he had enjoyed twice before, once when Boonesborough was in its prime, and later while he was living in Maysville. The records of the Assembly for 1791 show that he served on two then important committees — the committee on religion and the committee on propositions and licenses. But there is nothing to indicate that he took any part in the Assembly debates other than to vote on bills brought up for consideration.

Before the Assembly adjourned word arrived of the disaster that had overtaken Governor St. Clair's ill-starred expedition against the Indian towns on the Miami, and with praiseworthy promptitude it was voted to send a large supply of ammunition to the militia on the Monongahela and the Kanawha, who were to be called out to defend the frontier against the Indian raids which it was expected would immediately follow St. Clair's defeat. This drew from Boone another of his strangely misspelled, but historically valuable, letters.

"Sir," he wrote to the governor of Virginia, "as sum person Must Carry out the armantstion (ammunition) to Red Stone if your Exclency should have thought me a proper person I would undertake it on conditions I have the apintment to vitel the company at Kanhowway so that I Could take Down the flowre as I paste that place I am your Excelencey's most obedent omble servant Daniel Boone."

Five days later, December 18, 1791, his offer was accepted, and he set out for Red Stone, now Brownsville, Pennsylvania. But for some reason he failed to deliver the necessary rations to the Kanawha troops. Nor, unlike his old friend Simon Kenton, who had settled near Washington, Kentucky, does he seem to have participated in the Indian wars in Ohio. Scarcely anything, in fact, is known of his life during the years 1792-98, except that he moved his residence from Point Pleasant to a settlement farther up the Kanawha, near the site of Charleston, West Virginia; roamed and hunted as of old, and was a frequent visitor to the now rapidly growing towns on the Ohio, where his fame invariably drew about him a group of newcomers, eager to hear from his own lips the story of his adventures in Kentucky. Several of those who thus met him for the first time have left brief accounts of the impression he made on them.

"It is now," records one, writing in 1847, "fifty-four years since I first saw Daniel Boone. He was then about sixty years old, of a medium size, say five feet ten inches, not given to corpulency, retired, unobtrusive, and a man of few words. My acquaintance was made with him in the winter season, and I well remember his dress was made of tow cloth, and not a woollen garment on his body, unless his stockings were of that material...I slept four nights in the house of one West, with Boone; there were a number of strangers, and he was constantly occupied in answering questions."

Another writes that "his large head, full chest, square shoulders, and stout form are still impressed upon my mind. He was (I think) about five feet ten inches in height, and his weight say one hundred and seventy-five pounds. He was solid in mind as well as in body, never frivolous, thoughtless, or agitated; but was always quiet, meditative, and impressive, unpretentious, kind, and friendly in his manner. He came very much up to the idea we have of the old Grecian philosophers — particularly Diogenes."

The great naturalist Audubon, who happened to pass a night with Boone in a West Virginia cabin, declared that "the stature and general appearance of this wanderer of the Western forests approached the gigantic. His chest was broad and prominent; his muscular powers displayed themselves in every limb; his countenance gave indication of his great courage, enterprise, and perseverance; and when he spoke, the very motion of his lips brought the impression that whatever he uttered could not be otherwise than strictly true." [5]

But, popular and revered though he was, it cannot be said that Boone's life was a happy one. Even the Kanawha Valley, now filling up with population, had grown distasteful to him. He longed, as always, for the frontier, for the serenity of the unbroken forest, abounding with game. He missed the warm friendships, the close companionships, of the men by whose side he had lived and fought in the old Boonesborough days. To fill the cup of his unhappiness, his few remaining land-holdings in Kentucky, which had escaped the rapacity of the "claim-jumpers," were sold at auction in 1798 because of his inability to pay taxes on them. In his wrath and bitterness of heart he declared that he would no longer endure a civilization that had proved so cruel to him, but would advance again into the wilderness.

Westward once more, therefore, he made his way, embarking on the Kanawha with his family, to voyage by flatboat to Missouri, whither his oldest surviving son, Daniel Morgan, had already gone. It is said that on the day set for his departure there was a great gathering of pioneers to bid him an affectionate farewell. From the Kanawha he sailed leisurely down the Ohio, putting in at various river towns to buy provisions and visit old friends. At Cincinnati, the story goes, somebody asked him why, at his time of life, he wished to expose himself again to the dangers and hardships of the frontier.

"It is too crowded here," he grimly replied. "I want more elbow-room."

Sturdy, brave, self-reliant as ever, he journeyed on, steadily westward, in search of the contentment and peace of mind that had vanished with the ruin of his hopes in Kentucky.

[1] The importance of Danville in the early political history of Kentucky is well brought out in two Filson Club publications, "The Political Club of Danville" and "The Political Beginnings of Kentucky."

[2] It does not fall within the province of this book to deal with the exciting, but extremely complicated, political events in Kentucky involved in the efforts of the Kentuckians, during the closing years of the eighteenth century, to secure navigation rights through Spanish Louisiana to the mouth of the Mississippi, whence they could transmit their products by sea to the markets of the Atlantic States. For clear and interesting studies of this subject the reader may consult Mr. Roosevelt's "The Winning of the West," and Mr. Frederic Austin Ogg's "The Opening of the Mississippi."

[3] It may be noted in passing that in 1798, by merger with the Kentucky Academy, established near Lexington in 1796, Transylvania Seminary became Transylvania University. This name it retained until 1865 when, again by merger with another institution, it became Kentucky University. Its history is ably told in a Filson Club publication, Dr. Robert Peter's "Transylvania University."

[4] The reference is to the campaigns of Harmar, St. Clair, and Wayne against the Ohio Indians, 1790-94. The supplies for the troops were obtained largely from Kentucky.

[5] The first of these descriptions is quoted from Howe's "Historical Collections of Ohio," the second from Dr. Thwaites's "Daniel Boone," the third from Maria R. Audubon's "Audubon and his Journals."

Chapter Eighteen - Boone's Last Years

MISSOURI was then, and had been since 1763, a Spanish possession, but the majority of its white inhabitants were French. They were the same care-free, light-hearted, irresponsible type of people that George Rogers Clark had found at Kaskaskia, Cahokia, and Vincennes, dwelling in small log-cabin settlements, practising a crude agriculture, and apparently regarding life as though it were one long perpetual holiday. At first disposed to resent the enforced transfer of their allegiance from France to Spain, they soon reconciled themselves to the change, precisely as the French of the Illinois country had done after Clark's conquest. As Boone discovered on his arrival in Missouri, they were still leading an almost patriarchal existence, grazing their flocks and herds on pastures held in common by all, and supplying their further wants by hunting and trapping and by barter with the Indians, with whom they were on the most friendly terms. The simplicity of their nature was reflected in the appearance of their towns, the largest of which, St. Louis, was a mere village, extremely picturesque but quite unlike the bustling centres of industrial and commercial enterprise so rapidly arising on the American side of the Mississippi.

To Boone, however, fleeing from the hubbub and turmoil of the fast-peopling Middle West, the absence of all signs of progress was a welcome relief. He was still further gladdened by the reception given him by the Spanish authorities at St. Louis, the capital of Upper Louisiana, of which Missouri was a part. In answer to his request for a grant of land, he was given, free of charge, a farm of about eight hundred and fifty acres in the choice but sparsely inhabited Femme Osage District, where his son and some other adventurous Americans had located; and, in 1800, was appointed syndic, or magistrate, an office which he retained until the cession of Louisiana to the United States.

As syndic he was the most important official in Femme Osage, and dispensed justice with such an even hand as to win not only the respect of the French and American settlers, but the warm commendation of the lieutenant-governor of Upper Louisiana, Charles Dehault Delassus. In a list of syndics which he drew up in 1804, Delassus referred to Boone as "Mr. Boone, a respectable old man, just and impartial, who has already, since I appointed him, offered his resignation owing to his infirmities — believing I know his probity I have induced him to remain, in view of my confidence in him, for the public good."

As may be imagined, Boone's performance of his duties as syndic was most unconventional. He knew absolutely nothing of legal procedure, except what he had gained through his unpleasant experiences in the courts of Kentucky. There were no lawyers in the Femme Osage District, and if there had been, it is doubtful whether Boone would have allowed them to plead before him, so prejudiced was he against all lawyers, to whose cunning devices he attributed the loss of his lands. In every case, therefore, that came to him for settlement, he acted as judge, jury, and counsel. He examined and cross-examined the witnesses, without the slightest regard for the laws of evidence; imposed whatever penalties he saw fit, sometimes to the extent of a sound flogging; and permitted no appeal from his decisions. Withal, according to contemporary accounts, he conducted himself with the greatest dignity, and displayed such unfailing fairness and good sense that the longer he was a syndic, the more respected he became.

Only a small part of his time was taken up by the cares of office, leaving him with plenty of leisure for his favorite occupation of hunting and trapping. Every winter he left his cabin on Femme Osage Creek, and, accompanied by one or the other of his sons, wandered off to the great game fields that stretched for hundreds of miles north and south of the Missouri. Advancing years had somewhat dimmed his eyesight, and brought a slight tremor to his powerful hands; but despite the weaknesses of age, his marksmanship still excelled that of many far younger men. And he was still as keen for the chase as in the long-gone days of his boyhood when, a little lad of ten or twelve, he had wielded his knob-rooted sapling to such deadly effect against the squirrels and chipmunks of Oley Township. In the summer he travelled about, visiting friends, or holding court in various settlements. It was a life that exactly suited him. Indeed, he was afterwards heard to say that his first years in Missouri were the happiest he had known since his long hunt in Kentucky with John Finley.

In faraway Europe, however, important political events were transpiring that were destined to bring sorrow and suffering to him once more. In 1800 the mighty Napoleon, who dreamed of restoring France's lost empire in the New World, persuaded Spain to retrocede to France the whole of vast Louisiana in exchange for an Italian principality. Before the exchange was formally completed, it became certain that war would soon break out between France and England, and, lacking command of the sea, Napoleon at once realized that he would have to abandon his cherished colonial enterprise. Instead of handing Louisiana back to Spain, he offered to sell it to the United States, which had already sent commissioners to France to negotiate for the purchase of New Orleans and Florida. His offer was promptly accepted, and a treaty signed conveying Louisiana to the United States and thereby doubling the area of the youthful Republic at a cost of only fifteen million dollars.

It was a great day's work for the American people, but it was disastrous to Daniel Boone. With the raising of the Stars and Stripes at St. Louis, March 10, 1804, his authority and emoluments as a syndic ceased; and, what was a far more serious matter, the change of sovereignty involved him in a bitter struggle to keep possession of his farm in Femme Osage. According to the Spanish law regarding land grants, every settler was required, in order to insure a permanent holding, to occupy and cultivate his grant within a certain time. Boone, who had been living near but not on his farm, had failed to comply with this proviso, having been assured, as he told the American commissioners appointed to investigate the titles of Louisiana settlers, that syndics were exempt from the requirement of settlement and cultivation. But, after reserving judgment for some time, the commissioners finally decided that their instructions were too explicit to permit them to make any exception in his favor, and he was thus left, at the age of seventy-five, and after a career of exploration and pioneering unsurpassed by any man of his generation, without a foot of land that he could call his own.

Aid now came to him from an unexpected source. At the time of his removal to Missouri, Boone had a number of small debts outstanding against him in Kentucky, and in 1810, having had a most successful season trapping beavers, he made a last journey to his old haunts for the express purpose of settling these obligations. Tradition has it that he returned with only half a dollar in his pocket, but happy in the thought that, "No one can say, when I am gone, 'Boone was a dishonest man.'" He also brought back the cheering consciousness that the people of Kentucky were beginning to appreciate what they and the nation owed to his heroic labors as a pathfinder and defender of the West, and were willing to assist him in his efforts to regain his Missouri grant. He therefore addressed to the Kentucky Legislature, in 1812, a memorial begging that body to help him in securing from Congress a reversal of the commissioners' judgment.

In his petition, which was quite long, he declared that "the history of the settlement of the western country was his history," and reminded the legislators of his struggles "in the fatal fields which were dyed with the blood of the early settlers, amongst whom were his two oldest sons, and others of his dearest connections." He alluded briefly to his misfortunes in Kentucky, when, "unacquainted with the niceties of the law, the few lands he was enabled to locate were, through his ignorance, generally swallowed up by better claims." He then told of the similar loss he had recently suffered in Missouri, stated that he had appealed to Congress for relief, and added: —

"Your memoralist cannot but feel, so long as feeling remains, that he has a just claim upon his country for land to live on, and to transmit to his children after him. He cannot help, on an occasion like this, to look towards Kentucky. From a small acorn she has become a mighty oak, furnishing shelter to upwards of four hundred thousand souls. Very different is her appearance now from the time when your memorialist, with his little band, began to fell the forest and construct the rude fortification at Boonesborough."

Referred to a committee of the Senate, the memorial was made the basis of a resolution — which was adopted without a division by both branches of the Legislature — instructing Kentucky's representatives at Washington to use every effort to induce Congress "to procure a grant of land in said territory to said Boone," since "it is as unjust as it is impolitic that useful enterprise and eminent services should go unrewarded." Reenforced by this resolution, Boone's appeal to Congress was successful. December 24, 1813, the committee on public lands, which had taken his petition under consideration, reported to the House of Representatives that "as the petitioner was induced to omit settlement and cultivation by the suggestion of the said Delassus that it was unnecessary, his claim ought not on that account to be rendered invalid," and "it also appears to the committee that the petitioner is in his old age, and has in early life rendered to his country arduous and useful services; and ought not, therefore, to be deprived of this remaining resource by a rigorous execution of a provision of our statute, designed to prevent frauds on the Government." A few weeks later, by congressional enactment, Boone was confirmed in the possession of his Spanish grant. [1]

Before this act of justice was done him, he had sustained the greatest loss of his career, in the death, in 1813, of his faithful wife Rebecca, who had, no less courageously than he, braved the perils of Indian-infested Kentucky, had shared with him the horrors of the border wars, and had supported and cheered him with loving devotion throughout the years of his accumulating misfortunes. After her death Boone removed to the home of his daughter

Jemima, who, with her husband, Flanders Callaway, had come to Missouri from Kentucky soon after the cession of Louisiana to the United States. But, even in extreme old age, he was of too roving a disposition to remain long in any one place. Much of his time he spent at the homes of his sons, Daniel Morgan and Nathan. It was while he was on a visit to Nathan, in the autumn of 1816, that he wrote to his sister-in-law, Sarah Boone, wife of his brother Samuel, a letter now among the most treasured possessions of the Wisconsin State Historical Society, and valuable as providing the only personal account extant of his religious beliefs.

"Deer Sister," the aged pioneer began, "with pleasuer I Red a Later from your Sun Samuel Boone who informs me that you are yett Liveing and in good health Considing your age I wright to you to Latt you know I have Not forgot you and to inform you of my own Situation Sence the Death of your Sister Rabacah I live with flanders Calaway But am at present with my Sun Nathan and in tolerabel halth you can gass at my feilings by your own as we are So Near one age I Need Not write you of our Satuation as Samuel Bradley or James grimes Can inform you of Every Surcumstance Relating to our family and how we Live in this World and what Chance we Shall have in the next we know Not for my part I am as ignerant as a Child all the Relegan I have to Love and feer god believe in Jesus Christ Do all the good to my Nighbours and my Self that I can and Do as Little harm as I can help and trust on god's mercy for the rest and I beleve god never made a man of my prinspel to be Lost and I flater my Self Deer Sister that you are well on your way in Cristineaty gave my Love to your Childran and all my friends fearwell Deer Sister." [2]

To the last Boone retained his fondness for life in the open, and almost to the last continued his hunting excursions, making long trips into the Western wilderness. As late as 1816, when he was eighty-two, he was seen in Nebraska "in the dress of the roughest, poorest hunter." He even talked, when Missouri began to increase too rapidly in population to suit him, of removing still farther west, but his sons would not let him depart. They could not induce him, however, to forego his hunts, which, during and after the War of 1812, were by no means free from danger, owing to the increasing hostility of the trans-Mississippi Indians. According to his biographer, Dr. Peck, he was at least once attacked by a small party of Osages, but, with the aid of a negro servant, managed to beat them off. On another occasion he was forced to keep in hiding several days, to avoid discovery by a band of hostile reds, hunting in his vicinity.

To Dr. Peck we are indebted for an interesting pen-portrait of Boone in these closing years. "It was in the month of December, 1818," he says, "that the author of this memoir, while performing the duty of an itinerant minister of the gospel in the frontier settlements of Missouri, saw for the first time this venerable pioneer. The preceding day had been spent in the settlement of Femme Osage, where Mr. Callaway, with whom Boone lived, met and accompanied the writer to Charette village, a French hamlet situated on the north side of the Missouri, adjacent to which was his residence. On his introduction to Colonel Boone, the impressions were those of surprise, admiration, and delight. In boyhood he had read of Daniel Boone, the pioneer of Kentucky, the celebrated hunter and Indian fighter; and imagination had portrayed a rough, fierce-looking, uncouth specimen of humanity, and, of course, at this period of life, a fretful and unattractive old man.

"But in every respect the reverse appeared. His high, bold forehead was slightly bald, and his silvered locks were combed smooth; his countenance was ruddy and fair, and exhibited the simplicity of a child. His voice was soft and melodious. A smile frequently played over his features in conversation.

At repeated interviews an irritable expression was never heard. His clothing was the coarse, plain manufacture of the family; but everything about him denoted that kind of comfort which was congenial to his habits and feelings, and evinced a happy old age. His room was part of a range of log-cabins, kept in order by his affectionate daughter and granddaughters.

"Every member of the household appeared to delight in administering to his comforts. He was sociable, communicative in replying to questions, but not in introducing incidents of his own history. He was intelligent, for he had treasured up the experience and observations of more than fourscore years. In these interviews every incident of his life might have been drawn from his lips; but, veneration being the predominant feeling which his presence excited, no more than a few brief notes were taken.

"He spoke feelingly, and with solemnity, of being a creature of Providence, ordained by Heaven as a pioneer in the wilderness to advance the civilization and the extension of his country. He appeared to have entered into the wilderness with no comprehensive views or extensive plans of future improvement; he aimed not to lay the foundations of a state or nation; but still he professed the belief that the Almighty had assigned to him a work to perform, and that he had only followed the pathway of duty in the course he had pursued. He gave no evidence of superstition, manifested no religious credulity, told of no remarkable dreams and strange impressions, as is common with superstitious and illiterate people, but only expressed an internal satisfaction that he had discharged his duty to God and his country by following the direction of Providence."

Others who visited Boone at this time have confirmed Dr. Peck's highly favorable estimate. The Rev. James Welch, another frontier clergyman, says that he was "soft and quiet in his manner," with "but little to say unless spoken to, sociable and kind in his feelings, very fond of quiet retirement, of cool self-possession and indomitable perseverance." Timothy Flint — who, like Dr. Peck, was one of Boone's early biographers, and knew him in Missouri — pictures him as "five feet ten inches in height, of a very erect, clean-limbed, and athletic form — admirably fitted in structure, muscle, temperament, and habit for the endurance of the labors, changes, and sufferings he underwent. He had what phrenologists would have considered a model head — with a forehead peculiarly high, noble, and bold — thin and compressed lips — a mild, clear, blue eye — a large and prominent chin, and a general expression of countenance in which frankness and courage sat enthroned...Never was old age more green, or gray hairs more graceful."

But the most intimate view we possess of Boone in his last years is from the pen of the American artist Chester Harding, who, prompted by a patriotic impulse, made a long journey in 1819 for the purpose of painting Boone's portrait. At the time of Harding's visit Boone was temporarily living alone in an old cabin, having apparently left home on one of his periodical outings. The artist found him "engaged in cooking his dinner. He was lying in his bunk, near the fire, and had a long strip of venison wound around his ramrod, and was busy turning it before a brisk blaze, and using salt and pepper to season his meat.

"I at once told him the object of my visit. I found that he hardly knew what I meant. I explained the matter to him, and he agreed to sit. He was [nearly] ninety years old, and rather infirm; his memory of passing events was much impaired, yet he would amuse me every day by his anecdotes of his earlier life. I asked him one day, just after his description of one of his long hunts, if he never got lost, having no compass. 'No,' said he, 'I can't say as ever I was lost, but I was *bewildered* once for three days.'"

Boone's Cabin in Missouri

Harding painted his portrait none too soon. Little more than a year later, on September 21, 1820, Boone passed away, dying at the home of his son Nathan. The end, it is said, came gradually and peacefully, without the slightest suffering. When he died, the Missouri Legislature was holding its first session at St. Louis, and upon hearing the news of his death the representatives adjourned for the day, after adopting a resolution to wear a badge of mourning twenty days out of respect to his memory.

He was buried, in accordance with his often expressed desire, by the side of his well-loved Rebecca, in a grave on the bank of a small stream. But, twenty-five years afterwards, in response to a request from the Kentucky Legislature, the people of Missouri consented to allow the removal of the remains of both Boone and his wife for reinterment in the State so immeasurably indebted to their brave pioneering. September 18, 1845, in the presence of an enormous assemblage from all parts of Kentucky, and with most impressive funeral services, they were laid at rest in the public cemetery at Frankfort, their graves being marked in after years by a beautiful monument.

No monument is needed, though, to keep Boone's memory green in the hearts of his fellow-countrymen. His name will always live in the record of his bold adventurings, his historic explorations, his epoch-making road-building in the trans-Alleghany wilds, to which he above all other men led the advance of civilization.

[1] The documents relating to Boone's appeal are contained in "American State Papers — Public Lands," Vol. II. It appears that he first appealed to Congress as early as 1807, or before the commissioners had finally decided against him; and that his petition was favorably reported in 1810, but was not then followed by the necessary legislative action.

[2] This letter is quoted from Dr. Thwaites's "Daniel Boone," in which it is reproduced in facsimile.

www.ingramcontent.com/pod-product-compliance
Lightning Source LLC
LaVergne TN
LVHW091259080426
835510LV00007B/327